Business Companion:
GERMAN

TIM DOBBINS
PAUL WESTBROOK

Translation and culture notes by:
PETER KELLERSMANN

Edited by:
ZVJEZDANA VRZIĆ

LIVING LANGUAGE®
A Random House Company

ACKNOWLEDGMENTS

Special thanks to the Living Language staff: Lisa Alpert, Elizabeth Bennett, Christopher Warnasch, Suzanne McGrew, Helen Tang, Elyse Tomasello, Fernando Galeano, Pat Ehresmann, Linda Schmidt, Marina Padakis, and Denise DeGennaro. Thanks also to: Rita Wuebbeler.

AUTHOR INFORMATION

Timothy Dobbins, M Div., is a communications and strategic alignment specialist. As President of Leadership Technologies, Inc./Cultural Architects™.com, he provides advice, direction, and conflict management skills. An Episcopal priest, he was educated in the United States and Jerusalem, and had studied at the G.G. Jung Institute in Zurich. He lives in Philadelphia and New York City.

Paul Westbrook has a broad business background, and has worked for major corporations and business consulting firms. He is now running his own financial and retirement firm, WestBrook Financial Advisers, in Ridgewood, New Jersey. He is the author of *Word Smart for Business* and *Math Smart for Business*, both published by Random House.

To my sons, Matt and John Dobbins, for continuously teaching me the universal language of not taking one's self too seriously. To my parents, Christine and Peter, for letting me spend my most joyous years of childhood in the Spanish culture of Quito, Ecuador. To my brother, Dan, for his unconditional support of my vision to help others communicate beyond their differences. And finally, for his editorial contribution, Christopher Warnasch, who has never, until now, had a book dedicated to him. *Pax Domini.*

–*Tim Dobbins*

To business men and women around the globe who are practicing the noblest of professions: business.

–*Paul Westbrook*

Published by Living Language, A Random House
Company, New York, New York.
Living Language is a member of the Random House
Information Group.

Random House, Inc. New York, Toronto, London, Sydney,
Auckland

www.livinglanguage.com

Living Language and colophon are registered trademarks
of Random House, Inc.

Manufactured in the United States.

Design by Wendy Halitzer

Library of Congress Cataloging-in-Publication Data
available

ISBN 0-609-80627-0

10   9   8   7   6   5   4   3   2   1

First Paperback Edition

CONTENTS

3 Getting Out

4 Getting Around

5 Getting Businessized

6 Reference

Appendix A
Measurements 215

Appendix B
Useful Addresses,
   Telephone Numbers,
   and Web Sites 219

Appendix C
National and Religious
   Holidays 227

Appendix D
Grammar Summary
   and Verb Charts 229

Glossary of Industry-
   Specific Terms

General Glossary

Index 387

Acknowledgments
and Author Information ... 397

Preface

It can be said that business is the basis of human relationship. The opportunity to interact with people beyond our own "hometown experience" is both a growing necessity and a challenging adventure. Business never stops. Journeying from one country to another becomes easier every day. *Business Companion* is written for people in the global marketplace of today's world.

But you don't need to cross borders to experience the people and culture of other lands. In today's global marketplace, business is conducted without borders. The telecommunications revolution allows the businessperson to travel to distant lands measured not in miles but in megahertz.

Do business in Hong Kong, Mexico City, and Berlin, without ever leaving your desk. Of course, a great deal of global business is conducted in English. Yet these interactions are enhanced and strengthened by the strategic use of key words and phrases in the other's native tongue, and placed in letters, conversations and over the Internet.

The primary aim of this book, then, is to provide you with the tools to put language to work for you, even if you don't have the time for a traditional language course. Whether you travel to work in foreign lands by plane, train, ship, telephone, or computer, this book will increase your business self-confidence and help you develop the power of using a foreign language. After all, communicating on a global level will only continue to be essential in the workplace of the 21st century.

The second, and subtler purpose of this book is to offer you proven and effective ways to communicate the keywords and phrases themselves. This aim has to do with enhancing your global communication skills. Whenever business leaders ask me to help them and their companies create, shape, and sustain a new organizational culture, I try to help them use the talents, insights, and creative energy of their employees. In guiding this collective leadership effort, I am amazed at how broad and deep is the desire for learning one of the core competencies of global business today: key words and phrases in a foreign language. Developing your foreign language skills and practicing them in the context of the scenarios in this book, will improve your chances for business success.

To assume that English is the only language necessary for successful business interactions is to limit yourself to fewer growth possibilities and maybe even to offend potential clients or associates. In fact, speaking the words and phrases of another language is only part of the equation to more effective communication.

Just as important is your understanding of when they are used in dialogue. When you begin to "read, mark, learn, and inwardly digest" the material in this book, you will be seen as a person willing to expand your communication horizons beyond what's comfortable. You will reveal an intellectual curiosity that will gain the respect of your business partners and your colleagues. Now, let's go to work!

–Tim Dobbins

ORGANIZATION
OF THE PHRASEBOOK

Even if your German is only rudimentary, and you don't have the time (or will?) to immerse yourself in yet another general German course, this phrasebook is here to help you get by and get ahead in doing business in Germany. While this book provides you with basic phrases and expressions you need to make an appointment or introduce yourself in a meeting, it also contains a wealth of very specific business-related terminology and phrases that you would have a hard time finding even in a dictionary.

This book can be used either as a reference, where you will look up things of special interest, or as a continuous read, where you will find interesting commentary on doing business abroad and helpful cultural information in addition to abundant language material.

Before you start, here's how we organized it:

Pronunciation Chart

In order to avoid including cumbersome pronunciation transcriptions throughout the book, we give you this guide to German spelling and pronunciation, which will help you pronounce any German word without stumbling.

Chapters 1–6

These chapters provide several hundred phrases and sentences to be used when on the telephone, in a negotiating meeting, at the dinner table with your business associate, or when settling down in your office abroad. They also provide you with language basics, such as numbers, emergency expressions, and days of the week.

Dialogues

Each chapter has several dialogues recreating a variety of business situations to help you experience the language as it is really used.

Key Words

Here, we provide lists of the key terms you will need to remember from each section or subsection. In order to make them easy to locate, we put them into shaded boxes with a key icon in the upper right corner.

Culture Notes

Culture notes are interspersed throughout the chapters, and provide you with fascinating and useful information about business-related behavior abroad. Their location in the text is marked by a globe icon.

Appendices

If you feel that things have been missed in the chapters, appendices are here to make you change your mind. They provide such useful information as measurements used in the country of your interest, holidays celebrated, or interesting web sites. Appendix D also provides a grammar summary.

Industry-Specific Terms

This section contains a very thorough glossary of the terminology used in a wide range of different industries.

Glossary

Both English-German and German-English, the glossary lists both basic vocabulary words and specific business terminology used in the six chapters of the book.

CD

If you acquired our package including the CD, you will be able to listen to recordings of more than 500 phrases from the book. You can just listen, or listen and repeat during a pause provided between the recordings. All of the words, phrases, and sentences that are recorded come from Chapters 1–6 and appear in **boldface type.**

PRONUNCIATION CHARTS

The German spelling system is more regular and consistent than English, and you will have few problems pronouncing a German word when you see it, once you learn the conventions of German orthography. You may have a harder time pronouncing sounds represented as ö and ü (both with the "umlaut" symbol above the letters o and u), as these sounds do not exist in English. (Just remember to round your lips when you produce these sounds.) Most German words have the stress on the first syllable.

1. THE VOWELS

long **a**	as in first syllable of "father"	*Vater*
short **a**	as in "art"	*Ratte*
long **ä**	as in "hair"	*spät*
short **ä**	as in "men"	*Männer*
long **e**	as in "dare"	*gehen*
short **e**	as in "bent"	*Adresse*
unstressed **e**	as in "the"	*heute*
long **i, ie**	as in "meet"	*Liebe*
short **i**	as in "ship"	*Mitte*
long **o**	as in "tall"	*Bohne*
short **o**	as in "tall", but shorter	*kommen*
long **ö**	similar to **e** in *geben* but with rounded lips	*König*
short **ö**	like long **ö** only shorter	*könned*
long **u**	as in "mood"	*Buch*
short **u**	as in "bush"	*dumm*
long **ü**	similar to **i** *Liebe* but with rounded lips	*früh*
short **ü**	like long **ü** only shorter	*Brücke*
y	pronounced as long **u**	*Typ*

2. THE DIPHTHONGS

ai		as in "by"	*Kai*
ei			*Leine*
au		as in "house"	*Haus*
äu		as in "boy"	*häufig*
eu			*Freund*

3. THE CONSONANTS

b	as *b* in "bed"
	at the end of a word as *p* in "trap"
c	as *k* in "keep"
	rarely like *ts* in "cats"
d	as *d* in "date"
	at the end of a word as *t* in "but"
f	as *f* in "fly"
g	as *g* in "garden"
h	as *h* in "hundred"
	sometimes not pronounced at all
	as in *Schuh*—shoe
j	as *y* in "York"
k	as *c* in "cut"
l	as *l* in "life"
m	as *m* in "man"
n	as *n* in "never"
p	as *p* in "painter"
q	as *q* in "quality"
r	a little more rolled than in English
s	at the beginning of a word as *z* in "zoo"
	at the end of a word or syllable as *s* in "son"
t	as *t* in "tea"
v	as *f* in "fair"
w	as *v* in "vain"
x	as *x* in "mix"
z	like the English combination *ts*

4. SPECIAL LETTER COMBINATIONS

ch	as *k* in "character," e.g., *Charakter*
chs	as *ks* in "fox," e.g., *Fuchs*
ch	a sound near the English *h* in "hue," e.g., *Kirche*—church
ch	a guttural sound not existing in English but close to the Scotch "loch," e.g., *ach!*—ah!
ck	in final position pronounced *k*, e.g., *Scheck*—check
ig	as sound of *h* in "hue"
sch	as *sh* in "shoe"
sp or **st**	when placed at the beginning of the word also gives the initial sound of the *sh* as in "shoe," e.g., *Spanien*—Spain
ng	as *ng* in "sing"
tz	similar to the English *ts*, e.g., *Blitz*—lightning

5. THE ALPHABET

Letter	Name	Letter	Name	Letter	Name
a	ah	j	yot	s	ess
b	beh	k	kah	t	teh
c	tseh	l	ell	u	oo
d	deh	m	em	v	fauh
e	eh	n	en	w	veh
f	eff	o	oh	x	iks
g	geh	p	peh	y	üpsilon
h	hah	q	ku	z	tsett
i	ee	r	err		

In addition to the above letters, German also has special letters **ä, ö,** and **ü** for vowel sounds, and a letter *ß*—as in *Straße*—street—called an "ess-tseh," or esset, which is pronounced as an **s** sound (and can also be written as double **ss**).

1 GETTING STARTED

Business is global, business is fast-paced, and business is high-tech. There is an energy and urgency underlying our activities and communications.

High-tech tools give instant access to clients and associates. Finding the right way to communicate is the key to success in business as much as it is in our private lives. Learning the following greetings, introductions, or openers will go a long way. When you say "Hello!" to people in their native language, you show your willingness to make an effort in their tongue and you also make a great first impression.

We cover a bunch of subjects, all getting you started in doing business successfully overseas. Here is a summary of this chapter's sections:

Saying Hello
Introducing Oneself and
Getting Names Right
Introducing Others
Thank you and Please
Small Talk
Presenting Your Business and
Department
Telephone: Making a Call
Telephone: Getting Through
Telephone: Why You are Calling
Setting the Time for the
Appointment or Meeting
Talking to Machines: Voice-mail
or Answering Machines
Telling Time and Giving Dates
Business Letters
E-mail and Internet

So let's start with the basics—the opener, the ice-breaker, the hand offered in greeting.

SAYING HELLO

"Zur Begrüßung"

HERR SMITH: *Guten Tag, mein Name ist Smith.*
HERR SCHULZ: *Ich heiße Schulz. Ich hatte Sie um zehn Uhr erwartet.*
HERR SMITH: *Ja, bitte entschuldigen Sie meine Verspätung. Der Taxifahrer hatte Probleme Sie zu finden.*
HERR SCHULZ: *Nun, kommen Sie herein und nehmen Sie Platz.*

"Saying Hello"

MR. SMITH: *Hello, my name is Mr. Smith.*
MR. SCHULZ: *My name is Mr. Schulz. I was expecting you at ten.*
MR. SMITH: *Yes. I'm sorry to be late. The taxi didn't know how to find you.*
MR. SCHULZ: *Well, come in and have a seat.*

Key Words

Good-bye	*Auf Wiedersehen*
Hello	*Guten Tag/Hallo* (informal)
Introduce oneself/ someone (to)	*sich vorstellen/jemanden vorstellen*
Name	*der Name*
It's nice to meet you.	*Sehr nett Sie kennenzulernen.*

Repeat (to)	*wiederholen*
Thank you.	*Danke.*
You're welcome.	*Bitte./Bitteschön.*

Good morning/afternoon/ evening.	**Guten Morgen/Guten Tag/Guten Abend.**
Good-bye.	**Auf Wiedersehen.**
Hello.	**Hallo.** (*informal*)
See you soon/later.	**Bis bald./Bis später.**
See you tomorrow/next week/next year.	**Bis Morgen**/nächste Woche/nächstes Jahr.
It's a pleasure to see you again.	**Es freut mich Sie wieder zu sehen.**
It's great to see you again.	Wie schön Sie wieder zu sehen.
How are you?	**Wie geht es Ihnen?**
It's a pleasure to finally meet you.	Ich freue mich Sie endlich kennenzulernen.
I'm glad to meet you in person. (We've spoken on the phone so many times.)	**Sehr erfreut Sie persönlich kennenzu-lernen. (Wir haben ja so oft miteinander telefoniert.)**
Hi! How are you doing?	**Hallo! Wie geht's?** (*informal*)
I'm honored to be here.	**Es ist eine Ehre für mich hier anwesend zu sein.** (*very formal*)
I'm so glad to be here.	Ich freue mich sehr hier zu sein.

INTRODUCING ONESELF AND GETTING NAMES RIGHT

Names are important for a business relationship. Get them right! Since a person's name is critically important to that person, if you get it wrong it can mean an unsuccessful business connection.

The way of addressing another person is becoming less formal in Germany. However, the business world is something of an exception. To address another businessman or businesswoman by first name is very uncommon, not just for new contacts. Even long-standing business relationships are rarely on first name basis. The formal "you" (*Sie*) is by far the common form used in business. To ask a business partner for his or her shorter name or nickname would be, though common in America, quite inappropriate in Germany.

There are some "hip" companies in Germany with a less formal approach in business relations. Most of the emerging Internet companies are a good example. But even if many employees of those companies *are* on a first name basis, it is still highly uncommon to use the informal form "you" (*du*) in any business setting.

Remember also that you should greet somebody by shaking hands, not just the first time, but every time you meet. A short and firm shake is appropriate, but don't make it too firm.

My name is . . .	**Mein Name ist . . .**
I am . . . /I'm called . . .	Ich bin . . . /**Ich heiße . . .**
What is your name?	**Wie ist Ihr Name?**
You are?	**Wie heißen Sie?**
Can you please repeat your name/it?	**Würden Sie Ihren Namen**/das **bitte wiederholen?**
Can you please write your name/it down for me?	Würden Sie ihren Namen/ihn bitte für mich aufschreiben?
How do you spell that?	Wie buchstabieren Sie das?

My name is spelled . . .	**Meinen Namen schreibt man . . .**
My title/position is . . .	**Meine Firmenposition ist . . .**
How do you do!	Wie geht's?
It's a pleasure to meet you. I am . . .	Ich freue mich Sie kennenzulernen. Ich heiße . . .
It's nice to meet you. I'm . . .	**Sehr erfreut. Ich bin . . .**
So, we finally meet.	Endlich lerne ich Sie kennen.
Please call me.	**Bitte rufen Sie mich an.**
Please/Let's keep in touch.	**Lassen Sie uns den Kontakt aufrecht erhalten.**

INTRODUCING OTHERS

Mr. Pohl, may I introduce you to Ms. Kleinen?	Herr Pohl, darf ich Ihnen Frau Kleinen vorstellen?
I'd like to introduce you to Ms. Kleinen.	**Ich möchte Ihnen Frau Kleinen vorstellen.**
Ms. Ludwig, this is Mr. Schmidt.	Frau Ludwig, das ist Herr Schmidt.
Have you met Mr. Thoma?	**Kennen Sie Herrn Thoma bereits?**
It's important for you to meet Ms. Wilms.	Sie müssen unbedingt Frau Wilms kennenlernen.
You should meet Mr. Karsten.	**Sie sollten auch Herrn Karsten kennenlernen.**

Titles such as *Herr Direktor* are only used in written form in Germany today. It is very outdated to address someone in a conversation with a title, except for a professor in university or anyone with a doctorate degree. Someone with a doctorate would be addressed with Herr Dr./Frau Dr. and their last name. But be aware when doing business in Vienna, Austria. As a form of flattery many people are addressed (especially by hotel personnel) with a title they don't actually merit. It's just a part of the so called "Vienna charm."

THANK YOU AND PLEASE

Thank you (very much).	**Danke** (vielmals).
You're welcome.	**Bitte./Bitteschön.**
Please.	Bitte.
Excuse me.	**Entschuldigen Sie** (mich) bitte.
Sorry.	**Verzeihung.**
I'm so sorry.	**Das tut mir sehr leid.**
It doesn't matter.	**Das macht gar nichts./Kein Problem.**
That's fine/Okay.	**Schon gut so./Das ist schon in Ordnung.**
Here we go. (handing something over)	Bitte./Bitteschön.

SMALL TALK

When you make even a stumbling attempt at small talk, you show that you're willing to put yourself out there and make an effort. You don't need to be perfect, you just need to show you'll take a lead and try your best to make a great first impression. In most cases you will even discover that the attempt to make small talk in German will trigger your speaking partner to help you along with words, which might not only carry the conversation, but provide some humor and break barriers as well.

We Americans are a "chatty" bunch of people. People in other cultures do not feel so pressed to make "small talk" and keep the conversation going, even when there is not so much to be said. So don't get impatient or offended if there are moments when people don't have anything to say to you or push a conversation to others. Learning to communicate in other languages and cultures is like learning to dance—relax and let the music lead you. Don't forget to keep a certain business formality, though humor is also quite welcome when doing business in Germany.

"Small Talk"
HERR WARNER: *Wie war Ihr Flug?*
FRAU WEST: *Er war ein wenig turbulent, aber überraschenderweise war das Essen gut.*
HERR WARNER: *Aber wahrscheinlich doch nicht so gut wie in diesem Restaurant.*
FRAU WEST: *Haben Sie hier schon mal gegessen?*

"Small Talk"
MR. WARNER: *How was your flight?*
MS. WEST: *It was somewhat turbulent. But surprisingly the food was good.*
MR. WARNER: *Probably not as good as in this restaurant.*
MS. WEST: *Have you eaten here before?*

Key Words

English	Englisch
How do you say . . . ?	Wie sagt man . . . ?
Language	Sprache
Today	heute
Tomorrow	morgen
Weather	das Wetter

How are you?	Wie geht es Ihnen?
What's new?	Was gibt es Neues?

How are you feeling this morning?

Wie geht es Ihnen heute Morgen?

Very well./Fine. Thank you. And you?

Sehr gut, danke. Und Ihnen?

It's very hot/cold today. What beautiful/lousy weather.

Es ist sehr heiß/kalt heute. Was für ein schönes/ schreckliches **Wetter.**

It's supposed to rain/to snow/to be nice tomorrow.

Es soll morgen regnen/ schneien/recht schön werden.

Is it always this hot here?

Ist es hier immer so heiß?

I'm looking forward to working with you.

Ich freue mich darauf, mit Ihnen zusammen arbeiten zu dürfen.

I am looking forward to our time together.

Ich freue mich auf eine angenehme Zeit mit Ihnen.

Me too.

Gleichfalls.

I'd like to keep in touch with you.

Ich möchte in Kontakt bleiben.

I'll give you a call when I get back (to my office).

Ich rufe Sie an, wenn ich zurück (im Büro) **bin.**

Please call me.

Bitte rufen Sie mich an.

I want to try using your language.

Ich möchte gern Deutsch sprechen.

I'm afraid I'm not very good at it.

Ich fürchte nicht besonders gut damit zu sein.

Please be patient with me.

Bitte haben Sie Geduld mit mir.

Unfortunately, I speak only English.

Leider spreche ich nur Englisch.

I'd like to learn (some words in) your language.

Ich möchte gern (ein wenig) Deutsch lernen.

Can you teach me some words in your language?

Können Sie mir ein wenig Deutsch beibringen?

Of course, it will be my pleasure.

Natürlich, mein Vergnügen.

How do you say . . . ?	**Wie sagt man . . . ?**
Can you say that again?	**Würden Sie das bitte wiederholen?**
Repeat, please.	Wiederholen Sie bitte.
How do you write that?	Wie schreibt man das?

On Weather

The safest small talk? Yes, the weather. When in doubt, talking about the weather is the least controversial subject. It's non-political, non-religious, and non-business.

"Das Wetter"

FRAU PHILLIP: *Das Wetter ist ja ganz schön umgeschlagen.*

HERR LUDWIG: *Ja, gestern war es noch so klar und heute regnet es so stark.*

FRAU PHILLIP: *Regnet es zu dieser Jahreszeit oft?*

HERR LUDWIG: *Nicht unbedingt. Heute haben wir mal einen Regentag.*

"The Weather"

MS. PHILLIP: *The weather sure has changed.*

MR. LUDWIG: *Yes. Yesterday it was clear, but now it's raining very hard.*

MS. PHILLIP: *Is this the season for rain?*

MR. LUDWIG: *Not really. It's just a rainy day.*

Key Words	
Clear	klar, unbewölkt
Cold	kalt
Cool	kühl
Hot	heiß
Rain/rainy	der Regen/regnerisch
Snow	der Schnee

Stormy	*stürmisch*
Temperature	*die Temperatur*
Warm	*warm*
Weather	*das Wetter*

What's the temperature?[1]

Welche Temperatur haben wir?

It's 15 degrees Celsius.

Es ist fünfzehn* Grad Celsius.

What's the average temperature this time of year?

Was ist die Durchschnittstemperatur zu dieser Jahreszeit?

What's the weather report?

Was sagt der Wetterbericht?

What's the forecast for tomorrow?

Wie ist die Wettervorhersage für morgen?

It's going to stay nice.

Es soll schön bleiben.

It's going to be cloudy.

Es soll sich bewölken.

It should be sunny.

Es soll sonnig werden.

The forecast is for warm weather.

Der Wetterbericht sagt warmes Wetter voraus.

We're going to have beautiful weather.

Das Wetter soll schön werden.

We're going to have cold weather.

Es soll kalt werden.

We're going to have good weather.

Das Wetter soll gut werden.

We're going to have hot weather.

Es soll heiß werden.

We're going to have bad weather.

Das Wetter soll schlecht werden.

Will it . . .

Wird es . . .

rain?

regnen?

snow?

schneien?

---

[1]Please refer to the Appendix A for the conversion table between Celsius and Fahrenheit.

*Throughout the book, German numbers occurring in the phrases will be written out as words to indicate their pronunciation.

How are the road conditions between . . . and . . . ?	Wie ist der Straßenzustand zwischen . . . und . . . ?

It's very foggy.	**Es ist sehr neblig.**
It's very slippery.	**Es ist spiegelglatt.**
The roads have been plowed.	Die Straßen sind geräumt (von Schnee).

PRESENTING YOUR BUSINESS AND DEPARTMENT

Following the initial greetings and introductions, you may wish to identify your company, organization, group, and/or position in it. Never take for granted that others know your role.

Some titles and positions within German companies suggest a different responsibility for Americans, and of course vice versa. Some titles and positions within German companies suggest a different responsibility to Americans, and of course vice versa. The terms "director" (*der Direktor*) and "president" (*der Präsident*) are not normally used in German corporations. (The only time these are used with a related meaning in German is in *Bankdirektor*, "director of a bank," or *Bundespräsident*, "president of a country.") The term for the highest ranking person in a company, a "president" or a "CEO," is *Geschäftsführer/in*.

The name of my company is . . .	**Der Name meiner Firma ist . . .**
I/We specialize in . . .	**Ich habe mich/Wir haben uns auf . . . spezialisiert.**
My department is . . .	**Ich arbeite für die . . . Abteilung.**
I am with . . .	Ich komme von . . .

I work with . . .	Ich arbeite für . . .
I'm . . .	Ich bin . . .
president of . . .	Leiter(in) des/der . . .
vice-president of . . .	stellvertretende(r) Leiter(in) des/der . . .
in charge of operations.	betriebliche(r) Manager(in).
the chief financial officer.	der Finanzleiter/**die Finanzleiterin.**
the treasurer.	der Schatzmeister/die Schatzmeisterin.
a director.	Abteilungsdirektor(in).
a manager.	Manager(in).
the leader of our team.	unser(e) Teamleiter(in).
I work . . .	Ich arbeite . . .
in administration.	in der Verwaltung.
in customer service.	im Kundendienst.
in finance.	im Finanzwesen.
in human resources.	im Personalbüro.
in the legal department.	in der Rechtsabteilung.
in marketing.	**in der Marketingabteilung.**
in production.	in der Produktionsabteilung.
in sales.	im Verkauf.

Business Cards

When offering your business card (*die Visitenkarte*), pay attention to some cultural norms in Germany. In general, never force a card on a potential client. Try to sense if a potential business partner is interested. It is also not appropriate to use a social event to hand out business cards too generously, or during lunch or dinner. The safest way to hand out your card is always by first asking for theirs. Naturally, the person you speak to will ask for one in return. Don't stuff it into your pocket immediately! Don't write a restaurant's telephone number on the back of it (at least not in front of the person)! Be sure to actually take a look at it and note what's on it—to some people it actually matters. Then, put it away in a careful manner. One last point: You may be passing out more business cards than at home, so bring plenty.

"Ein Treffen im Büro"

FRAU JONAS: *Frau Hendel, hier ist meine Karte. Meine Telefonnummer ist 134 23 24 [eins vierunddreißig dreiundzwanzig vierundzwanzig]. Meine E-Mail–Adresse steht auch darauf.*

FRAU JONAS: *Frau Hendel, kann ich auch Ihre Karte bekommen.*

FRAU HENDEL: *Sicherlich, bitteschön.*

FRAU JONAS: *Oh, ich sehe, dass Sie im Büro in Stuttgart arbeiten. Ah, hier ist ja auch Ihre E-Mail–Adresse.*

"A Meeting at the Office"

MS. JONAS: *Ms. Hendel, this is my card. You will see that my phone number is 134 23 24. My e-mail address is also included.*

MS. JONAS: *Ms. Hendel, may I have one of your cards?*

MS. HENDEL: *Sure. Here you go.*

MS. JONAS: *Oh, I see that you work out of the Stuttgart office. Also, I see your e-mail address.*

Here is my business card.	**Bitte, hier ist meine Karte/ Visitenkarte.**
Our telephone number is . . .	**Unsere Telefonnummer ist . . .**
Our address is . . .	**Unsere Adresse ist . . .**
My e-mail address is . . .	**Meine E-Mail–Adresse ist . . .**

May I have one of your business cards?	**Hätten Sie eine Visitenkarte für mich?**
Do you have a business card?	Haben Sie eine Karte?
Your company has very nice business cards.	**Ihre Firma hat recht attraktive Visitenkarten.**
Your card looks very nice.	Ihre Visitenkarte ist sehr ansprechend.
Your logo is very nice.	Ihr Firmenlogo ist sehr ansprechend.
Could you pronounce your name for me?	**Wie spricht man Ihren Namen aus?**
Could you repeat your name?	Würden Sie Ihren Namen wiederholen?
Could you repeat the name of your firm?	Würden Sie den Namen Ihrer Firma wiederholen?

TELEPHONE: MAKING A CALL

When you're trying to be understood in another language, using a telephone is not as simple as picking up the receiver. Here are the vocabulary and phrases you will need to make this common business activity a success, even in German.

Germans commonly answer the phone by just stating their last name. In companies they first mention the name of the company or the department followed immediately by their last name. Remember that Germans never say *Auf Wiedersehen!* (Goodbye!) on the phone, but *Auf Wiederhören!*, which means literally, "Until we hear each other again." Note that this expression is only used on the phone and is without substitute when making a professional call.

A cellular phone has, for some strange reason, another English name; it's called a *Handy*. Legend has it that one European businessman attended a technology conference where the first cellular phone was introduced—and everyone was impressed by how "handy" it was.

Keep in mind that making a call from a hotel in Germany is always about 5 to 10 times more expensive than from a public or private phone. This could be quite expensive when making long-distance calls. International calling cards work, but many hotels have a surcharge for these type of calls as well.

"Am Telefon"
HERR SIMON: *Würden Sie bitte die Nummer wiederholen?*
VERMITTLUNG: *Die Nummer ist 134 23 24 [eins vierunddreißig dreiundzwanzig vierundzwanzig]. Ich verbinde Sie jetzt.*
HERR SIMON: *Danke.*

"On the Phone"
MR. SIMON: *Would you repeat that number, please?*
OPERATOR: *The number is 134 23 24. Let me transfer you now.*
MR. SIMON: *Thank you.*

Key Words

Answer (to)	antworten
Answering machine	der Anrufbeantworter
Be on hold (to)	warten
Busy	beschäftigt
Call (to)	anrufen
Calling card	die Telefonkarte
Cellular phone	das Handy
Dial (to)	wählen
Extension	der Apparat

15

Hang up (to)	*auflegen*
Line	*die Leitung*
Local call	*das Ortsgespräch*
Long-distance call	*das Ferngespräch*
Message	*die Nachricht*
Number	*die Nummer*
Operator	*die Vermittlung*
Put on hold (to)	*an der Leitung bleiben*
Telephone	*das Telefon*
Transfer (to)	*verbinden*
Voice mail	*das Sprachspeichersystem* (also: *die Voicemailbox*)

I'd like to place a call.

Ich möchte ein Telefongespräch führen.

How can I make a phone call?

Wie kann ich einen Anruf machen?

Where can I make a phone call?

Wo kann ich telefonieren?

Is there a telephone booth here?

Gibt es hier eine Telefonzelle?

How much does a local call cost?

Wieviel kostet ein Ortsgespräch?

Can I use my calling card on this phone?

Kann ich meine Telefonkarte mit diesem Telefon benutzen?

How can I make a local call?

Wie kann ich ein Ortsgespräch führen?

How can I make a long-distance call?

Wie kann ich ein Ferngespräch führen?

How can I make a conference call?

Wie kann ich ein Konferenzgespräch per Telefon führen?

How do I get an outside line?

Wie bekomme ich einen Freiton für ein Gespräch nachaußerhalb?

How can I call the United States?	Wie kann ich in die Vereinigten Staaten anrufen?
Please . . .	**Bitte . . .**
call this number.	rufen Sie diese Nummer an.
dial this number.	wählen Sie diese Nummer.
forward this call.	leiten Sie dieses Gespräch weiter.
get an operator.	rufen Sie die Vermittlung an.
redial this number.	wählen Sie die Nummer noch einmal.
transfer this call.	**verbinden Sie mich.**
I need to call Ms. Müller.	Ich muss Frau Müller anrufen.
I would like to leave a message.	**Ich möchte eine Nachricht hinterlassen.**
No one is answering.	**Niemand antwortet.**
Please hang up.	**Bitte legen Sie auf.**
My party hung up.	Mein Gesprächspartner hat aufgelegt.
I was put on hold.	**Ich sollte an der Leitung bleiben.**
Please put me on speaker.	**Schalten Sie mich auf Lautsprecher.**
I have you on speaker.	Ich habe Sie auf Lautsprecher geschaltet.
How do I redial?	Wie mache ich Wahlwiederholung?
How do I forward/transfer this call?	Wie leite ich dieses Gespräch weiter?
I'd like to check my voice mail.	**Ich möchte meinen Anrufbeantworter checken.**
How do I make a recording?	Wie mache ich eine Aufnahme?[2]

---

[2]*Aufnahme* could also mean "a photo" or "an inventory."

Do you have . . .	**Haben Sie . . .**
an answering machine?	einen Anrufbeantworter?
a calling card?	eine Telefonkarte?
a direct line?	**eine direkte Telefonverbindung nach außen?**
a switchboard?	eine Vermittlung?
a telephone directory?	eine Telefonliste/ein Telefonbuch?
a contact list?	eine Kontaktliste?
I would like to buy . . .	Ich möchte gern . . .
a car phone.	ein Autotelefon kaufen.
a cellular phone.	ein Handy kaufen.
a portable phone.	ein schnurloses Telefon kaufen.
a video phone.	ein Videotelefon kaufen.
Does your office have . . .	**Gibt es hier in Ihrem Büro . . .**
e-mail capability?	**die Möglichkeit für E-Mail?**
Internet?	einen Internet-Anschluss?
Web access?	Zugang zum Web?
The line is busy.	**Die Leitung ist besetzt.**
We have a bad connection.	**Wir haben eine schlechte Verbindung.**
We got cut off.	**Wir sind unterbrochen worden.**

TELEPHONE: GETTING THROUGH

"Eine Verbindung bekommen"
HERR SMITH: *Hallo?*
HERR TANZER: *Hallo. Tanzer am Apparat.*
HERR SMITH: *Hallo. Ich möchte gern mit Herrn Huber sprechen.*

HERR TANZER: *Moment bitte. Tut mir leid, aber Herr Huber ist außer Haus. Möchten Sie eine Nachricht hinterlassen?*

HERR SMITH: *Ja. Bitte sagen Sie ihm, er möchte doch so bald wie möglich Herrn Smith im Hilton Hotel unter Nummer 123 45 46 [eins dreiundzwanzig fünfundvierzig sechsundvierzig] anrufen. Meine Zimmernummer ist 523 [fünfhundert dreiundzwanzig].*

HERR TANZER: *Ich werde ihm die Nachricht geben.*

"Getting Through"

MR. SMITH: *Hello?*

MR. TANZER: *Hello. This is Mr. Tanzer speaking.*

MR. SMITH: *Hello. I would like to speak to Mr. Huber.*

MR. TANZER: *Please hold . . . I'm sorry, but Mr. Huber is not here. May I take a message?*

MR. SMITH: *Yes. Please tell him to call Mr. Smith as soon as possible at the Hilton Hotel, number 123 45 46. My room number is 523.*

MR. TANZER: *I will give him this message.*

Hello?	**Hallo?**
This is Hans Keller calling/speaking.	**Hans Keller am Apparat.**/ Hier spricht . . .
I'd like to speak to Mr. Lehmann.	Ich möchte gern mit Herrn Lehmann sprechen.
Could I speak to Ms. Sommer?	**Kann ich mit Frau Sommer sprechen?**
Do I have the office of Mr. Winter?	Bin ich mit dem Büro von Herrn Winter verbunden?
Could you connect me with Ms. Adams?	Würden Sie mich bitte mit Frau Adams verbinden?

Extension 345 please.	**Apparat drei vier fünf bitte.**
Please put me through to Ms. Seger.	**Bitte verbinden Sie mich mit Frau Seger.**
I don't mind holding.	**Ich warte gern.**
Is Mr. Lager available?	**Ist Herr Lager zu sprechen?**
Is Ms. Weigel in the office?	**Ist Frau Weigel im Haus?**
When do you expect Mr. Martin to return?	**Wann erwarten Sie Herrn Martin zurück?**
He/she is busy/not available right now.	**Er/Sie ist gerade beschäftigt/** nicht abkömmlich im Moment.
He/she is not at his desk.	**Er/Sie ist momentan nicht am Schreibtisch.**
He/she is . . .	**Er/Sie ist . . .**
in a meeting.	in einer Besprechung.
out to lunch.	zu Mittag.
out of town/away from the office.	auf Geschäftsreise/**nicht im Büro.**
Yes, I understand	**Ja, ich verstehe.**
I'm sorry, I did not understand.	**Es tut mir leid, ich habe nicht ganz verstanden.**
Could you please repeat that?	Würden Sie das bitte wiederholen?
Okay.	In Ordnung.
Could you repeat your name?	Können Sie Ihren Namen wiederholen?
Could I ask you to spell that please?	Darf ich Sie bitten, das zu buchstabieren?

TELEPHONE: WHY YOU ARE CALLING

I'm calling to follow-up with/on . . .	**Ich rufe an, um an . . . anzuknüpfen.**
I would like to arrange an appointment with . . .	**Ich möchte gern einen Termin mit . . . vereinbaren.**

The reason for my call is . . .	Der Grund meines Anrufes ist . . .
I'm calling at the request of . . .	Ich rufe auf Anfrage von . . . an.
I'm calling to tell you . . .	Ich rufe an, um Ihnen mitzuteilen, dass . . .
This call is in reference to . . .	Dieser Anruf ist in Bezug auf . . .
. . . asked me to call him/her this morning.	. . . hat mich gebeten, ihn/sie heute Morgen anzurufen.
I'm returning . . . call.	Ich rufe . . . zurück.
You may remember . . .	Sie erinnern sich vielleicht an . . .
Who's calling?	Wer ist am Apparat?
Hold the line.	Bitte bleiben Sie am Apparat.
You have a call on line one.	Sie haben ein Gespräch auf Leitung eins.
You have the wrong number.	Sie haben die falsche Nummer.

SETTING THE TIME FOR THE APPOINTMENT OR MEETING

Appointments are generally made over the telephone. While it is true that more arrangements are now being made by e-mail, it's to your advantage to speak to the person directly, to his or her secretary, or through voice mail. These days, busy people receive many e-mails per day. You don't want your request for an appointment to get lost in that sea of e-mail.

"Einen Termin machen"
FRAU KARSTEN: *Wir möchten die Besprechung gern um zehn beginnen.*

21

HERR HANSEN: *Könnten wir früher anfangen, vielleicht um neun Uhr dreißig?*
FRAU KARSTEN: *Gut. Wir werden ein paar Minuten vor neun Uhr dreißig in Ihrem Büro sein.*
HERR HANSEN: *Bis dann.*

"Setting the Appointment"
MS. KARSTEN: *We would like to start the meeting at ten.*
MR. HANSEN: *Could we start earlier, say 9:30?*
MS. KARSTEN: *Fine. We'll be in your office a few minutes before 9:30.*
MR. HANSEN: *See you then.*

Key Words

Appointment	der Termin
Beginning/End	der Beginn/das Ende
Calendar	der Kalender
Cancel an appointment (to)	einen Termin absagen
Day	der Tag
Earlier	früher
Later	später
Make an appointment (to)	einen Termin machen
Meeting	die Besprechung/das Meeting/ die Sitzung
Okay	in Ordnung
Schedule	der Zeitplan
Start	der Beginn/der Anfang
Time	die Zeit
Week	die Woche

Time

I'd like to meet with you tomorrow.	Ich möchte mich morgen mit Ihnen treffen.
Would next week be okay?	Wäre nächste Woche in Ordnung?
How does Thursday/next week look?	Wie sieht's mit Donnerstag/nächster Woche aus?
Does he/she have room on her calendar for . . .	Hat er/sie Platz im Kalender für . . .
It's important to meet soon.	Ein baldiges Treffen ist wichtig.
I can't meet next week.	Ich kann Sie nächste Woche nicht treffen.
I'm not available/busy tomorrow.	Ich bin morgen nicht abkömmlich/beschäftigt.
At what time will the meeting begin?	Um wieviel Uhr beginnt die Besprechung?
What time do we begin?	Um wieviel Uhr beginnen wir?
When will the meeting be over?	Wann ist die Besprechung vorbei?
When do we finish?	Wann sind wir fertig?
Tomorrow is fine/excellent.	Morgen passt mir gut/hervorragend.

Place and Directions

Where shall we meet?	Wo sollen wir uns treffen?
Do you wish to meet in my office?	Möchten Sie sich in meinem Büro treffen?
Shall I come to your office?	Soll ich zu Ihrem Büro kommen?
Where is your office/hotel?	Wo ist Ihr Büro/Hotel?
Could you fax me a map please?	Können Sie mir einen Straßenplan faxen?

Please wait while I get a pencil and some paper.	**Bitte warten Sie, ich hole einen Bleistift und Papier.**
Do you need directions to my office?	Brauchen Sie eine Wegbeschreibung zu meinem Büro?
I will meet you in my office/the lobby of the hotel.	**Ich treffe Sie in** meinem Büro/**im Foyer des Hotels.**
Where is the hotel?	Wo ist das Hotel?

Completing the Conversation

Thank you very much for your assistance.	**Herzlichen Dank für Ihre Hilfe.**
It's been a pleasure/great to talk to you.	**Das Gespräch mit Ihnen war mir ein Vergnügen/** ausgezeichnet.
I'm very glad we were able to talk.	Ich freue mich, dass wir die Gelegenheit zu einem Gespräch hatten.
I can't believe we finally connected!	Schließlich haben wir uns doch noch getroffen!
I look forward to the meeting.	**Ich sehe dem Treffen mit Erwartung entgegen.**
I look forward to hearing from/talking to you again.	Ich hoffe bald von Ihnen zu hören. Ich hoffe bald wieder mit Ihnen sprechen zu dürfen.
Take care, and I hope to see you soon.	Alles Gute. Hoffentlich sehen wir uns recht bald wieder.

Other Helpful Phrases While on the Telephone

Yes, I understand.	**Ja, ich verstehe.**
I'm sorry. I did not understand you.	**Tut mir leid. Ich habe Sie nicht verstanden.**

Could you please repeat that/your name?	Würden Sie das/Ihren Namen bitte wiederholen?
Could you please spell your/the name for me?	Würden Sie bitte Ihren/den Namen für mich buchstabieren?
All right./Okay.	**Sehr gut./In Ordnung.**
Sure.	**Sicher.**
May I read the number back to you?	Kann ich die Nummer wiederholen?
Could you please speak louder?	**Würden Sie bitte lauter sprechen?**
This is a bad line. Let me call you back.	**Wir haben eine schlechte Verbindung. Lassen Sie mich zurückrufen.**

TALKING TO MACHINES: VOICE MAIL OR ANSWERING MACHINES

Remember to speak slowly and repeat important information, such as telephone numbers, names, and specific times.

"Eine Nachricht hinterlassen"

HERR JONAS: *Herr Sanders, hier spricht Karl Jonas von der Firma Amalgamated. Ich wohne im Hilton Hotel. Die Telefonnummer hier ist 123 45 67 [eins dreiundzwanzig fünfundvierzig siebenundsechzig]. Ich würde Sie gern zum Abendessen um acht Uhr treffen, wie wir vorher besprochen hatten. Könnten Sie mich im Hotel abholen? Noch einmal: Ich bin im Hilton, Telefon 123 45 67 [eins dreiundzwanzig fünfundvierzig siebenundsechzig]. Lassen Sie mich wissen, ob acht Uhr Ihnen passt.*

"Leaving a Message"

MR. JONAS: *Mr. Sanders, this is Karl Jonas of Amalgamated. I'm staying at the Hilton Hotel. The telephone here is 123 45 67. I would like to meet you for dinner at 8:00 P.M. as we had talked about. Could you pick me up at the hotel? Again, I'm at the Hilton, telephone number 123 45 67. Let me know if eight o'clock works for you.*

Key Words

Answering machine	der Anrufbeantworter
Dial (to)	wählen
Leave a message (to)	eine Nachricht hinterlassen
Message	die Nachricht
Pound key	die Rautentaste/die Nummerntaste
Voice mail	die Voicemailbox

I would like to leave a message.	Ich möchte eine Nachricht hinterlassen.
Could you transfer me to his voice mail?	Können Sie mich mit seinem Anrufbeantworter verbinden?
Please tell . . . I will call later/at a later date.	Richten Sie . . . aus, dass ich später/zu einem späteren Zeitpunkt anrufe.
Please tell . . . to give me a call as soon as possible.	Richten Sie . . . aus, mich so bald wie möglich zurückzurufen.
I will call back again later.	Ich werde später zurückrufen.
May I ask who is calling?	Darf ich fragen wer am Apparat ist?
Would you like to leave a message?	Möchten Sie eine Nachricht hinterlassen?

Would you like to leave your name and number?	Möchten Sie Ihren Namen und Ihre Telefonnummer hinterlassen?
Please hold while I try that extension.	Bitte bleiben Sie am Apparat während ich seine Leitung versuche.
Is there anything you would like me to tell . . . ?	Gibt es etwas, das ich . . . ausrichten kann?
This is . . . I'm away from my desk.	**Hier spricht . . . Ich bin momentan nicht an meinem Schreibtisch.**
You have reached . . .	Sie sind mit dem Anschluss von . . . verbunden.
I'm away from the office until . . .	**Ich bin bis zum . . . nicht im Büro.**
I'm on vacation until . . .	Ich bin im Urlaub bis zum . . .
I'm on the other line.	**Ich spreche auf der anderen Leitung.**
Please call back after nine A.M. on Monday, June 1.	Bitte rufen Sie zurück ab Montag, dem ersten Juni, nach neun Uhr.
Please leave a message.	**Bitte hinterlassen Sie eine Nachricht.**
Leave a message after the tone.	Bitte hinterlassen Sie eine Nachricht nach dem Ton.
Please leave your name, number, and a brief message, and I will call you back.	Bitte hinterlassen Sie Ihren Namen, Ihre Nummer und eine kurze Nachricht und wir rufen Sie zurück.
If you wish to speak to my assistant, please dial extension . . .	**Wenn Sie mit meinem Assistenten/meiner Assistentin sprechen möchten, wählen Sie den Anschluss . . .**

To return to an operator, please press zero now.	Bitte wählen Sie Null für die Vermittlung.
To return to the main menu, please press four.	Iür das Hauptmenü wählen Sie vier.
To leave a message, press . . . now.	Wenn Sie eine Nachricht hinterlassen möchten, wählen Sie jetzt . . .
To speak to an operator, press zero now.	Für die Vermittlung wählen Sie die Null.

TELLING TIME AND GIVING DATES[3]

"Die Uhrzeit angeben"

HERR LEHMANN: *Wieviel Uhr haben Sie?*
HERR ABEL: *Es ist zehn Uhr dreißig hier. Ich glaube Sie sind uns sechs Stunden voraus.*
HERR LEHMANN: *Ja. Es ist sechzehn Uhr dreißig hier. Ich bin gerade sehr beschäftigt. Könnte ich Sie in einer Stunde zurückrufen?*
HERR ABEL: *Ja, aber lassen Sie mich in einer Stunde zurückrufen, um siebzehn Uhr dreißig deutsche Zeit.*

"Telling Time"

MR. LEHMANN: *What time do you have?*
MR. ABEL: *It is 10:30 A.M. here. I believe you are six hours ahead of us.*
MR. LEHMANN: *Yes. It is 4:30 P.M. here. I'm busy right now. Could I call you back in one hour?*
MR. ABEL: *Yes, but let me call you back in one hour, at 5:30 P.M. German time.*

---

[3]Please refer to the section Telling Time in Chapter 6, for additional ways of expressing time.

What time is it?	Wieviel Uhr ist es?
It's 10:30 A.M.	Es ist zehn Uhr dreißig.
What day is it?	Welchen Wochentag haben wir heute?
It's Monday.	Es ist Montag.
What month is it?	Welchen Monat haben wir?
It's November.	Es ist November.
What year is it?	Welches Jahr haben wir?
It's the year 2002.	Es ist das Jahr zweitausendundzwei.
It's morning.	Es ist Morgen.
It's noon.	Es ist Mittag.
It's afternoon.	Es ist Nachmittag.
It's evening.	Es ist Abend
It's midnight.	Es ist Mitternacht.
five minutes/two hours ago	vor fünf Minuten/vor zwei Stunden
in twenty minutes/a half hour/an hour	in zwanzig Minuten/in einer halben Stunde/ in einer Stunde
What time do we begin?	Wann beginnen wir?
When is the meeting over?	Wann ist die Besprechung vorbei?

BUSINESS LETTERS

No, the business letter is not completely a relic of the pre-Internet era. A well-written letter on your company's letterhead is still an effective means of communication, and in fact, may never go out of style.

The business letter is also effective as a follow-up thank you, which is especially important when doing business in Germany. People appreciate receiving even a short personalized business note. It says that you care. It tends to build relationships, which is the bedrock of success in business or in any walk of life.

There is an art to writing a business letter. The first rule is to express yourself as clearly as possible. The second rule is to write well. Use proper grammar and sentence structure, and of course, there is no excuse for misspellings with spell checking. The third and most crucial rule is to write persuasively. That's the most important type of business letter. In business, non-profit, or governmental agencies, you are often trying to win people over to do something, or to take action.

When addressing people in a German business letter, it is always better to know their name with its correct spelling, of course. For example, if a man has a title, it is very common to address him with Mr., then add the title, and then the last name (*Sehr geehrter Herr Direktor Schulz*).

It is also quite important to remember, that most unmarried women today don't like to be addressed as *Fräulein* (Miss), but rather as Frau (Mrs.), which is now becoming equivalent to English "Ms." The reason is mainly that the term *Fräulein* is grammatically a diminutive; it means literally "a little woman." So, unless you are sure you are speaking or writing to a girl under eighteen years of age, it is safer to address every woman as *Frau*.

The Greeting

Dear Mr. Schulz	Sehr geehrter Herr Schulz
Dear Mrs. Kleinen	Sehr geehrte Frau Kleinen
Dear Ms. Schwarz	Sehr geehrte Frau Schwarz
Dear Miss Wunderlich	Sehr geehrtes Fräulein Wunderlich

Dear Sirs/Madams	Sehr geehrte Herren/Damen
Dear Sir(s) or Madam(s)	Sehr geehrte Damen und Herren[4]
Dear Doctor Wendel	Sehr geehrter Herr Doktor Wendel
Dear Professor Weiner	Sehr geehrter Herr Professor Weiner
Dear Director Reber	Sehr geehrter Herr Direktor Reber

Stating the Purpose

This should be done right up front, but don't forget the necessary courtesy, which is expected in German business letters.

The reason for my letter is . . .

to accept . . .	Hiermit möchten wir die Annahme . . . bestätigen.
to ask . . .	Der Grund dieses Schreibens ist die Frage nach . . .
to answer . . .	Mit diesem Schreiben möchten wir auf . . . antworten.
to apologize . . .	Hiermit möchten wir uns für . . . ganz herzlich entschuldigen.
to confirm . . .	Mit diesem Schreiben bestätigen wir . . .
to commend . . .	Der Grund dieses Schreibens ist die Stellungnahme zu . . .
to inform . . .	Hiemit möchten wir Sie darüber informieren, dass . . .

---

[4]This expression is most commonly used if the name is not known.

to provide . . .	Hiemit bieten wir Ihnen . . .
to recommend . . .	Mit diesem Brief möchten wir Ihnen . . . empfehlen.
to reject . . .	Hiemit müssen wir . . . leider ablehnen.
to request . . .	Der Grund unseres Schreibens ist die Anfrage nach . . .
to submit . . .	Mit diesem Scheiben lassen wir Ihnen . . . zukommen.
to thank you for . . .	Der Grund dieses Schreibens ist, Ihnen ganz herzlich für . . . zu danken.

You may wish to start more informally.

In connection with . . .	Im Zusammenhang mit . . .
In regard to . . .	. . . betreffend, . . .
In response to . . .	Als Antwort auf . . .
Instead of calling . . .	Statt eines Telefonanrufes . . .
On behalf of . . .	Im Auftrag von . . .
With reference to . . .	In Bezug auf . . .

You may wish to organize your letter with bullets, which is not the traditional form of German business letters, but is becoming more common recently.

• This is the first point
• This is the second point

Or, perhaps a long hyphen, which is the traditional form in German letters.

—this is the first point
—this is the second point

Other Important Phrases

The purpose of this letter is . . .	Der Grund dieses Schreibens ist . . .

The mission of our business/organization is . . .	Das Ziel unsere Organisations/ Unternehmens ist . . .
Our strategic goals include . . .	Unser strategisches Ziel beinhaltet . . .
The quality assurance team wishes to present its report on . . .	Unser Team der Qualitäts kontrolle präsentient seinen Report über . . .
It has come to our attention that . . .	Wir haben erfahren, dass . . .
We regret to inform you . . .	Leider müssen wir Ihnen mitteilen . . .
Could you please provide me/us with . . . ?	Würden Sie mich/uns bitte . . . zur Verfügung stellen?
Unfortunately, we cannot accept/agree/complete . . .	Leider können wir . . . nicht akzeptieren/zustimmen/ beenden.
In consultation with . . .	Nach Beratung mit . . .
In reviewing your proposal . . .	Nach eingehender Prüfung Ihres Angebots . . .
In going over the contract, I/we discovered . . .	Bei der Prüfung des Vertrags habe ich/haben wir festgestellt, dass . . .
While reviewing the financial statements . . .	Bei der Prüfung der Bilanz . . .
It is our pleasure to accept your proposal.	Wir freuen uns, Ihr Angebot annehmen zu können.
Would you contact us at your earliest convenience?	Bitte setzen Sie sich möglichst bald mit uns in Verbindung.
Enclosed is:	Anlage:
Enclosed please find . . .	Anliegend erhalten Sie . . .

The Closing

Thank you for your attention to this matter.	Herzlichen Dank für Ihre Aufmerksamkeit in dieser Sache.

33

I look forward to hearing from you.	Ich hoffe auf eine baldige Antwort.
Please let me (us) know if I can provide further information.	Bitte lassen Sie mich (uns) wissen, ob wir Ihnen mit weiteren Informationen behilflich sein können.
Please contact me (us) at the following telephone number.	Bitte rufen Sie mich (uns) unter folgender Rufnummer an.
I look forward to . . .	Ich treue mich auf . . .
your response to this letter.	eine baldige Antwort.
your/the proposal.	Ihr/ein baldiges Angebot.
the contract.	baldige Zusendung des Vertrags.
your evaluation.	ihre baldige Beurteilung.
your call.	Ihren baldigen Anruf.
your order.	Ihre Bestellung.
the samples.	die Zusendung der Muster.
the corrected statements.	die Zusendung Ihrer Korrekturen.
additional information.	zusätzliche Information.

Salutations

Sincerely,	Hochachtungsvoll,
Signed,	Gezeichnet,
Yours truly,	Ich verbleibe Ihr, (*outdated*)
Yours sincerely,	Mit vorzüglicher, Hochachtung
With friendly regards,	Mit freundlichen Grüßen, (*most common*)
Best wishes,	Mit besten Wünschen,

34

15. Oktober 2002

Herrn Karl Wagner
Fa. ABC
Hauptstraße 112
6000 Frankfurt 1

Sehr geehrter Herr Wagner:

Vielen Dank für Ihre Zusätze zum Vertragsvorschlag.
Wir sind ganz der Meinung, dass sie eine Verbesserung
bedeuten. Die entgültige Version des Vertrages werden wir Ihnen in wenigen Tagen zur Unterschrift
zukommen lassen.

Wenn Sie weitere Fragen haben, so lassen Sie es mich
umgehend wissen.

Mit freundlichen Grüßen,

Jennifer Smith

October 15, 2002

Mr. Karl Wagner
Fa. ABC
Hauptstraße 112
6000 Frankfurt 1

Dear Mr. Wagner:

Thank you for the additions to the proposed contract.
We agree that this will improve the contract. We will
be sending the final version of the contract to you for
your signature in a couple of days.

If you have any questions, please let me know.

Sincerely,

Jennifer Smith

E-MAIL AND INTERNET

In a few short years the e-mail and the Internet have gone from curiosities to an essential part of our existence. Internet access is in Germany as common today as it is in America, even though it is much more expensive than in the States. Besides access to the Internet, people need a special data line, which is very fast, but the regular telephone connection is not compatible and cannot be used for Internet access. It is predicted that all Internet access in Germany will be free eventually because of the commercial value of the Internet.

When it comes to e-mail, use complete sentences and proper grammar. Avoid so-called cyber slang or chat room abbreviations, which often differ in Germany from the American terms anyway. Using correct language and grammar communicates that you're a professional. And spell-check your messages! Spelling errors could show carelessness or a poor education more so in Germany than in the United States.

There are many English terms used in Germany when it comes to computer language or the Internet. However, sometimes the meaning differs. A home page in Germany could be the same as in America, but the term is also widely used to refer to a Web site. In crucial situations make sure that you are talking about the same thing.

Key Words

Browser	der Web-Browser
CD-ROM disk	die CD-Rom Disk
Check/download e-mail (to)	die E-mail checken/herunter laden
Computer disk	die Diskette

Desktop computer	*der PC*
E-mail or electronic mail	*die E-Mail*
Laptop computer	*das Notebook*
Send/receive e-mail (to)	*E-mail schicken/einpfangen*
Server	*der Server*

More Computer Talk

Cyberspace	der Cyberspace (*also:* die Netzwelt)
Database	die Datenbank
download (to)	herunterladen (*also:* downloaden)
File	die Datei
Flat-panel display	der Flachbildschirm
Help	Hilfe
Home page	die Homepage
Hypertext	der Hypertext
Internet	das Internet
Link	der Link
Mailing list	die Mailing-Liste/die Adressenliste
Mainframe	der MainFrame-Computer
Modem	das Modem
Multimedia	die Multimedia
Network	das Netzwerk (*also:* das Network)
Online service	der Online-Dienst
portable	tragbar
reboot	rebooten/wieder hochfahren
Search engine	die Suchmaschine (*also:* der Search-Engine)
surf	surfen
Technical support	der technische Kundendienst
URL	der URL/der Universelle-Resourcen-Lokalisator

Videoconference	die Videokonferenz
Virtual reality	die virtuelle Realität
Web page/site	der Web-Site (*also:* Homepage)
World Wide Web	das WorldWideWeb

What you need to do

to log on/off	einloggen/ausloggen
to forward e-mail	eine E-Mail weiterleiten
to open a file	eine Datei öffnen
to reply to an e-mail	auf eine E-Mail antworten
to search the Internet/Web	im Internet/Web suchen
to send a file	eine Datei schicken
How do I turn the computer on?	**Wie schalte ich den Computer an?**
How do I dial up/log on?	**Wie logge ich ein?**
Do I need a password?	**Brauche ich ein Passwort?**
What is the password?	**Was ist das Passwort?**
Do you have an IBM compatible computer?	**Haben Sie einen IBM-kompatiblen Computer?**
Do you have a Mac computer?	Haben Sie einen Mac-Computer?
What word processing software do you use?	**Welche Textverarbeitungs-programme benutzen Sie?**
What spreadsheet software do you use?	**Welche Software für Matrixbilanzen benutzen Sie?**
What database software do you use?	Welche Software für Datenbanken benutzen Sie?
What presentation software do you use?	Welches Präsentations-programm benutzen Sie?
How can I get Word/WordPerfect on this computer?	Wie kann ich Word/WordPerfect auf diesen Computer bekommen?

How can I get Excel/ Lotus 1-2-3 on this computer?	Wie kann ich Excel/Lotus eins-zwei-drei auf diesen Computer bekommen?
How can I get PowerPoint on this computer?	Wie kann ich PowerPoint auf diesen Computer bekommen?
How can I get Dbase on this computer?	Wie kann ich Dbase auf diesen Computer bekommen?
Do you have Internet capability?	**Haben Sie Zugang zum Internet?**
Do you have e-mail capability?	**Gibt es Möglichkeiten für E-Mail?**
How can I get AOL on this computer?	**Wie kann ich AOL auf diesen Computer laden?**
How do I . . .	**Wie kann ich . . .**
log on?	**einloggen?**/anloggen?
check my e-mail?	meine E-Mail checken?
access a Web site?	einen Web-Site anwählen?
search the Web?	eine Suche im Netz beginnen?
bookmark a Web site?	einen Web-Site mit Lesezeichen versehen?
print this page?	diese Seite ausdrucken?
print this document?	dieses Dokument ausdrucken?
send an e-mail?	eine E-mail schicken?
send this document to someone?	dieses Schreiben an jemanden schicken?
forward this message to someone?	diese Nachricht an jemanden weiterleiten?
attach a file to an e-mail?	eine Datei der E-Mail beifügen?
Do I leave the computer on?	**Soll ich den Computer laufen lassen?**
How do I turn the computer off?	**Wie schalte ich den Computer aus?**

39

2 GETTING INVOLVED

Conducting business overseas adds an unusual dimension to your work. Not only do you need to transact sales, negotiate contracts, communicate plans, receive feedback on products and services, but you now need to do it in a foreign place and in a foreign tongue.

As a general principle, don't assume that your own ways of doing business apply in other countries and cultures. Be cautious until you know the culture you're dealing with, and take an active role in learning about it. For example, in some cultures, it is bad form to be overly assertive, a common U.S. business trait. In the course of this chapter, and indeed, this whole book, we'll give you tips on how to proceed.

Business Companion, however, is not content to just help you with the language and culture, we also want to remind you of how to handle your business successfully. For instance, in talking about business presentations, we not only give you words like *easel*, *slide projector*, or *refreshments*, but we also provide you with a review of what makes a presentation successful. Thus, we mix language and culture with ideas on how to make your business dealings successful.

Here are the most common business situations you'll be confronting in your work and learning about in this chapter:

> **The General Business Meeting**
> **The Presentation or Speech**
> **The Sales Call**
> **The Negotiating Meeting**
> **The Training Session**

The Trade Show
Attending a Conference or
Seminar
Conducting an Interview

Now, let's get involved.

THE GENERAL BUSINESS MEETING

What's the purpose of the meeting? If you're in charge, make it clear. If you're a participant, find out ahead of time, so you can successfully contribute.

If you are leading the meeting, you need to make sure things are organized on two levels: the *purpose* of the presentation and the *details*, such as announcements, agenda, room arrangements, presentation equipment, and any refreshments.

A last-minute question to ask is: Is there anything else that needs to be on the agenda to make the meeting more successful?

Finally, during the meeting, make sure you encourage the participation of everyone. By the end of the meeting, call on those who have not participated much or not at all for their comments.

So, let's go have a meeting.

"In einer Besprechung"

HERR SCHMIDT: *Warum sind die Stichtage auf der Agenda nicht vermerkt?*

FRAU JONAS: *Das ist eine gute Frage. Lassen Sie uns das für den Spätnachmittag einplanen, nachdem wir unsere Diskussion über den Bericht des Team Force Komitees beendet haben.*

HERR KARSTEN: *Warum können wir das nicht als ersten Punkt morgen früh besprechen? Wir werden vielleicht mit dem Bericht des Komitees erst sehr spät am Nachmittag fertig werden und einige werden dann nicht mehr hier sein.*

FRAU JONAS: *Die Idee ist sogar noch besser. Wir werden es als Erstes morgen früh besprechen.*

— — — — — — —

"At the Meeting"

MR. SCHMIDT: *Why were deadlines left out of the agenda?*

MS. JONAS: *That's a good point. Let's put that in for later this afternoon, after we finish our discussion on the Team Force committee report.*

MR. KARSTEN: *Why not discuss it first thing tomorrow morning? We may not finish the committee report until late this afternoon and not everyone will be here.*

MS. JONAS: *That's an even better idea. We'll discuss it first thing tomorrow morning.*

— — — — — — —

Key Words	
Agenda	*die Agenda/ Tagesordnung*
Answer	*die Antwort*
Cancel a meeting (to)	*eine Besprechung/Tagung absagen*
Committee	*das Komitee*
Deadline(s)	*der/die Stichtag(e)*, (also: *die Deadline*)
Decision(s)	*die Entscheidung(en)*
Discussion	*die Diskussion/die Debatte*
Facilitator	*der Tagungskoordinator*
Feedback	*das Feedback*
Information	*die Information*
Have a meeting (to)	*eine Besprechung (Tagung) haben*

Lead a meeting (to)	*eine Besprechung/Tagung leiten*
Materials	*die Materialien/Unterlagen* (if documents)
Meeting	*die Besprechung* (small), *die Tagung, das Meeting*
Participant	*der Teilnehmer/die Teilnehmerin*
Problem solving	*die Problemlösung*
Purpose	*der Zweck/Grund*
Question	*die Frage*
Schedule	*der Zeitplan*
Schedule a meeting (to)	*eine Besprechung einplanen*
Set an agenda (to)	*eine Agenda aufstellen*
Team building	*die Teamarbeit/die Teamaufstellung*

Hello.	Hallo.
Good morning/ afternoon/evening.	Guten Morgen/Tag/Abend.
Welcome to Oratel GmbH.	**Herzlich willkommen bei der Firma Oratel GmbH.**
My name is Müller.	Mein Name ist Müller.
I am Ms. Wendel.	Ich bin Frau Wendel.
I want to introduce . . .	**Darf ich . . .**
myself.	**mich vorstellen.**
the participants.	**die Teilnehmer vorstellen.**
the secretary.	den Sekretär/die Sekretärin vorstellen.
the administrative assistant.	den Verwaltungsassistenten/ die Verwaltungsassistentin vorstellen.
the recorder.	den Protokollanten/die Protokollantin vorstellen.
Please introduce yourself.	Bitte stellen Sie sich vor.

Before we begin the meeting, let's introduce ourselves.	**Bevor wir die Besprechung** (*also:* das Meeting) **beginnen, sollten wir uns gegenseitig vorstellen.**
Beginning on my left/right please state your name, company, and position/title.	**Links/**Rechts **von mir beginnend nennen Sie bitte Ihren Namen, Ihre Firma und Ihre Stellung/**Ihren Titel.

Remember that in Germany most people smoke, sometimes even cigars, during a meeting. If smoke bothers you, try to speak to the meeting coordinator beforehand in order to find out which people smoke less or do not smoke, so you can sit next to them. According to some non-smoking victims of smoke-filled conference rooms overseas, drinking a sour lemonade or tea with lemon should ease the discomfort of heavy second-hand smoke.

Agenda: **Komitee der Teamaufstellung**

9:00 A.M.	*Einleitung*
9:10 A.M.	*Zusammenfassung der letzten Besprechung*
9:20 A.M.	*Diskussion zur Zusammenlegung der beiden*
	Verwaltungsabteilungen
	Vorgangsausführungen
	Schaubild der neuen Organisation
	Hilfestellung für gekündigte Arbeitnehmer
10:30 A.M.	*Kaffeepause*
10:45 A.M.	*Gruppenarbeit—Richtlinien zur Problemlösung*
11:45 A.M.	*Bericht der einzelnen Gruppen*
12:00 P.M.	*Mittagessen*

1:00 P.M.	*Diskussion der neuen Vorgangsrichtlinien*
4:30 P.M.	*Schlusswort*

Agenda: **Team Force Committee**

9:00 A.M.	*Opening*
9:10 A.M.	*Review of last meeting*
9:20 A.M.	*Discussion of merging the two administrative departments*
	Handling of procedures
	New organization chart
	Outplacement
10:30 A.M.	*Coffee break*
10:45 A.M.	*Breakout sessions—Handling problems*
11:45 A.M.	*Reporting on the sessions*
12:00 noon	*Lunch*
1:00 P.M.	*Discussion of new procedures*
4:30 P.M.	*Close*

Purpose of Meeting

The purpose of this meeting is . . .	Der Grund dieser Besprechung/Tagung ist . . .
Today's meeting concerns itself with . . .	In unserer heutige Besprechung wollen wir uns auf . . . konzentrieren.
I've been asked to lead this discussion about . . .	**Man hat mich gebeten, die Leitung der Diskussion über . . . zu übernehmen.**
This morning/afternoon/ evening we'll be discussing . . .	Heute Morgen/Nachmittag/ Abend werden wir . . . diskutieren.
I'm sure you all know why we are here.	**Ich bin sicher, dass Ihnen allen der Grund unseres Hierseins bekannt ist.**
Let's begin by going over the agenda.	**Lassen Sie uns beginnen mit einem Blick auf die Agenda.**

Are there any questions about the agenda?	**Haben Sie irgendwelche Fragen zur Agenda?**
Yes, I have a question.	**Ja, ich habe eine Frage.**
Yes, please, what is your question?	**Ja bitte, was ist Ihre Frage?**
Who determined/set the agenda?	**Wer hat die Agenda festgelegt/**aufgestellt?
I set the agenda.	Ich habe die Agenda aufgestellt.
The agenda was determined by the committee.	Die Agenda wurde vom Komitee festgelegt.
The agenda was determined in our last meeting.	**Die Agenda wurde bei unserer letzten Besprechung/**Tagung **festgelegt.**
Is the agenda complete?	Ist die Agenda vollständig?
Does everyone have a copy of the agenda?	Hat jeder eine Kopie der Agenda?
Does anyone need a copy of the agenda?	**Braucht jemand eine Kopie der Agenda?**
Is there anything that needs to be added to the agenda?	**Gibt es irgendetwas, das der Agenda beigefügt werden muss?**
Has everyone received the materials?	**Hat jeder die Materialien/**Unterlagen **erhalten?**

Scheduling

 Germans are known to stick almost religiously to a schedule, and there is definitely some truth to it when it comes to business. Meetings are usually well prepared, and the starting times are not delayed. There is little tolerance for latecomers, even after a break or lunch. On the other hand, it is common for a meeting to run over the scheduled time. But once the business is done, German businessmen and -women like to enjoy their leisure time over a good meal and beer or wine.

We will have a coffee break at . . .[5]	**Wir machen eine Kaffeepause um . . .**
10:15 A.M.	**Viertel nach zehn** (zehn Uhr fünfzehn).
10:30 A.M.	halb elf (zehn Uhr dreißig).
2:30 P.M.	halb drei (vierzehn Uhr dreißig).
3:00 P.M.	drei Uhr (fünfzehn Uhr).
Lunch will be served at . . .	**Das Mittagessen wird um . . .**
12:00 noon.	**zwölf Uhr Mittag serviert.**
12:30 P.M.	zwölf Uhr dreißig serviert.
Lunch will last . . .	**Die Mittagspause ist . . .**
one hour.	**eine Stunde.**
one hour-and-a-half.	anderthalb Stunden (neunzig Minuten).
The meeting will continue at 2:00 P.M.	**Die Besprechung/**Tagung **wird um zwei Uhr/**vierzehn Uhr **fortgesetzt.**
The meeting should be over at . . .	**Die Besprechung/**Tagung **soll planmäßig bis . . .**
4:30 P.M.	**halb fünf/**sechzehn Uhr dreißig **dauern.**
5:00 P.M.	fünf Uhr (siebzehn Uhr) dauern.
Let's begin.	**Lassen Sie uns beginnen.**
Does anyone have any questions before we begin?	**Hat jemand noch Fragen bevor wir beginnen?**

---

[5]For more on how to tell time, please refer to section "Telling Time" in Chapter 6.

Does anyone have a question on the first subject?

Hat jemand eine Frage zum ersten Punkt?

Not everyone has spoken.

Nicht jeder hat dazu etwas gesagt.

Mr. Weber, do you have something to add?

Herr Weber, möchten Sie etwas hinzufügen?

We have not heard from everyone.

Nicht jeder hat dazu Stellung genommen.

Does anyone else have a comment or a question?

Hat sonst noch jemand eine Stellungnahme oder eine Frage?

Can we move on to item number two?

Können wir dann zum zweiten Punkt übergehen?

Who will take responsibility for this item?

Wer möchte die Verantwortung für diese Sache übernehmen?

Has everyone spoken on this point?

Hat sich jeder zu diesem Punkt geäußert?

Do we need to vote on this item?

Müssen wir über diesen Punkt abstimmen?

Those in favor, raise your hand.

Bitte heben Sie Ihre Hand, wenn Sie dafür sind.

Those opposed, raise your hand.

Bitte heben Sie die Hand, wenn Sie dagegen sind.

The agenda passes.

Die Agenda ist damit angenommen.

The agenda loses.

Die Agenda ist damit abgelehnt.

The motion passes.
The motion fails.

Der Antrag ist angenommen.
Der Antrag ist abgelehnt.

Would you like to discuss this topic at a later meeting?

Möchten Sie dieses Thema in einer späteren Besprechung diskutieren?

Let's table discussion on this matter.	Lassen Sie uns diesen Punkt in einer Diskussionsrunde besprechen.

The Closing

Do we need a follow-up meeting?	Ist eine Nachfolgebeschprechung/ Tagung notwendig?
Before we leave, let's set a date for the next meeting.	Lassen Sie uns den Termin für die nächste Besprechung/ Tagung festlegen, bevor wir enden.
Thank you for being here today.	Herzlichen Dank für Ihre heutige Teilnahme.

THE PRESENTATION OR SPEECH

How can you tell if the content of your presentation or speech is sound? Perhaps the most successful way is to answer this question: *Does it tell a logical story?* If it does, people will follow you step by step. If not, you will probably confuse your audience, and have questions raised that will sidetrack your main purpose.

Give your presentation or speech ahead of time to those you can count on to provide you with constructive comments. Where do they ask questions? That's where your clarity of thought may be weak. Go over each point and make sure you know the information and can articulate it.

One final thought: Assume that there will always be something wrong about the physical aspects of the presentation or speech, such as arrangements, handouts, equipment, or the refreshments. Why? Because there usually is.

"Eine Präsentation geben"

FRAU OLIVER: *Wir haben die Ehre Herrn Sanders von unserem Hauptbüro heute bei uns begrüßen zu dürfen. Bitte heißen Sie Herrn Sanders willkommen.*

HERR SANDERS: *Vielen Dank für die Einladung. Bereits seit mehreren Monaten habe ich die Absicht, Ihr Büro zu besuchen und endlich war es mir diese Woche möglich. Darf ich während meiner Darstellung Ihre Fragen entgegennehmen, oder möchten Sie damit bis zum Ende warten?*

FRAU OLIVER: *Bitte halten Sie es nach Ihrem Belieben.*

"Giving a Presentation"

MS. OLIVER: *We are so fortunate to have Mr. Sanders from our central office here today. Please welcome Mr. Sanders.*

MR. SANDERS: *Thank you for having me. I've wanted to come to visit your office for several months, and finally I was able to do so this week. May I take questions during my talk or do you want me to wait until the end?*

MS. OLIVER: *You can do it either way.*

Key Words

Clarification question	die klärende Frage
Discussion	die Diskussion
Discussion question	die Diskussionsfrage
Introduction	die Einführung
Microphone	das Mikrofon
Mission	das Endziel
Point/s	der Punkt/die Punkte
Presentation	die Präsentation

Q&A period	*die Fragerunde*
Question	*die Frage*
Subject	*der Punkt/der Hauptpunkt*
Talk	*das Gespräch*
Topic	*das Thema*
Vision	*die Vision/die Zielsetzung*

Audiovisual Presentation Aids

Here are the common aids that you may need.

Audio	das Audio
Board	die Tafel
Chalk	die Kreide
Chart	das Schaubild
Computer	der Computer
Diagram	das Diagramm
Easel	der Präsentationsständer/die Staffelei
Extension cord	die Verlängerungsschnur
Folder	die Mappe
Handouts	die Informationsblätter
Illustrations	die Illustrationen
Marker	der Textmarker
Microphone	das Mikrofon
Model	das Modell/das Muster (*sample*)
Monitor	der Monitor
Note pad	der Notizblock
PowerPoint presentation	die PowerPoint-Präsentation
Screen	der Bildschirm/die Leinwand
Slide projector	der Diaprojektor
Tape recorder	der Kassettenrecorder/das Tonbandgerät
Television	der Fernseher
Transparency	die Transparenz/die Folie (*overhead*)
Video	das Video

Video recorder	das Videogerät
Thank you for having me.	**Herzlichen Dank für die Einladung.**
I want to thank Mr. Wagner for that nice introduction.	**Ich möchte Herrn Wagner für die freundliche Einführung danken.**
I want to thank Mr. Wagner for inviting me to tell you about . . .	Ich möchte Herrn Wagner für die Einladung danken, Ihnen etwas über . . . zu berichten.
I want to thank your organization for having me.	**Ich möchte Ihrer Firma für die Einladung danken.**
It's an honor to be with you today.	**Es ist eine Ehre für mich, hier heute teilnehmen zu dürfen.**
It's my pleasure to speak to you today.	Es ist ein besonderes Vergnügen, heute zu Ihnen sprechen zu dürfen.
I'm grateful for the opportunity to speak to you.	**Ich bin sehr dankbar für die Möglichkeit, hier heute zu Ihnen sprechen zu können.**

The Subject

The purpose of this presentation/speech/talk is . . .	**Der Grund dieser Präsentation/dieser Rede/dieses Gesprächs ist** . . .
This morning/afternoon/ evening I'm going to talk about . . .	Ich werde heute Morgen/ heute Nachmittag/heute Abend über . . . sprechen.
The major point of my presentation/speech/talk is . . .	**Der wesentliche Punkt in meiner Präsentation/meiner Rede/des Gesprächs ist** . . .
In this presentation/ speech/talk, I'd like to . . .	In dieser Präsentation/dieser Redediesem Gespräch / möchte ich . . .

My topic today is . . .	Mein heutiges Thema ist . . .
The subject of my presentation is . . .	Der Hauptpunkt meiner Präsentation ist . . .
I'd like to begin by telling you my conclusion.	Ich möchte damit beginnen, Ihnen meine Schlussfolgerung darzulegen.
I'd first like to tell you about the concept behind by presentation/speech/talk.	**Zu erst möchte ich Ihnen das Grundkonzept meiner Präsentation/meiner Rede/ des Gesprächs darlegen.**
Please feel free to interrupt me with any questions.	**Bitte zögern Sie nicht, mich mit Ihren eventuellen Fragen zu unterbrechen.**

The Major Points

I'd like to begin with a story.	Ich möchte mit einer kurzen Geschichte beginnen.
There are three issues I would like to cover today.	**Es gibt drei Themen, die ich heute besprechen möchte.**
There are three points that I would like to make/cover today.	Es gibt drei Punke, die ich heute aufzeigen/erledigen möchte.
I want to make several points today.	**Ich möchte heute mehrere Punkte aufzeigen.**
First I want to cover . . .	**Zuerst möchte ich . . . erledigen/ansprechen.**
Second I want to discuss . . .	**Als zweiten Punkt möchte ich über . . . diskutieren.**
There is a growing need to be aware of . . .	Es gibt eine steigende Notwendigkeit, auf . . . aufmerksam zu machen.
My/our mission is . . .	**Mein/unser Hauptziel ist . . .**
My/our vision is . . .	Meine/unsere Vision ist . . .

The following . . .	Die folgenden . . .
data	Daten
financial figures	finanziellen Angaben
findings	Funde (*physical findings*)/ Ergebnisse
information	Informationen
results	Resultate
provide support for my central thesis.	unterstützen meine Zentralthese.
Now, on to the second point.	Nun zum zweiten Punkt.
Next, I would like to discuss . . .	Weiterhin möchte ich . . . besprechen.
Moving along, let's now consider . . .	Als nächstes lassen Sie uns . . . in Betracht ziehen.
Before I move on, are there any questions?	Gibt es noch irgendwelche Fragen, bevor ich fortfahre?
I hope you'll understand . . .	Ich hoffe, Sie verstehen . . .
You should be able to see . . .	Sie werden in der Lage sein, . . . zu sehen.
To support my point, I would like to . . .	Um meinen Standpunkt zu unterstützen, möchte ich . . .
demonstrate	demonstrieren
display	abbilden
distribute	verteilen
illustrate	mit . . . untermalen
provide	Ihnen . . . zur Verfügung stellen
reveal	Ihnen . . . zeigen
show	Ihnen . . . aufzeigen

The Summary and Conclusion

| I would like to review my main points/items/ ideas now. | Ich möchte meine wesentlichen Punkte/ Sachpunkte/Ideen jetzt noch einmal wiederholen. |

Finally, I want to say . . .	Abschließend möchte ich noch sagen . . .
In summary, I would like to reiterate . . .	Zusammenfassend möchte ich noch einmal wiederholen, . . .
In conclusion . . .	Abschließend . . .
This concludes my main points.	Damit bin ich am Ende meiner Hauptpunkte.
This ends my remarks.	Hiermit enden meine Anmerkungen.
I hope this presentation has convinced you of . . .	Ich hoffe, diese Präsentation hat Sie von . . . überzeugt.
It has been a pleasure talking to you.	Es war mir ein Vergnügen, zu Ihnen sprechen zu dürfen.
It has been a pleasure being with you today.	Es war mir ein Vergnügen, heute bei Ihnen zu sein.
I have enjoyed presenting my . . .	Es hat mich sehr gefreut, Ihnen meine . . .
activities	Arbeit
experience(s)	Erfahrung(en)
ideas	Ideen
paper	Dokumente
thesis	These
theories	Theorien
to you.	präsentieren zu dürfen.
I hope you have . . .	Ich hoffe . . .
enjoyed . . .	meine Präsentation hat Ihnen gefallen.
found these ideas helpful from . . .	Sie fanden die Ideen in meiner Präsentation hilfreich.
gained insight from . . .	Sie haben ein wenig Einsicht während meiner Präsentation gewonnen
gained knowledge from . . .	Sie haben zusätzliche Kenntnisse in meiner Präsentation gewonnen

learned something from . . .	meine Präsentation war lehrreich
my presentation.	
Thank you for your attention.	**Vielen Dank für Ihre Aufmerksamkeit.**

Don't be confused about people knocking with their knuckles on the table after a presentation or speech. This is a common form of appreciation in Germany. Applause is only common if a very large audience is present.

THE SALES CALL OR MEETING

The basis of successful sales is building relationships, i.e., establishing the trust that allows for the free flow of information. Selling skills also involves the ability to understand and match customer needs with the features of your product or service.

The absolute crucial element of sales, and the most difficult to learn, is the ability to close, or ink, the deal. That's where passion and motivation on your part can make a difference.

"Der Verkauf Ihrer Produkte"
HERR JASPER: *Dann möchten Sie also entweder fünfundzwanzig oder fünfzig unserer neuen Pumpen, je nach Ihrem Wartungsplan?*
HERR KURT: *Nun, ich habe Ihnen nicht zugesagt, dass ich Ihre Pumpen kaufe.*
HERR JASPER: *Was würde Sie zum Kauf bewegen? Der Preis, die Lieferbedingungen, die Zuverlässigkeit?*
HERR KURT: *Hauptsächlich der Preis.*

HERR JASPER: *Ich kann Ihnen fünfzehn Prozent Rabatt einräumen, wenn Sie sich jetzt für den Kauf von fünfzig entschließen.*
HERR KURT: *Dann sind wir im Geschäft.*

"Selling Your Products"

MR. JASPER: *Then, you would like either 25 or 50 of our new pumps depending on your maintenance schedule?*

MR. KURT: *Well, I haven't said that I would buy your pumps.*

MR. JASPER: *What would it take for you to purchase them? Price, delivery, reliability?*

MR. KURT: *Mainly price.*

MR. JASPER: *I am prepared to offer you a 15 percent discount if you buy 50 now.*

MR. KURT: *We have a deal.*

According to a survey made in Germany, more than 80 percent believe that salespeople would have a higher quota if they didn't talk so much and instead listened more to the wishes and concerns of the customer. Another survey revealed that Americans are viewed as one of the most talkative cultures.

Key Words	
Brochure	die Broschüre
Buy (to)	kaufen
Close a deal	ein Geschäft abschließen
Cold call	der Überraschungsanruf/der unerwartete Anruf

Deal	der Handel
Delivery	die Lieferung
Delivery date	der Liefertermin
Discount	der Preisnachlass/der Rabatt
Follow-up	der Nachfassanruf (call)/der Nachfassbrief (letter)
Option(s)	die Wahlmöglichkeit(en)
Price	der Preis
Product	das Produkt
Quality	die Qualität
Quantity	die Menge/die Quantität
Sell (to)	verkaufen
Service	der Service/die Dienstleistung
Shipping costs	die Versand/die Lieferungskosten
Specification(s)	die Spezifikation(en)/die Einzelheiten

My name is Berger. I am from Huber Inc.	Mein Name ist Berger. Ich komme von der Firma Huber.
Here is a brochure on our products/services.	**Hier ist eine Broschüre unserer Produkte/unserer Dienstleistungen.**
Here is a folder with firm/company/ organization.	Hier ist eine Informationsmappe unserer Firma/Gesellschaft/ Organisation.
Here is our company's brochure.	**Hier ist die Broschüre unserer Firma.**

Questions to Ask

Is everything working okay?	Läuft alles einwandfrei?
Would you like to improve your current business?	**Möchten Sie den Status Quo Ihres Geschäfts verbessern?**

Would you like to increase your productivity?	Möchten Sie Ihre Produktivität erhöhen?
What problems are you having?	Welche Probleme haben Sie?
What are your concerns?	Was sind Ihre Vorbehalte?

Your Product or Service

Our product was designed by our engineers with our customers' needs in mind.	Unser Produkt wurde von unseren Ingenieuren unter besonderer Berücksichtigung der Anforderungen unserer Kunden entworfen.
Our services were designed by our experts.	Unsere Dienstleistungen wurden von unseren Experten gestaltet.
Our products/services have proved to be highly successful.	Unsere Produkte/Dienstleistungen haben sich als außerordentlich erfolgreich erwiesen.
We are able to tailor the product/services to your needs.	Wir sind in der Lage das Produkt/die Dienstleistungen auf Ihre Anforderungen zuzuschneiden.
We can alter our product/services to your specifications.	Wir können unser Produkt/unsere Leistungen nach Ihren Spezifikationen abändern.
Here are testimonials from our customers.	Hier sind einige Empfehlungsschreiben unserer Kunden.

Handling Acceptance, Skepticism, Indifference

Yes, I agree we have an excellent track record.

Ja, wir sind auch der Meinung, dass wir eine ausgezeichnete Erfolgsquote haben.

Yes, we are proud of our product/services.

Ja, wir sind stolz auf unser Produkt/unsere Dienstleistungen.

Our company is very satisfied with our product(s)/service(s).

Unsere Firma ist sehr mit unserem Produkt (unseren Produkten)/unserer Dienstleistung (unseren Dienstleistungen) zufrieden.

Thank you for that compliment.

Vielen Dank für das Kompliment.

Perhaps you are not aware of the problems in your operations department.

Vielleicht sind Ihnen die Probleme in Ihrer Produktionsabteilung/ betrieblichen Abteilung **nicht bekannt.**

Perhaps you are not aware that our customers find our product/service very effective.

Vielleicht ist Ihnen nicht bekannt, dass unsere Kunden unser Produkt/ unseren Service für sehr effektiv halten.

Our product/service has been successful in most companies/organizations.

Unser Produkt/unser Service ist in den meisten Firmen/ Organisationen **bisher sehr erfolgreich gewesen.**

Let me explain what this product/service can do for your company.

Lassen Sie mich erläutern, was unser Produkt/unsere Dienstleistung **für Ihre Firma tun kann.**

Our prices are extremely competitive.

Unsere Preise sind außerordentlich wettbewerbsfähig.

Do you realize what this product/service can do for your organization?	Können Sie sich vorstellen, was dieses Produkt/diese Dienstleistung für Ihre Organisation bedeuten kann?
Do you know how much this product/service could save you each year?	Wissen Sie, wieviel Sie durch dieses Produkt/diese Dienstleistung jährlich einsparen können?
Are you aware of what this could do for your company?	Können Sie sich vorstellen, wie sehr das Ihrer Firma helfen kann?

The Close

May I order you this product/service?	Darf ich dieses Produkt/diese Dienstleistung für Sie bestellen?
How many do you want?	Wie viele möchten Sie?
When would you like it installed?	Wann möchten Sie es installiert haben?
When would you like it delivered?	Wann möchten Sie es geliefert haben?

THE NEGOTIATING MEETING

Reading people is key. Who's the decision maker? Is he a take-charge type, or is he looking for you to take the lead? Listening is a critical skill, whether you are leading the negotiations or are a member of a negotiating team.

While your German language skills seem still weak to you, pay attention to the body language and make sure you do not miss the heads that nod in agreement. It may just mean that there is, after all, an understanding of what you said. Another piece of advice: Try to be patient, because in some cultures, unlike ours, there is often a painstakingly slow process to reach a conclusion or an agreement.

Also, look for the bottom line. What are the key issues, on each side? Is what you are negotiating perceived as a zero-sum game? Turn it into a win-win game.

"Vertragsverhandlung"

HERR JONAS: *Wir möchten, dass in der Garantie steht: 'Neben den genannten sind keine weiteren Garantien inbegriffen.'*

FRAU HENDEL: *Wir müssen darauf bestehen, dass dort steht: 'Neben den genannten werden keine weiteren Garantien vorausgesetzt.'*

HERR JONAS: *In den meisten unserer Verträge benutzen wir inbegriffen.*

FRAU HENDEL: *In unserem Land benutzen wir vorausgesetzt.*

HERR JONAS: *In Ordnung. Wir stimmen dem Wort vorausgesetzt zu.*

"Negotiating the Contract"

MR. JONAS: *We would want the warranty to say 'No warranty is* implied *other than what is stated.'*

MS. HENDEL: *We must insist that it says 'No warranty is* assumed *other than what is stated.'*

MR. JONAS: *Most of our contracts use* implied.

MS. HENDEL: *In our country the word* assumed *is used.*

MR. JONAS: *Okay. We'll agree to the word* assumed.

Key Words

Accept (to)	*akzeptieren*
Acceptable	*akzeptabel*
Agree (to)	*zustimmen*

Agreement	*die Übereinkunft* (mutual)/*die Zustimmung* (one side with the other)
Conflict	*der Konflikt*
Contract	*der Vertrag*
Disagree (to)	*widersprechen/anderer Meinung sein* (more polite)
Guarantee	*die Garantie*
Issue(s)	*die Angelegenheit(en)*
Item(s)	*der (die) Sachpunkt(e)* (not physical items)
Key issues	*die Hauptpunkte*
Lawyer(s)	*der Anwalt/die Anwälte*
Negotiate (to)	*verhandeln*
Offer	*das Angebot*
Point(s)	*der (die) Punkt(e)*
Proposal	*der Antrag*
Propose (to)	*vorschlagen*
Reject (to)	*ablehnen*
Rejection	*die Ablehnung*
Unacceptable	*unannehmbar/nicht akzeptabel*
Warranty	*die Gewährleistung/die Zusicherung*

I want to introduce my partner.

Ich möchte meinen Geschäftspartner/meine Geschäftspartnerin **vorstellen.**

I want to introduce our lawyer.

Ich möchte unseren Firmenanwalt vorstellen.

Please introduce yourself.

Bitte stellen Sie sich vor.

Please introduce the other people.

Bitte stellen Sie die anderen Personen vor.

Has everyone arrived?

Sind alle eingetroffen?

Is everyone here?

Sind wir vollzählig?

Is everyone comfortable?

Ist alles zu Ihrer Zufriedenheit?

Could we begin?	**Könnten wir anfangen?**
May we begin?	Dürfen wir anfangen?
Can we begin?	Können wir anfangen?

| Let's begin. | Lassen Sie uns anfangen. |
| Are there any questions before we begin? | Gibt es irgendwelche Fragen, bevor wir anfangen? |

Stating the Issues

| Let's each of us state the issues. | **Lassen Sie uns jeder unsere Punkte vortragen.** |
| Let's each of us present our positions. | Lassen Sie uns jeder Stellung nehmen. |

What are the issues we need to cover in this meeting?	**Was sind die Punkte, die wir in dieser Besprechung erledigen müssen?**
What is the purpose of this meeting?	**Was ist der Zweck dieser Besprechung?**
What objectives would you like to accomplish in this meeting?	Welche Ziele möchten Sie in dieser Besprechung erreichen?
Why is this meeting necessary?	Warum ist diese Besprechung notwendig?

| What are the key issues as you see them? | **Was sind Ihrer Meinung nach die Hauptpunkte?** |
| What is missing? | Was fehlt (noch)? |

| Is anyone confused about our purpose here today? | Hat irgendjemand ein unklares Bild über den Grund unseres heutigen Zusammentreffens? |

| What is it you need us to do? | **Was erwarten Sie von uns?** |

| Which points are not clear? | **Welche Punkte sind nicht klar?** |

| Let's go over the details again. | **Lassen Sie uns noch einmal über die Details gehen.** |

Has everything been covered?	Haben wir alle Punkte angesprochen?
We have a problem with . . .	Wir haben ein Problem mit . . .
credits and payments.	den Krediten und Zahlungen.
deadlines.	den Stichtagen.
deliveries and terms.	Lieferungen und Lieferbedingungen.
guarantees.	den Garantien.
licensing.	den Lizenzen.
warranties.	den Gewährleistungen.

Disagreement, Ambivalence, and Reaching an Agreement

We disagree with these points.	Wir stimmen diesen Punkten nicht zu.
We don't agree.	Wir stimmen nicht zu.
That's unacceptable.	Das ist unannehmbar/ unakzeptabel.
Why do you disagree with this provision?	Warum stimmen Sie dieser Vorkehrung nicht zu?
Why do you reject this provision?	Warum lehnen Sie diese Vorkehrung ab?
There is still too much keeping us apart.	Es gibt immer noch zu viel, was uns von einer Einigung trennt.
We must continue to negotiate.	Wir müssen weiter verhandeln.
We must continue our efforts.	Wir müssen unsere Bestrebungen weiterführen.
You certainly don't expect us to accept that?	Sie werden doch sicherlich nicht von uns erwarten, dass wir das akzeptieren?
Unfortunately you are not offering enough.	Leider bieten Sie uns nicht genug.

We need more.	**Wir brauchen mehr.**
Who will pay for delivery?	**Auf wessen Kosten geht die Lieferung?**
Who will pay for insurance?	Auf wessen Kosten geht die Versicherung?
We wish to propose . . .	**Wir möchten . . . vorschlagen.**
We wish to counter propose . . .	Wir möchten den Gegenvorschlag machen . . .
What is your counter offer?	**Was ist Ihr Gegenvorschlag?**
We are prepared to . . .	**Wir sind in der Lage . . .**
You should know the following . . .	Sie sollten folgenden Aspekt wissen . . .
Our lawyers have informed us . . .	Unser Anwalt hat uns informiert, dass . . .
We expect payment in thirty/sixty/ninety days.	**Wir erwarten die Zahlung in dreißig/sechzig/neunzig Tagen.**
Is there any discount for early payment?	**Bieten Sie irgendeinen Rabatt für die vorzeitige Bezahlung?**
Can you open a letter of credit for us?	**Können Sie ein Akkreditir für uns eröffnen?**
What is your guarantee?	**Was ist Ihre Garantie?**
We are getting close.	**Wir sind nicht weit von einer Einigung entfernt.**
I'm beginning to see your point.	**Ich beginne Ihren Standpunkt zu verstehen.**
Now I understand your point.	Jetzt verstehe ich Ihren Standpunkt.
Give us some time to think this over.	**Geben Sie uns ein wenig Zeit, das zu überdenken.**
Let's plan another meeting.	**Lassen Sie uns eine weitere Besprechung/Sitzung einplanen.**

We agree except for . . .	**Wir stimmen zu, außer was . . .**
the cost.	**die Kosten . . .**
the delivery date.	den Liefertermin . . .
the guarantee.	die Garantie . . .
the legal costs.	die Rechtskosten . . .
the price.	den Preis . . .
the shipping.	die Versandkosten **. . . betrifft.**
We agree with some of your points.	**Wir stimmen einigen Ihrer Punkte zu.**
We seem to agree in general.	**Wir scheinen generell einander zuzustimmen.**
We agree with your point.	Wir stimmen Ihnen in diesem Punkt zu.
What is left to discuss?	**Was haben wir weiterhin zu diskutieren?**
This is our final offer.	Das ist unser letztes Angebot.
Is that your final offer?	**Ist das Ihr letztes Angebot?**

To Americans, German business people might seem overly straightforward in negotiations, almost to a degree of being impolite. Keep in mind that frankness ranks higher than courtesy in the German culture. Many business people view it as part of their integrity not to hold back on their honest opinions, even when they are negative. American business negotiations are often much more careful and diplomatic, and negative aspects are generally expressed in a subtler way.

Inking the Deal

Once a deal is reached, you'd want to celebrate, of course. But note that people may celebrate and congratulate each other in different ways in different cultures: bowing, shaking hands, offering a drink or toast, and so forth. If you are not sure of the cultural norms, the rule of thumb as usual is to follow your hosts.

We agree.	Wir stimmen zu.
We accept your offer.	**Wir akzeptieren Ihr Angebot.**
This point/offer is acceptable.	Dieser Punkt/**dieses Angebot ist akzeptabel.**
We have an agreement.	**Wir haben eine Übereinkunft.**
We have the deal.	Wir sind im Geschäft.
We worked hard, let's have an agreement.	Wir haben hart gearbeitet. Lassen Sie uns eine Übereinkunft erzielen.
We need a written document by Friday.	**Wir brauchen ein schriftliches Dokument bis Freitag.**
The document must be signed by all parties.	**Das Dokument muss von allen Parteien unterschrieben sein.**
Who will draft the agreement?	**Wer wird einen Entwurf dieser Übereinkunft auf Papier bringen?**
We will draft/type the document.	Wir werden das Dokument entwerfen/tippen.
We will send you a draft of the agreement.	**Wir werden Ihnen einen Entwurf dieser Übereinkunft zuschicken.**
We will send a draft of the agreement for your comments.	Wir schicken einen Entwurf dieser Übereinkunft für Ihre Stellungnahme.
Thank you for your efforts.	Vielen Dank für Ihre Mühe.
It was very nice working with you.	**Es war sehr nett, mit Ihnen zusammenarbeiten zu dürfen.**

| If you have any questions, please let us know. | Wenn Sie irgendwelche Fragen haben, lassen Sie es uns bitte wissen. |
| We will be in touch. | Wir werden in Kontakt bleiben. |

Because German business people tend to be more reserved and use less body language, they may often appear as less passionate about a deal than they actually are. Furthermore, it is viewed as a sign of confidence and trust to be physically closer (often not more then a foot apart) to a partner during negotiation. What is viewed as a violation of personal space in America is just normal in Germany. Also, steady eye contact is important to German business people as well.

THE TRAINING SESSION

Are you conducting the session, or are you there to be trained? If you're giving the session, make sure the training is constructed from the participant's point of view. Too often training is organized more for the expert than the learner.

Then again, there may be a cultural aspect to consider when designing training programs. It's important to know how best to provide information to those in other business cultures. Advanced discussions with those in the country, or region of a country, eliminate most of the surprises and difficulties.

You may wish to review two of the sections in this chapter for words and phrases to begin and open the training session with: *The General Business Meeting* and *The Presentation or Speech.*

"Schulung"

HERR SCHMAL: *Wir werden jetzt über die "Entwicklung einer gemeinsamen Vision" sprechen. Wenn Sie in Ihrem Arbeitsbuch auf Seite siebenundzwanzig schauen, sehen Sie die wesentlichen Ideen hinter diesem Konzept. Herr Hendel, würden Sie darüber spekulieren, wie dieser Prozess beginnen könnte?*

HERR HENDEL: *Ja. Ich denke, dass eine gemeinsame Vision damit beginnt, dass das Management der Gesellschaft eine Zielerklärung festlegt, eine Liste der Hauptziele im Management, welche die treibende Kraft der Organisation ist.*

HERR SCHMAL: *Sehr gut. Herr Hendel, wie erreicht man es dann aber, dass die Angestellten diese Organisationsziele anerkennen?*

HERR HENDEL: *Ich möchte annehmen durch einen interaktiven Prozess, wie in einer Projektgruppe oder Komiteebesprechung, in der Angestellte mitdiskutieren können, wie diese Ziele auf der tatsächlichen Arbeitsebene implementiert werden können.*

"Being Trained"

MR. SCHMAL: *We are now going to talk about "Developing a Shared Vision." If you look in your workbook on page 27, you'll see a list of the principal ideas behind this concept. Mr. Hendel, could you speculate on how this process begins?*

MR. HENDEL: *Yes. I believe a shared vision starts with the management of the organization establishing a mission statement, and a list of management objectives that will drive the organization.*

MR. SCHMAL: *Very good. Mr. Hendel, how then do you get employees to buy into these organizational objectives?*

MR. HENDEL: *I would guess by having some interactive process, like a task force or a series of committee meetings where employees can participate in determining how these objectives can be implemented at the actual work level.*

Key Words

Ask/have a question (to)	fragen/eine Frage haben
Be confused (to)	unklar darüber sein/verwirrt sein (quite confused)
Classroom	der Schulungsraum
Course	der Kursus
Group work	die Gruppenarbeit
Note pad	der Notizblock
Pencil/pen	der Bleistift/der Kugelschreiber
Seminar	das Seminar
Train (to)	trainieren/anlernen
Training session	die Schulungsperiode
Understand (to)	verstehen
Workbook	das Arbeitsbuch
Workshop	der Workshop/die Arbeitstagung

Today, I'm conducting training in . . .	**Heute halte ich eine Schulung über . . .**
our policies.	**unsere Firmenvorschriften**
our procedures.	unsere Richtlinien/ Verfahrensweisen.

The training program today covers our new . . . financial reports.	Das Lehrprogramm bezieht sich auf . . . **unsere neuen Finanzberichte.**
marketing reports.	unsere neuen Absatzberichte.
organization.	unsere neue Organisation.
sales reports.	unsere neuen Verkaufsberichte.
system(s).	unser neues System/unsere neuen Systeme.

I would like to . . .	**Ich möchte . . .**
convince you . . .	Sie von . . . überzeugen.
discuss . . .	. . . mit Ihnen diskutieren.
encourage dialogue on . . .	**einen Meinungsaustausch über . . . unterstützen.**
give feedback regarding . . .	Ihnen ein Feedback über . . . geben.
lead a discussion on . . .	eine Diskussion über . . . anregen.
participate in . . .	mich an . . . beteiligen.
provide information on . . .	Informationen zu . . . zur Verfügung stellen.

Is there any question on the agenda?	Stehen irgendwelche Fragen auf der Agenda?
Does everyone have all the materials?	**Hat jeder die vollständigen Unterlagen?**
Do you have any questions before we begin?	Haben Sie irgendwelche Fragen, bevor wir beginnen?
Could you repeat that question?	**Würden Sie die Frage wiederholen?**
Does everyone understand the question?	Ist die Frage allgemein verständlich?
Does everyone understand the issues?	Sind die Sachpunkte allgemein verständlich?

72

Let's begin.	Lassen Sie uns anfangen.
Can I clarify anything?	**Kann ich irgendetwas verdeutlichen?**
What do you think about this?	**Was halten Sie davon?**
Would anyone like to respond?	**Möchte sich jemand dazu äußern?**
Are there any other ideas?	Gibt es noch weitere Ideen?
Let's break out into teams to solve this problem.	**Lassen Sie uns dieses Problem in Teamarbeit lösen.**
Who will report on your solutions?	**Wer wird über Ihre Lösungen berichten?**
That concludes the training on . . .	**Damit kommen wir zum Abschluss der Schulung über . . .**
I'll be happy to answer any questions.	Ich beantworte gern alle Fragen.
If you have any further questions, I'll be here for awhile.	Wenn Sie noch weitere Fragen haben, ich werde noch eine Weile hier sein.
Please contact me if you have further questions.	Bitte setzen Sie sich mit mir in Verbindung, wenn Sie noch weitere Fragen haben.
Thank you for your attention.	Vielen Dank für Ihre Aufmerksamkeit.

Types of Room Setup or Style[6]

Classroom	der Schulungsraum/ das Klassenzimmer (*for pupils*)

---

[6]Please refer back to the section *The Presentation or Speech* to find the terms for common audio-visual aids.

Conference table	der Konferenztisch
Dais	das Podium
Podium	das Podium/das Podest
Theater	das Theater
U-shaped	u-förmig

Types of Charts and Graphs

Bar chart	das Balkendiagramm/das Histogramm
Display	die Darstellung
Dotted line	die punktierte Linie
Exponential	exponential
Histogram	das Histogramm
Horizontal bar chart	das waagerechte Säulendiagramm
Line graph	das Liniendiagramm
Linear	linear
Logarithmic scale	die logarithmische Skala
Organization chart	das Organisationsschema/Orgaingrainm
Pie chart	das Tortendiagramm
Regression	die rückläufige Entwicklung/der Rückgang
Solid line	die ungebrochene Linie
Stacked	aufgestockt
Table	das Verzeichnis/die Tabelle (*as a chart table only*)
3-D chart	das dreidimensionale Diagramm
XY scatter	die XY-Streuung

Parts of Charts and Graphs

Arc	der Bogen
Area	die Zone/die Fläche (*surface area*)
Arrow	der Pfeil
Beginning	der Anfang

Bell-shaped	glockenförmig
Box	der Kasten/die Box
Bullet	das Aufzählungszeichen[7] der Spiegelstrich
Circle	der Kreis
Column	die Spalte
Curve	die Kurve
Dash	der Bindestrich
Diagram	das Diagramm
Dotted line	die punktierte Linie
Edge	der Rand
Ellipse	die Ellipse
End	das Ende
First	das Erste
Grid	das Gitter
Heading(s)	die Kopfzeile/die Überschrift
Label(s)	das Etikett(s)
Last	das Letzte
Layout	die Anordnung/die Skizze/das Layout
Line	die Linie
Logo	das Firmenzeichen/das Logo
Map	die Karte/die Übersichtstafel
Maximum	das Maximum
Middle	die Mitte
Minimum	das Minimum
Numbers	die Zahlen
Object	das Objekt
Origin	die Herkunft
Percentage	der Prozentsatz
Polygon	das Vieleck
Right angle	der rechte Winkel
Row	die Zeile
Scale	die Skala
Shadow	der Schatten

---

[7]Bullets are not frequently used in Germany. Hyphens are used instead to list items.

Slice	der Schnitt/das Teil/das Stück
Space	das Leerfeld/der Abstand
Square	das Viereck
Rectangle	das Rechteck
Shadow	der Schatten
Table	das Verzeichnis/die Tabelle
Text	der Text
Triangle	das Dreieck
Title	der Titel
Values	die Werte

Positions

Bottom	unten
Center	zentral
Horizontal	waagerecht/horizontal
Inside	innen
Left	links
Outside	außerhalb
Right	rechts
Side	seitlich
Top	oben
Touching	berührend
Vertical	senkrecht/vertikal
X-axis	die Abzissenachse
Y-axis	die Ordinatenachse
Z-axis	die Z-Achse

Other Symbols and Formatting Designs[8]

Asterisk	das Sternchen
Blank	die Leerstelle
Bold	fettgedruckt
Crosshatched	mit gekreuzter Schraffur
Dash	der Bindestrich
Pound sign	das Rautenzeichen/ das amerikanische Nummernzeichen

---

[8]When it comes to terms used by major software programs, English terms are very often used in Germany. If you don't know a German word, just try using English.

Shaded	schattiert
Solid	voll (*for color*)/durchgehend (*for line*)
Star	der Stern
Underlined	unterstrichen

You Can See the Color

Aqua	hellblau
Black	schwarz
Blue	blau
Brown	braun
Green	grün
Orange	orange
Purple	purpur
Red	rot
Yellow	gelb

THE TRADE SHOW

The trade show is a cross between a sales call and a mass presentation. If you are part of the team presenting your company's products or services, you usually have only a brief time to talk about them. If you are just attending to learn about what companies are offering, then being organized is helpful. So many exhibits to see, so many people to meet, so many contacts to make.

You might also like to review the section *The Sales Call* in this chapter, and the section on *Business Cards* in Chapter 1.

- - - - - - - - - - - - -

"Informationen geben"
FRAU SCHMIDT: *Möchten Sie eine Broschüre?*
TEILNEHMER: *Ja. Kann ich eine Veranschaulichung Ihrer Dienstleistungen sehen?*
FRAU SCHMIDT: *Sie können das Menu auf dem Monitor sehen. Wir klicken einfach auf Option zwei.*

TEILNEHMER: *Ist Ihr System mit Microsoft Windows kompatibel?*

"Giving Information"

MS. SCHMIDT: *Would you like a brochure?*

ATTENDEE: *Yes. Can I see a demonstration of your service?*

MS. SCHMIDT: *You can see the menu on the monitor. We'll just select option two.*

ATTENDEE: *Is your system compatible with Windows?*

Key Words

Badge	der Messeausweis
Booth	der Messestand
Brochure	die Broschüre
Demonstrate (to)	demonstrieren/zeigen
Demonstration	die Demonstration
Exhibit	die Ausstellung
Literature	die Literatur/das Informationsmaterial
Message center	das Nachrichtenzentrum
Register (to)	registrieren/sich anmelden
Registration	die Anmeldung
Trade show	die Handelsmesse

I want to register for the trade show.	**Ich möchte mich für die Handelsmesse anmelden.**
Where do I get my badge?	**Wo bekomme ich meinen Messeausweis?**
Where is . . . the business center?	**Wo ist . . . das Geschäftszentrum?**[9]

---

[9] In business it is quite common that English names are used for certain facilities, even if a German translation exists. More people use, for instance, the name *business center* for such business facilities in a hotel than the German word *Geschäftszentrum*.

check-in?	der Schalter zum Einchecken?
the information desk?	der Informationsschalter?
the message center?	das Nachrichtenzentrum?
the shipping center?	das Verschickungszentrum?
ticket sales office?	das Verkaufsbüro für Eintrittskarten?

I would like to reserve . . .	Ich möchte gern . . .
a booth.	einen Messestand
a room at the conference center.	einen Raum im Konferenzzentrum
	. . . reservieren.

I would like to rent . . .	Ich möchte gern . . . mieten.
a color monitor.	einen Farbmonitor
a computer.	einen Computer
a computer cable.	ein Computerkabel
a microphone.	ein Mikrofon
a slide projector.	einen Diaapparat
a sound system.	ein Vertonungssystem
a speaker.	einen Lautsprecher
a table.	einen Tisch
a television.	einen Fernseher

There is a problem with . . .	Es gibt ein Problem mit . . .
the electrical line.	der elektischen Leitung.
my booth.	meinem Stand.
the location of my booth.	dem Standort meines Standes.

I need . . .	Ich benötige . . .
chairs.	Stühle.
display tables.	Präsentationstische.
electricity.	Strom.
easels.	Staffeleien.
extension cords.	Verlängerungskabel.

| My materials have not arrived. | Mein Material ist noch nicht hier. |

Please deliver these to booth number 124.	Bitte liefern Sie diese zum Stand einhundert vier-undzwanzig.
Hi, my name is . . . What's yours?	Hallo, mein Name ist . . . Wie heißen Sie?
My name is Lorenz. My company/ organization is Telecom. My position is Technical Advisor.	Mein Name ist Lorenz. Ich komme von der Firma/Gesellschaft Telecom. Ich arbeite dort als technischer Berater/ techniche Beraterin.
Are you familiar with our products/services? What can I tell you about them? Can I explain anything to you?	**Sind Ihnen unsere Produkte/ Dienstleistungen bekannt? Was darf ich Ihnen darüber erzählen? Kann ich Ihnen irgendetwas erklären?**
Please take a brochure.	**Bitte nehmen Sie eine Broschüre.**
Please write your name, address, and phone number.	Bitte schreiben Sie Ihren Namen, Ihre Adresse und Ihre Telefonnummer auf.
Do you have any questions? Can I help you?	Haben Sie irgendwelche Fragen? Kann ich Ihnen helfen?
May I have your business card? What is your e-mail address?	Darf ich um Ihre Visitenkarte bitten? Was ist Ihre E-Mail-Adresse?
You can visit our Web site . . .	**Sie können unseren Web-Site besuchen . . .**
Would you like to see . . . a brochure? a demonstration?	**Möchten Sie gern . . .** eine Broschüre sehen? **eine Demonstration sehen?**

Do you have a brochure in . . .	Haben Sie eine Broschüre auf . . .
English?	**Englisch?**
Chinese?	Chinesisch?
German?	Deutsch?
Spanish?	Spanisch?
What can I tell you about the product/services?	**Was darf ich Ihnen über die Produkte/**Dienstleistungen **erzählen?**
My company will be giving a demonstration in the conference room.	**Meine Firma wird eine Demonstration im Konferenzzimmer geben.**
We will be demonstrating the product/service . . . [10]	Wir werden das Produkt/die Dienstleistung . . .
later.	später demonstrieren.
tomorrow.	morgen demonstrieren.
at 10:00 a.m.	um zehn Uhr demonstrieren.
at 2:00 p.m.	um vierzehn Uhr demonstrieren.
Can you come back tomorrow at . . .	Könnten Sie morgen um . . .
11:00 a.m.?	elf Uhr wiederkommen?
3:00 P.M.?	fünfzehn Uhr wiederkommen?
Can I contact you to keep you informed about our products/services?	**Darf ich mit Ihnen Kontakt aufnehmen, um Sie über unsere Produkte/**Dienstleistungen **auf dem Laufenden zu halten?**
Can I have . . .	Könnte ich . . .
a list of your products/services?	eine Auflistung Ihrer Produkte/Dienstleistungen bekommen?
your business card?	Ihre Karte bekommen?
your catalog?	Ihren Katalog bekommen?

[10]See *Telling Time* in Chapter 6.

Can you tell me more about . . .	**Können Sie mir mehr über . . .**
the delivery options.	**die Lieferungsbedingungen sagen?**
next year's model.	das Modell des kommenden Jahres sagen?
your new system.	Ihr neues System berichten?
your company's history.	die Geschichte Ihrer Firma?
your other products.	Ihre anderen Produkte?
your system being developed.	die Entwicklung Ihres Systems?
Please explain your guarantee/warranty.	**Bitte erklären Sie mir Ihre Garantie/**Gewährleistung.
Please speak more slowly.	Würden Sie bitte langsamer sprechen?
Could you repeat that?	Würden Sie das wiederholen?
I understand.	Ich verstehe.
I am not interested.	**Ich bin leider nicht daran interessiert.**[11]
May I give you a call?	Darf ich Sie anrufen?
I'll give you a call.	Ich werde Sie anrufen.
Please call me.	Bitte rufen Sie mich an.
It was nice meeting you.	Es war mir ein Vergnügen, Sie kennengelernt zu haben.
Perhaps I'll see you later.	Vielleicht werde ich Sie später sehen.
Thank you for stopping by.	Vielen Dank für Ihren Besuch.
Thank you for showing me your products.	Vielen Dank, dass Sie mir Ihre Produkte gezeigt haben.

---

[11]*Leider* must be added to avoid being inpolite.

ATTENDING A CONFERENCE OR SEMINAR

You can accomplish several objectives by attending a conference or seminar. Obviously, you can learn new information, points of view, or better ways of doing something. You can also make important contacts within your industry or field. Also, through questions you can provide the conference or seminar with your own experiences, information, or express your own or your company's opinions.

Conferences can be large auditorium affairs or small seminars. Taking good notes is key. Also, check with others on information that you weren't sure of. This can also be a way to make interesting and useful contacts.

Remember to write a note to your new contacts as soon as you can after the conference. A personal note, a phone call, or an e-mail goes a long way to continue and solidify a contact.

"Kontakte knüpfen"

FRAU JASPER: *Ich sehe Sie arbeiten für Amalgamated?*
HERR TALER: *Ja, ich hoffe während meiner Teilnahme mehr über den Markt in diesem Land zu lernen. Hätten Sie eine Visitenkarte für mich?*
FRAU JASPER: *Ja. Ich hätte gern auch Ihre. Wie hat Ihnen die Rednerin beim Mittagessen gefallen?*
MR. TALER: *Geht so. Ich hätte es gern gesehen, wenn sie genauer auf die Lösung der technischen Probleme eingegangen wäre.*

"Making Contacts"

MS. JASPER: *I see you're with Amalgamated?*
MR. TALER: *Yes, I'm attending hoping to learn*

*more about how to market in this country. May
I have your business card?*

MS. JASPER: *Yes. I would like one of yours as well.
How did you like the speaker at lunch?*

MR. TALER: *So-so. I would have liked it if she had
been more specific about how she solved the tech-
nical problems.*

Key Words

Ballroom	der Ballsaal
Business cards	die Visitenkarte
Conference room	das Konferenzzimmer
Cocktail party	die Cocktail-Party
Introductions	die Vorstellungen (people)/die Einleitungen (introductions to material)
Luncheon	das Geschäftsessen
Make contacts (to)	Kontakte knüpfen
Message(s)	die Nachricht(en)
Presentation/Talk/ Speech	Die Präsentation/das Gespräch/die Rede

Among German business people, humor is
the best icebreaker as long as it is contained
and does not take over the entire conversation or
negotiation. Avoid humor that is targeted toward a
certain person or has a political or religious conno-
tation. Light humor will make negotiations easier,
since it allows the other side to be a little less serious
and relaxed as well. However, moderation is the key.

Please introduce yourself.	Bitte stellen Sie sich vor.
Before we begin the meeting, let's introduce ourselves.	Bevor wir mit der Besprechung beginnen, lassen Sie uns gegenseitig vorstellen.

Beginning on my left/right please state your name, company, and position/title.	Links/rechts von mir angefangen Sie bitte nennen Ihren Namen, Ihre Firma und Ihre Stellung/Ihren Titel.
My name is Wagner.	Mein Name ist Wagner./ Ich heiße Wagner.
My company/organization is Teleport.	Meine Firma/Gesellschaft ist Teleport.
My position is . . .	Ich bin . . .
I hope to get . . .	**Ich hoffe in dieser Konferenz/ diesem Seminar . . .**
information	Informationen zu bekommen.
a better understanding	**ein besseres Verständnis zu bekommen.**
useful data	hilfreiche Daten zu erhalten.
out of this conference/seminar.	

Questions

Could you please repeat what you just said?	**Würden Sie bitte wiederholen, was Sie gerade gesagt haben?**
I didn't understand your second point?	**Ich habe den zweiten Punkt nicht verstanden.**
Why/How did you reach that conclusion?	**Warum/Wie sind Sie zu dieser Schlussfolgerung gekommen?**

Close

Could we receive a tape of this conference/seminar?	Können wir eine Kassettenaufnahme dieser Konferenz/dieses Seminars bekommen?
Thank you for the information.	Vielen Dank für die Information.

CONDUCTING AN INTERVIEW

Are you interviewing someone for your own department? Or, are you in human resources and screening people for a job position? Getting beyond the details of a resume is the key to a successful interview.

Remember that punctuality is a big issue in Germany. Being punctual for an interview means being at least ten to fifteen minutes early.

"Das Vorstellungsgespräch"

FRAU SCHMIDT: *Warum möchten Sie Ihren derzeitigen Arbeitsplatz verlassen?*

HERR HORN: *Es gibt keine Aufstiegsmöglichkeiten für mich. Ich bin in meiner Stellung festgefahren. Und es gibt keine Herausforderungen für mich.*

FRAU SCHMIDT: *Welche Art von Herausforderung suchen Sie?*

HERR HORN: *Ich möchte gern für ein ganzes Software-Projekt verantwortlich sein. Derzeit bin ich nur einer von vielen Progammierern.*

"The Interview"

MS. SCHMIDT: *Why do you want to leave your present job?*

MR. HORN: *There are no advancement possibilities for me. I'm stuck in my position. And, there are no challenges for me.*

MS. SCHMIDT: *What kind of challenges are you seeking?*

MR. HORN: *I would like to be in charge of an entire software project. Now I'm only one of the many programmers.*

Key Words

Ad	die Stellenanzeige
Benefits	die Sozialleistungen
Boss	der Chef/die Chefin
Career	die berufliche Laufbahn/der berufliche Werdegang
Experience	die Erfahrung
Goals	die Ziele
Job	die Arbeitsstelle
Interview	das Vorstellungsgespräch
Objective	die Zielsetzung
Offer	das Angebot
Organization	die Organisation/die Firma
Reference	die Empfehlung/die Referenz
Resume	der Lebenslauf
Salary	das Gehalt (monthly)
Skills	die Fähigkeiten

In Germany, a resume (*der Lebenslauf*) is traditionally written as a narrative that tells the main story of someone's life chronologically, including the date of birth, parents' information, schooling, college, work experience, and any other important aspect of a person's life. The modern version of the resume looks more like an American resume (*der tabellarische Lebenslauf*), except that it starts with a complete educational history and continues with work experience presented chronologically. Variations have become more popular recently, but are more acceptable in fast-changing professions like advertising, technology, publishing, and other creative fields.

Lebenslauf

Julia Doering
Hauptstraße 123
60123 Frankfurt
(069) 123 45 67

geb. 20.7.1961 in Frankfurt/M

Schulausbildung:
1974–1979   Grundschule Niederrath
1979–1988   Käthe-Kollwitz-Gymnasium,
Frankfurt/M

**Hochschul-
ausbildung:**   Universitätsabschluss in Buchhaltung
und Finanzwesen,
1988–1993   Freie Universität Berlin.

**Arbeits-
erfahrung:**

1994–1996   **Daimler Benz** AG, Stuttgart
<u>Hauptfinanzanalytikerin</u> in der be-
trieblichen Finanzabteilung.
Entwurf und Anwendung eines
kostenreduzierenden Programms
firmenweit. Einsparung von zwei Mil-
lionen DM in der Inventur.

ab 1996   **Deutsche Föderationsbank GmbH,**
Frankfurt
<u>Finanzanalytikerin</u> in der Buchhal-
tungsabteilung der Gesellschaft.
Standart- und Spezialanalysen von Fi-
nanzberichten, die von der
Gesellschaft an die Aktionäre aus-
gestellt werden.

Referenzen: Kurt Weiner, Schatzmeister, Deutsche
Bank GmbH, Tel. (069) 987 65 43

Julia Doering
123 Hauptstraße
6000 Frankfurt 1
(069) 123 45 67

Professional Experience:	**Deutsche Föderationsbank GmbH,** Frankfurt 1996–Present

<u>Senior Financial Analyst</u> in the Corporate Finance Department. Designed and Implemented a cost-cutting program company wide. Saved 2 million marks in inventory.

Daimler Benz, Stuttgart 1994–1996

<u>Financial Analyst</u> in the Corporate Accounting Department. Handled routine and special analysis of financial reports issued by the company to shareholders.

Education:	B.S. Degree in Accounting, Freie Universität Berlin.

Professional References:	Kurt Weiner, Treasurer, Deutsche Bank GMbH, Tel. (069) 987 65 43

Do you have a resume?	**Haben Sie einen Lebenslauf?**
Could you review your work experience for me?	**Würden Sie mir Ihre Arbeitserfahrungen darlegen?**
Please tell me about your education.	**Bitte erzählen Sie uns etwas über Ihren Bildungsweg.**
Please tell me about your jobs.	Bitte erzählen Sie uns etwas über Ihre bisherige Arbeitserfahrung.

What do you feel were your biggest accomplishments at each of your jobs?	**Was glauben Sie sind Ihre wesentlichen Erfolge in jeder Ihrer Stellungen?**
What was your salary/compensation at each of your jobs?	Wie hoch war Ihr Gehalt/Ihre Vergütung bei jeder Ihrer Arbeitsstellen?[12]
What is your salary/compensation now?	Wie hoch ist Ihr Gehalt/Ihre Vergütung jetzt?
Do you receive any . . . bonus? deferred compensation?	Bekommen Sie . . . einen Jahresbonus? spätere Vergütungen?
Do you have a . . . 401(k)–type plan? pension?	**Bieten Sie . . . Firmenzulagen zum Sechshundert vierundzwanzig–Mark-Gesetz?** zusätzliche Altersversorgung?

Every employer is bound by law to contribute to a pension plan in Germany. There are, however, some differences and some companies have extra contributions. The plan that comes closest to the American 401(k) is the 624–Mark-Gesetz (624–Marks-Law). An employee can choose to participate in the governmental savings plan, and the employee and/or the government contributes or matches a certain amount. Even though it is not invested in the stock market, it guarantees a very high fixed return.

Why did you leave Hansen Inc. and join Molarcon Ltd.?	Warum haben Sie die Firma Hansen verlassen und sind zur Molarcon GmbH gegangen?

---

[12]In Germany, a salary quoted is always quoted on a monthly rather than a yearly basis.

Why do you want to leave Molarcon Ltd. now?

Warum möchten Sie die Molarcon GmbH verlassen?

An welcher Stellung sind Sie interessiert?

What position are you looking for?

Was ist wichtig für Sie in einer Stellung?

What are you looking for in a position?

Was sind Ihre Gehaltsvorstellungen?

What salary/compensation are you looking for?

Auf welche Probleme sind Sie gestoßen?

What were some of the problems you experienced?

Wie sind Sie diese Probleme angegangen?

How did you deal with them?

Wie sind Sie mit Ihrem Chef zurecht gekommen?

How well did you get along with your boss(es)?

Wie sind sie mit Ihren Arbeitskollegen zurecht gekommen?

How well did you get along with your peers?

Haben Sie irgendwelche Referenzen?

Do you have any references?

Können wir diese Referenzen überprüfen?

Can we check with any of these references?

Haben Sie irgendwelche Fragen für mich?

Do you have any questions for me?

Welche Fragen haben Sie?

What questions do you have?

Wie können wir uns mit Ihnen in Verbindung setzen?

How can we be in touch with you?

Hier ist meine Karte.

Here is my card.

Rufen Sie mich an, wenn Sie weitere Fragen haben.

If you have any questions please call me.

Meine E-Mail-Adresse ist . . .

My e-mail address is . . .

Sie werden von uns innerhalb von . . . hören.

You will hear from us within . . .

We will be in touch with you within . . .	Wir werden uns innerhalb von . . .
two days.	zwei Tagen
one week.	einer Woche
two weeks.	zwei Wochen
three weeks.	drei Wochen
one month.	eines Monats
	. . . bei Ihnen melden.

Do you have any further questions?	**Haben Sie noch weitere Fragen?**
I enjoyed talking to you.	**Es war mir eine Freude mit Ihnen sprechen zu dürfen.**
It was a pleasure talking to you.	Das Gespräch mit Ihnen war mir ein Vergnügen.
Thank you for seeing us.	Ich danke Ihnen, dass Sie uns die Zeit geopfert haben.
Good luck to you.	Ich wünsche Ihnen viel Glück.

Finally, here is some general advice for businesswomen doing business in Germany. It is still the case that only a relatively small percentage of managerial positions in the country is held by women. Therefore, stereotypes still exist about women in business. There are a few tactics one can use to ensure that business will run smoothly regardless of gender. To establish credibility, outline the purpose of your business plans, and restate this purpose to ensure they understand you have a definite goal. Be assertive and firm in your demands, but do not overdo it, and also, don't be emotional. Follow the general rules for doing business in Germany: be punctual and formal.

3 GETTING OUT

Dining out, attending a sporting event or going to a movie, or just doing some pleasant sightseeing can offer a welcome break from meetings and conferences. It's a chance to relax after an intense or just busy business day. It's also an opportunity to see and learn about the country, culture, and people.

However, when you do these activities with business associates, you have to be as attentive and businesslike as when you are in the office. After all, you are merely extending your selling or negotiating from the office to a more casual setting. Thus, you must be very conscious of crossing the boundary between business and personal. If you do cross that line, do it deliberately.

But this more casual setting can offer the chance to establish or cement relationships more easily than in the office. It offers a chance to better know your business associates or people you are doing business with. This can build trust, the bedrock of successful business relationships.

Thus, getting out can mean different things to different people. We cover a number of different situations:

> **Getting a Taxi**
> **At the Restaurant**
> **Social Conversation**
> **Sporting Events, Movies,**
> **Theater, and Clubs**
> **Visiting the Partner's or**
> **Associate's Home**

For most of these activities, we need a taxi. Taxi!

GETTING A TAXI

There are usually plenty of taxis in all German cities. Sometimes, if you are near a designated taxi stand, a taxi driver will not stop when you hail him. Taxi stands are clearly marked, and taxis are waiting there for their passengers. You can also call a taxi to pick you up, but this is more expensive. Tipping is approximately 10 percent.

"Ein Taxi nehmen"
FAHRER: *Wohin möchten Sie?*
HERR JONAS: *Ich möchte gern in ein nettes franzö-sisches Restaurant. Gibt es eines in der Nähe?*
FAHRER: *Ja, es gibt einige. Möchten Sie in ein teures oder eines der mittleren Preisklasse?*
HERR JONAS: *Ich denke, mittlere Preisklasse.*

"Taking a Taxi"
DRIVER: *Where do you want to go?*
MR. JONAS: *I would like to go to a nice French restaurant. Is there one close by?*
DRIVER: *Yes, there are several. Do you want an expensive one, or only a moderate one?*
MR. JONAS: *A moderate one, I guess.*

Taxi!	Taxi!
I need a taxi.	Ich brauche ein Taxi.
Please call a taxi.	Bitte rufen Sie ein Taxi.

Take me to . . .	Fahren Sie mich . . .
this address . . .	zu dieser Adresse . . .
the restaurant called . . .	zu dem Restaurant mit dem Namen . . .
the hotel . . .	zum Hotel . . .
Please take me to the . . .	Bitte fahren Sie mich . . .
concert hall.	zur Konzerthalle.
conference center.	zum Konferenzzentrum.
dock/pier.	zur Anlegestelle/an die Pier.
museum.	zum Museum.
opera house.	zur Oper.
Turn here.	Biegen Sie hier ab.
Stop here.	Halten Sie hier.
Could you wait ten minutes?	Können Sie zehn Minuten warten?
How much do I owe?	Was bin ich Ihnen schuldig?
Keep the change.	Stimmt so.

AT THE RESTAURANT

Here's a chance to learn about the culture you're visiting—through food. If you're adventuresome, you may try a number of dishes indigenous to the country or region. If you are timid, then stay with the foods you know with perhaps one or two dishes that your host may recommend. But even if you don't try too many of the local dishes, you can ask about them and in doing so you will show your interest in the local culture, which will give your host/s a good impression.

"Ein Restaurant finden"
HERR SANDER: *So, in was für ein Restaurant möchten Sie heute Abend?*

HERR JONAS: *Entweder ein deutsches oder ein französisches.*

HERR SANDER: *Es gibt ein großartiges französisches Restaurant am Hafen.*

HERR JONAS: *Ist das nicht sehr weit?*

HERR SANDER: *Ja, aber wir nehmen ein Taxi.*

HERR JONAS: *Ausgezeichnet. Auf geht's.*

"Finding a Restaurant"

MR. SANDER: *So, what kind of restaurant do you want to go to tonight?*

MR. JONAS: *Either German or French.*

MR. SANDER: *There is a great French restaurant at the wharf.*

MR. JONAS: *Isn't that far?*

MR. SANDER: *Yes, but we'll take a taxi.*

MR. JONAS: *Great. Let's go.*

Key Words

Coats	*die Mäntel*
Check/Bill	*die Rechnung*
Drinks	*die Getränke*
Menu	*die Karte/die Speisekarte*
Order (to)	*bestellen*
Restaurant	*das Restaurant*
Rest room(s)	*die Toilette(n)*
Smoking/non-smoking	*Raucher/Nichtraucher*
Table	*der Tisch*
Waiter!/Waitress!	*Herr Ober!/Bedienung!*
Wine list	*die Weinkarte*

Waitresses were traditionally addressed as *Fräulein* (Miss). Since this term is not so well accepted by women today, to get the attention of a waitress, you can say *Bedienung bitte!* (Service, please!). To call a waiter, one used to say *Herr Ober!* However, the most common way to get the attention of either a waiter or a waitress is to just raise your right hand, or say *Entschuldigung!* (Excuse me!).

Good evening.	**Guten Abend.**
My name is Mueller. I have a reservation for two/three/four/five.	**Mein Name ist Mueller. Ich habe eine Reservierung für zwei/drei/vier/fünf personen.**
Can I/we check our coat(s)?	Kann ich/Können wir meinen Mantel/unsere Mäntel checken?
Could we have a drink at the bar first?	**Können wir erst etwas an der Bar trinken?**
Could we be seated promptly?	**Können wir sofort einen Tisch bekommen?**
Could we have a smoking/non-smoking table area?	**Können wir einen Tisch in der Raucherecke/** Nichtraucherecke **bekommen?**
Do you have a table . . . at a window? in a corner? in a smoking/non-smoking area? in a quiet area? in the other room?	Haben Sie einen Tisch . . . am Fenster? in einer Ecke? in der Raucherecke/ Nichtraucherecke? in einer ruhigen Ecke? im anderen Zimmer?
Could we have that table there?	Können wir dort einen Tisch bekommen?
We don't have much time, could we order quickly?	**Wir haben nicht viel Zeit; können wir gleich bestellen?**
Could we have a menu?	**Können wir die Karte bekommen?**

Do you have a wine list?	Haben Sie eine Weinkarte?
Here is the menu.	Hier ist die Karte.
Here is the wine list.	Hier ist die Weinkarte.
Do you mind if I have a cocktail/a drink?	Haben Sie etwas dagegen, wenn ich erst einen Cocktail/einen Drink bestelle?

Ordering Drinks

In some countries, giving a toast is expected. Thus, give some thought ahead of time about what toast you would offer. Even write it down. This will greatly impress your host/s, and go a long way toward establishing you as a world traveler.

I would like to order . . .	**Ich hätte gern . . .**
an aperitif.	**einen Aperitif.**
a drink.	einen Drink.
a beer.	ein Bier.
a cocktail.	einen Cocktail.
a glass of wine.	ein Glas Wein.
a juice.	einen Saft.
a Coke.	eine Cola.
mineral water with carbonation.	Mineralwasser mit Kohlensäure.
mineral water without carbonation.	Mineralwasser ohne Kohlensäure.
What types of wines do you have?	Was für Weine haben Sie?
Could you recommend a local wine?	**Können Sie einen hiesigen Wein empfehlen?**
Do you have Beaujolais Nouveau?	Haben Sie Beaujolais Nouveau?

I would like a glass of	Ich hätte gern ein Glas
white/red wine.	Weißwein/Rotwein.
I would like to make a	Ich möchte gern anstoßen.
toast.	

In general, don't order red wine or beer with seafood. While this rule is not strictly followed in the United States, it is still considered against good taste in Germany. Beer should only be ordered with a hearty meat dish. White wine goes with everything, unless the dish has been prepared in a wine sauce. In this case, it is best to ask the waiter about which wine complements the food.

Ordering Dinner

"Essen bestellen"

OBER: *Darf ich Ihre Bestellung aufnehmen?*
HERR RIEGER: *Haben Sie regionale Spezialitäten?*
OBER: *Oh ja, wir haben originale Weinwurst.*
FRAU SINGER: *Die ist sehr gut. Die nehme ich.*
HERR RIEGER: *Also, ich denke ich nehme das Steak, medium-rare.*
OBER: *Danke sehr.*

"Ordering Dinner"

WAITER: *May I take your order?*
MR. RIEGER: *Do you have any local specialties?*
WAITER: *Yes, we have original white sausage.*
MS. SINGER: *That's very good. I think I'll have that.*
MR. RIEGER: *Actually, I think I'll have the steak, medium rare.*
WAITER: *Thank you.*

Key Words

Appetizer	die Vorspeise
Dessert	die Nachspeise
Entrée	das Hauptgericht
Fruit	das Obst
Prix fixe	der Tagesteller/das Tagesgericht
Salad	der Salat
Soup	die Suppe
Vegetable	das Gemüse

Waiter!/Waitress!

Herr Ober!/Bedienung!

Do you have any specialties?

Haben Sie irgendwelche Spezialitäten?

What are your specialties of the day?

Was ist die Tagesspezialität?

I/We are ready to order.

Ich bin/Wir sind bereit zu bestellen.

Would like an appetizer?

Möchten Sie eine Vorspeise?

Yes, I would like an appetizer.

Ja, ich möchte eine Vorspeise.

No, I would like just a main course.

Nein, ich möchte nur ein Hauptgericht.

I recommend . . .
the chicken.
the fish.
the pork.
the steak.
the vegetarian platter.

Ich empfehle . . .
das Huhn/Hähnchen.
den Fisch.
das Schweinefleisch.
das Steak.
die vegetarische Platte.

I would like the prix-fixe meal.

Ich möchte gern einen Tagesteller.

What are you going to order?

Was möchten Sie bestellen?

I'm saving room for dessert.	Ich lasse Platz für die Nachspeise.
I would like my meat . . .	Ich möchte das Fleisch bitte . . .
medium.	medium.
medium rare.	medium-rare.
medium well.	medium-durch.
rare.	englisch.
well done.	durch/well done.
Could we have some . . .	Können wir etwas . . .
butter?	Butter . . .
bread?	Brot . . .
horseradish?	Meerrettich . . .
ketchup?	Ketchup . . .
lemon?	Zitrone . . .
mayonnaise?	Mayonnaise . . .
mustard?	Senf . . .
pepper?	Pfeffer . . .
salt?	Salz . . .
sugar?	Zucker . . .
water?	Wasser . . .
	. . . bekommen?

Don't try to ask for ketchup in a restaurant that is not a fast-food place. You not only insult the chef, but the person who suggested the restaurant as well. However, asking for pepper or salt is quite all right.

Could we have a little more?	Können wir etwas mehr bekommen?
Could we have a . . .	Können wir . . .
cup?	eine Tasse . . .
glass?	ein Glas . . .
fork?	eine Gabel . . .
knife?	ein Messer . . .

napkin?	eine Serviette . . .
plate?	einen Teller . . .
saucer?	eine Untertasse . . .
spoon?	einen Löffel . . .
teaspoon?	einen Teelöffel . . .
toothpick?	einen Zahnstocher . . .
	. . . bekommen?

It is considered bad manners not to use the fork and the knife at the same time during a meal, even if the knife is not really needed. The fork is in the left hand at all times, knife stays in the right hand. If the knife isn't needed to cut, it is used to help place food on the fork.

Appetizers	Vorspeisen
Antipasto	die Antipasto
Bisque	die Bisque
Broth	die Brühe
Cold cuts	der Aufschnitt
Pasta	die Pasta/die Teigspeisen
Rice	der Reis
Salad	der Salat
Snails (Escargots)	die Schnecken
Soup	die Suppe

Main Courses	Hauptspeisen
Chicken	das Huhn/Hähnchen
Clams	die Muscheln
Duck	die Ente
Fillet of beef	das Filetsteak
Goose	die Gans
Ham	der gekochte Schinken
Lamb	das Lamm
Liver	die Leber
Lobster	der Hummer
Pork	das Schweinefleisch

Oysters	die Austern
Quail	die Wachtel
Roast beef	das Roastbeef
Salmon	der Lachs
Sausages	die Würstchen
Scallops	die Jacobsmuschel (*small*)
Shrimp	die Shrimps
Sole	die Seezunge
Steak	das Steak
Tuna	der Tunfisch
Turkey	der Truthahn/die Pute
Veal	das Kalbsfleisch
Venison	der Rehbraten/das Wildbret

Your food can be done . . .

baked	gebacken
braised	geschmort
boiled	gekocht
fried	gebraten
grilled	gegrillt
marinated	mariniert
roasted	geröstet
poached	pochiert
sautéed	geköchelt
steamed	gedämpft
stewed	in der Sauce geschmort

Vegetables	Gemüse
Artichoke	die Artischocke
Asparagus	der Spargel
Beans	die Bohnen
Beets	die roten Beeteh
Cabbage	der Kohl
Carrots	die Karotten/die Möhren/die Wurzeln
Cauliflower	der Blumenkohl
Celery	der Sellerie
Corn	der Mais

Cucumbers	die Gurken
Eggplant	die Aubergine
Leek	der Lettich
Lettuce	der grüne Salat
Lentils	die Linsen
Mushrooms	die Pilze
Onions	die Zwiebeln
Peas	die Erbsen
Potatoes	die Kartoffeln
Spinach	der Spinat
Tomato	die Tomate
Turnips	die Rüben
Zucchini	die Zucchini

Herbs and Spices — Kräuter und Gewürze

Anise	der Anis
Basil	das Basilikum
Bay leaf	das Lorbeerblatt
Capers	die Kapern
Caraway	der Kümmel
Chives	der Schnittlauch
Cinnamon	der Zimt
Dill	der Dill
Garlic	der Knoblauch
Ginger	der Ingwer
Marjoram	der Majoran
Mint	die Minze
Nutmeg	die Muskatnuss
Oregano	der Oregano
Parsley	die Petersilie
Pepper	der Pfeffer
Pimento	das Piment
Rosemary	der Rosmarin
Saffron	der Safran
Sage	der Salbei
Tarragon	der Estragon
Thyme	der Thymian

I would like my potato . . .	Ich möchte die Kartoffeln . . .
baked.	gebacken.
boiled.	gekocht./
	Salzkartoffeln.
creamed.	in Sahnesauce.
french fried.	als Pommes Frites.
mashed.	als Kartoffelbrei.
pureed.	als Püree.

Fruits — Obst

Apple	der Apfel
Apricot	die Aprikose
Banana	die Banane
Blueberries	die Blaubeeren
Cherries	die Kirschen
Dates	die Datteln
Figs	die Feigen
Grapes	die Trauben
Grapefruit	die Pampelmuse
Kiwi	die Kiwi
Mango	die Mango
Melon	die Melone
Nectarine	die Nektarine
Orange	die Orange/Apfelsine
Peach	der Pfirsich
Pear	die Birne
Pineapple	die Ananas
Plum	die Pflaume
Prune	die Pflaume
Raisins	die Rosinen
Raspberries	die Himbeeren
Strawberries	die Erdbeeren
Watermelon	die Wassermelone

Nuts — Nüsse

Almonds	die Mandeln
Cashews	die Cashewnüsse

Chestnuts	die Kastanien
Hazelnuts	die Haselnüsse
Peanuts	die Erdnüsse
Pistachios	die Pistazien

In Germany, it is considered bad table manners to keep a hand underneath the table. Both hands should be on the table, or at least visible, at all times.

"Ordering Dessert"
FRAU KLEIN: *Herr Ober, wir möchten gern eine Nachspeise bestellen.*
FRAU JONAS: *Haben Sie irgendwelche Spezialitäten?*
OBER: *Ja, wir haben heißen Apfelstrudel mit Schlagsahne und Schwarzwälder Kirschtorte.*
FRAU JONAS: *Ich nehme das erste.*
FRAU KLEIN: *Hört sich gut an. Ich nehme das gleiche.*

"Ordering Dessert"
MS. KLEIN: *Waiter, we would like to order dessert.*
MS. JONAS: *Do you have any specialties?*
WAITER: *Yes, we have hot apple strudel with whipped cream and we have Black Forest cake.*
MS. JONAS: *I'll have the first.*
MS. KLEIN: *Sounds good. I'll have the same.*

| Would you like to order dessert? | **Möchten Sie eine Nachspeise bestellen?** |
| No, I think I've had enough. | **Nein, ich habe genug gegessen.** |

Yes, do you have a dessert menu?	Ja, haben Sie eine Nachspeisenkarte?
Yes, I would like to order . . .	Ja, ich hätte gern . . .
a piece of cake.	ein Stück Torte/Kuchen.
ice cream.	Eis.
We have . . .	Wir haben . . .
chocolate ice cream.	Schokoladeneis.
strawberry ice cream.	Erdbeereis.
sorbet.	Sorbet.
vanilla ice cream . . .	Vanilleeis.
Would you like to have some coffee?	**Möchten Sie gern Kaffee?**
No thank you.	Nein danke.
Yes, I would like . . .	**Ja, ich möchte gern . . .**
coffee.	**einen Kaffee.**
espresso.	einen Espresso.
cappuccino.	einen Cappuccino.
tea.	einen Tee.
Would you like your coffee . . .	Möchten Sie Ihren Kaffee . . .
black?	schwarz?
with cream?	mit Sahne?
with milk?	mit Milch?
Do you have decaffeinated coffee?	**Haben Sie koffeinfreien Kaffee?**
What kind of tea?	Was für einen Tee?
Black	schwarzen
Earl Grey	Earl Grey
English breakfast	English Breakfast
Green	grünen
Oolong	Oolong
Do you have . . .	**Haben Sie . . .**
cream?	**Sahne?**
a sweetener?	**Süßstoff**
sugar?	Zucker?

Every announced price has to be an end price in Germany, so additional charges are not allowed under German law. The prices on restaurant menus include service and tax. However, keep in mind that most waiters are paid little in Germany and depend on tips. In regular restaurants it is appropriate to leave a few marks (round up the bill to the next five or zero); in better restaurants a ten to fifteen percent tip is common. More than ten percent is considered very generous and would only be appropriate if the food and the service were outstanding.

Paying the Bill

Bill please!	**Die Rechnung bitte!**
Allow me to pay the bill.	**Erlauben Sie mir die Rechnung zu zahlen.**
Please be my guest.	**Bitte seien Sie mein Gast.**
Is service included?	Ist die Bedienung eingeschlossen?
Do you take credit cards?	**Nehmen Sie Kreditkarten?**
Which credit cards do you take?	Welche Kreditkarten nehmen Sie?
Can I pay by check/ traveler's check?	Kann ich mit Scheck/Reisescheck zahlen?

A lunch or dinner with German business people might seem a lot more formal than in United States. Keep in mind that Germans are generally not as outgoing as Americans. In most cases, however, Germans appreciate and even admire the social behavior of Americans.

Complaints

I didn't order this.	**Das habe ich nicht bestellt.**
What is this item on the bill?	Was ist dies hier auf der Rechnung?
This is too cold.	**Das ist zu kalt.**
This must be a mistake.	**Da muß Ihnen ein Fehler unterlaufen sein.**
May I see the headwaiter please?	Kann ich bitte den Oberkellner sprechen?

The Rest Room

Where is the rest room/lavatory?	**Wo ist das WC/die Toilette?**
Where is the men's room?	Wo ist die Herrentoilette?
Where is the ladies' room?	Wo ist die Damentoilette?

SOCIAL CONVERSATION

Caution here—in some cultures there is little business discussed during the main part of dinner, only during coffee. In others, there is no prohibition against discussing business at any time. Follow the lead of your hosts or ask if it's proper.

"Eine kurze Unterhaltung"

FRAU WENDEL: *So, wie war Ihr Flug?*
FRAU JONAS: *Er war recht gut.*
FRAU WENDEL: *Könnten Sie im Flugzeug schlafen?*
FRAU JONAS: *Ja, es gab keine Turbulenzen. Was für ein großartiges Wetter Sie hier haben.*
FRAU WENDEL: *Ja, wir mögen diese Jahreszeit sehr.*
FRAU WENDEL: *Lassen Sie uns etwas essen gehen, ja?*
FRAU JONAS: *Ich bin fast am verhungern.*

"A Social Conversation"

MS. WENDEL: *So, how was your flight?*

MS. JONAS: *It was just fine.*

MS. WENDEL: *Were you able to sleep on the plane?*

MS. JONAS: *Yes. It was a smooth flight. What great weather you have here!*

MS. WENDEL: *Yes. We enjoy this time of year.*

MS. WENDEL: *Let's go eat, shall we?*

MS. JONAS: *I'm starving.*

Key Words

Children	*die Kinder*
Family	*die Familie*
Hobby	*das Hobby*
Husband	*der Ehemann*
Interests	*die Interessen*
Sports	*der Sport*
Weather	*das Wetter*
Wife	*die Ehefrau*

Soccer (*Fußball*) is the national sport in Germany, and many German business people can and will forget business over it. If there is a major game, don't expect to be able to do any business—at least not in the evening when most games take place.

Please tell me about your . . .	Bitte erzählen Sie mir etwas über . . .
I'd like to hear about your . . .	**Ich möchte gern etwas wissen über . . .**
child/children.	**Ihr Kind/Ihre Kinder.**
daughter(s).	Ihre Tochter/Töchter.
family.	Ihre Familie.

grandparents.	Ihre Großeltern.
husband.	Ihren Ehemann.
parents.	Ihre Eltern.
son(s).	Ihren Sohn/Ihre Söhne.
wife.	Ihre Ehefrau.

Germans tend not to ask personal questions in a business context. So be careful in how you approach these issues.

Please give your family my regards.	**Bitte grüßen Sie die Familie von mir.**
How do you spend your weekends?	Wie verbringen Sie Ihre Wochenenden.
Do you like to garden?	Arbeiten Sie gern im Garten?
Do you have pets?	Haben Sie Haustiere?
I have a . . .	Ich habe . . .
cat.	eine Katze.
dog.	einen Hund.
horse.	ein Pferd.
Do you like sports?	**Gefällt Ihnen Sport?**
Yes, I like . . .	**Ja, mir gefällt . . .**
basketball.	**Basketball.**
football.	amerikanischer Fußball.
karate.	Karate.
ping pong.	Tischtennis.
rugby.	Rugby.
skiing.	Skifahren.
scuba.	Tauchen.
soccer.	Fußball.
Are you interested in . . .	**Haben Sie Interesse an . . .**
art?	**Kunst?**
books?	Büchern?

111

classical music?	klassischer Musik?
film?	Film?
history?	Geschichte?
hobbies?	Hobbies?
movies?	Filmen?
museums?	Museen?
music?	Musik?
opera?	Oper?
philosophy?	Philosophie?
plays?	Theaterstücken?

Saying Goodbye

The food was excellent.	**Das Essen war ausgezeichnet.**
Will it be difficult to find a taxi?	Ist es schwer ein Taxi zu finden?
Please excuse me, but I must go.	**Entschuldigen Sie bitte, aber ich muß gehen.**
Thank you for a wonderful evening.	**Vielen Dank für den ausgezeichneten Abend.**
I enjoyed very much our conversation.	Ich habe unsere Unterhaltung sehr genossen.
It was nice talking to you.	**Es war sehr nett, mich mit Ihnen zu unterhalten.**
I look forward to seeing you . . .	**Ich freue mich auf unser Treffen . . .**
at the office.	**im Büro.**
tomorrow.	morgen.
tomorrow morning.	morgen früh.
tomorrow night.	morgen Abend.
Please be my guest tomorrow night.	Morgen Abend werden Sie mein Gast sein.
It will be my pleasure.	Es wird mir ein Vergnügen sein.
Good night.	Schönen Abend.

The expression *Gute Nacht!* (Good night!) is only used right before you go to sleep. To wish somebody a nice (rest of) the evening just say *Schönen Abend!* (Have a nice evening!), which is not to be confused with *Guten Abend!* (Good evening!) to be used when you meet someone in the evening hours.

SPORTING EVENTS, MOVIES, THEATER, AND CLUBS

Do you have an evening or weekend free? Then enjoy the country you're visiting. Don't just eat at the hotel restaurant and watch television in your room. Get out.

Part of doing business in another culture is to learn and appreciate what that culture has to offer. What you learn can get you closer to your business contacts.

Finally, seeing a movie, going to the theater, or seeing a sporting event can be a welcome break from an arduous business day.

"Im Theater"

HERR SANDER: *Dieses Musical wird Ihnen gefallen. Es ist eine Liebesgeschichte.*
HERR JONAS: *Ist es sehr bekannt?*
HERR SANDER: *Nein, aber die Musik ist sehr schön. Es wird wahrscheinlich im nächsten Monat schließen.*
HERR JONAS: *Nun, dann lassen Sie es uns anschauen.*

"At the Theater"

MR. SANDER: *You'll like this musical. It's a love story.*

113

MR. JONAS: *Is it a popular one?*
MR. SANDER: *No, but it has very nice music. It may close next month.*
MR. JONAS: *Well, then, let's go see it.*

Being late for music, opera, or theater performances is not tolerated in Germany. If you are just a few minutes late, you will have to wait until the next major applause or even until the break. There is no formal dress code to visit any theater, opera, or concert hall, but dressing up for the occasion is very common.

Key Words

Program	das Programm
Teams	die Mannschaften
Ticket(s)	die Eintrittskarte(n)
What's playing?	Was wird gespielt?
Who's playing?	Wer spielt?

I would like to go to a . . .	Ich möchte gern zu einem . . .
basketball game.	Basketballspiel.
boxing match.	Boxkampf.
soccer match.	Fußballspiel.
tennis match.	Tennisspiel.
How much do tickets cost?	Wieviel kostet der Eintritt?
I would like one/two tickets.	Ich möchte gern eine/zwei Eintrittskarte(n).
When does the match/play/movie begin?	Wann beginnt das Spiel/die Vorstellung/der Film?

Who's playing?	Wer spielt?
What are the teams?	Was sind die Mannschaften?
May I buy a program?	Kann ich ein Programm kaufen?

I would like to go to the . . .	Ich möchte gern . . .
ballet.	ins Ballett.
cinema.	ins Kino.
concert.	ins Konzert.
museum.	ins Museum.
movies.	in einen Film.
opera.	in die Oper.
theater.	ins Theater.

I would like a seat in the . . .	Ich möchte gern einen Platz . . .
balcony.	im zweiten Rang.
box seats.	in der Loge.
front row.	in der ersten Reihe.
gallery.	im obersten Rang.
mezzanine.	im ersten Rang.
orchestra.	im Parkett.

I would like to see a . . .	Ich möchte gern . . .
action movie.	einen Abenteuerfilm sehen.
comedy.	eine Komödie sehen.
drama.	ein Drama sehen.
love story.	eine Liebesgeschichte anschauen.
musical.	ein Musical sehen.
mystery.	einen Krimi sehen.
romance.	einen romantischen Film sehen.
science fiction.	einen Science-Fiction-Film sehen.
western.	einen Western sehen.

115

Does the film have English subtitles?	Hat dieser Film englische Untertitel?
May I have a program please?	Kann ich bitte ein Programm bekommen?
What's playing at the opera tonight?	Was wird heute Abend in der Oper aufgeführt?
Who is the conductor?	Wer ist der Dirigent?
I would like to go to a . . . disco. jazz club. jazz concert. nightclub.	Ich möchte gern in . . . eine Diskothek. einen Jazzclub. ein Jazzkonzert. einen Nachtclub.
I'd like to go dancing.	Ich möchte gern tanzen gehen.
Would you like to dance?	Möchten Sie gern tanzen?
Is there a cover charge?	Gibt es Getränkeeintritt/ein Mindestgedeck?
Is there a floor show?	Gibt es eine Vorstellung?
What time does the floor show start?	Um wieviel Uhr beginnt die Vorstellung?

Participatory Sports

Is there a gym in the hotel?	Gibt es ein Fitnesscenter im Hotel?
Where is the closest gym?	Wo ist das nächste Fitnesscenter?
Is there a place to jog?	Wo kann ich hier joggen?
Where is the pool? Is it heated?	Wo ist der Swimmingpool? Ist er geheizt?
Are there towels?	Gibt es dort Handtücher?
I would like to play . . . golf. racquetball.	Ich möchte gern . . . Golf spielen. Rackettball spielen.

116

tennis.	Tennis spielen.
volleyball.	Volleyball spielen.

I would like to visit a . . .	Ich möchte . . .
beach.	an den Strand gehen
lake.	an einen See.

Is swimming allowed?	Ist das Schwimmen gestattet?
Are there life guards?	Gibt es Rettungsschwimmer?

Are there . . .	Gibt es . . .
beach chairs	Strandkörbe . . .
rowboats	Ruderboote . . .
sailboats	Segelboote . . .
towels	Handtücher . . .
umbrellas	Sonnenschirme . . . (for sun only)
for rent?	zu mieten?

Are there changing rooms?	Gibt es Umkleidekabinen?

And don't forget to bring . . .	Und vergessen Sie nicht, . . .
sunglasses.	eine Sonnenbrille . . .
suntan lotion.	Sonnenschutz . . .
	. . . mitzubringen.

I would like to go . . .	Ich möchte gern . . .
ice-skating.	Schlittschuh laufen.
skiing.	Ski fahren.
cross-country skiing.	Skilanglauf machen.

VISITING THE PARTNER'S OR ASSOCIATE'S HOME

Here's a chance to get closer to a business host or associate. Check with your contacts or the hotel concierge if flowers or gifts are appropriate. In some cultures, flowers for the wife can be misunderstood. Usually, a gift from home is safe and most welcome.

If your host has children, bringing a small present for them is the best move.

"Zu Hause"

FRAU HEIDER: *Willkommen bei uns!*
FRAU JONAS: *Vielen Dank für die Einladung.*
FRAU HEIDER: *Das ist mein Mann Heinz.*
FRAU JONAS: *Sehr nett Sie kennenzulernen.*
FRAU HEIDER: *Und hier sind unsere beiden Kinder, Iris und Michael.*
FRAU JONAS: *Hier sind ein paar kleine Geschenke für die Kinder.*
FRAU HEIDER: *Das ist sehr aufmerksam von Ihnen. Lassen Sie uns ins Wohnzimmer gehen.*

"At the Home"

MRS. HEIDER: *Welcome to our home.*
MS. JONAS: *Thank you for having me.*
MRS. HEIDER: *This is my husband, Heinz.*
MS. JONAS: *Very nice to meet you.*
MRS. HEIDER: *And, here are our two children, Iris und Michael.*
MS. JONAS: *Here are small gifts for your children.*
MRS. HEIDER: *That's very thoughtful of you. Let's move into the living room.*

If you are invited for dinner to someone's home, keep in mind that punctuality is very important in Germany. If your host invited you for 7:30 P.M., don't be even ten minutes late, or you might miss the appetizers.

If you are the host of a dinner party, don't step out of the shower at seven, if you've invited your German associates for that time. They are most likely to be at your door at seven o'clock sharp. Of course, this does not apply to open parties or receptions.

This is my wife/husband.	**Das ist meine Frau/mein Mann.**
This is our child.	**Das ist unser Kind.**
These are our children.	Das sind unsere Kinder.
This is our pet cat/dog.	Das ist unser(e) Hauskatze/ Haushund.
Here is a small gift (from the United States).	**Hier ist ein kleines Geschenk (aus Amerika).**
Make yourself at home.	**Machen Sie es sich gemütlich.**
What a pretty house. What a beautiful house you have.	**Was für ein schönes Haus.** Was für ein wundereschönes Haus Sie haben.
This is a very nice neighborhood.	Das ist eine sehr nette Gegend hier.
Please sit here. Please take a seat. Please come in the dining room.	**Bitte setzen Sie sich hierher.** Bitte nehmen Sie Platz. Bitte kommen Sie ins Esszimmer.
Would you like a drink before dinner?	**Möchten Sie einen Drink vor dem Essen?**
Dinner was great.	**Das Essen war großartig.**
It was a pleasure having you in our home.	Es war uns ein Vergnügen, Sie als Gast zu haben.
Thank you for inviting me to your home.	**Vielen Dank für die Einladung.**

 It is nice to bring flowers for the hostess, but don't bring red roses, carnations, or chrysanthemums as they all have special symbolic value that is not appropriate for the situation. Chocolates or nicely wrapped candy used to be common, but in the age of weight watching it is becoming less and less popular. If there are children in the house, an original, non-political and non-harmful toy might be appropriate. Don't bring candy for the children!

SIGHTSEEING

"An der Hotelrezeption"
HERR JONAS: *Welche Sehenswürdigkeiten sollte man hier gesehen haben?*
REZEPTIONIST: *Da wäre das Museum und die Katakomben.*
HERR JONAS: *Wo sind die?*
REZEPTIONIST: *Das Museum ist nur drei Straßen von hier, aber die Katakomben sind auf der anderen Seite der Stadt. Sie müssen ein Taxi nehmen um dort hinzukommen.*
HERR JONAS: *Ich werde die Katakomben besichtigen. Können Sie mir ein Taxi besorgen?*

"At the Hotel Reception"
MR. JONAS: *What kinds of sights are worthwhile to see here?*
HOTEL CLERK: *There is the museum and there are the catacombs.*
MR. JONAS: *Where are they?*
HOTEL CLERK: *The museum is only three blocks from here, but the catacombs are on the other side of the city. You need a taxi to get to them.*
MR. JONAS: *I'll go and see the catacombs. Can you get me a taxi?*

What are the main attractions?	**Was sind die Hauptsehenswürdigkeiten?**
Do you have a guidebook of the city?	**Haben Sie einen Stadtführer?**
Do you have a map of the city?	Haben Sie einen Stadtplan?
Is there a tour of the city?	**Gibt es eine Stadtrundfahrt?**
Where does it leave from?	**Wo beginnt sie?**
How much is it?	**Wieviel kostet sie?**
How long is it?	Wie lange dauert sie?
I would like to see . . .	Ich möchte gern . . .
an amusement park.	einen Vergnügungspark besuchen.
an aquarium.	ein Aquarium besuchen.
an art gallery.	eine Kunstgalerie anschauen.
a botanical garden.	einen botanischen Garten sehen.
a castle.	ein Schloß sehen.
a cathedral.	eine Kathedrale/einen Dom sehen.
a cave.	eine Höhle besichtigen.
a church.	eine Kirche besuchen.
a flea market.	einen Flohmarkt besuchen.
a library.	eine Bibliothek besuchen.
a museum.	ein Museum besichtigen.
a park.	einen Park besuchen.
a planetarium.	ein Planetarium besuchen.
a synagogue.	eine Synagoge besuchen.
a zoo.	einen Zoo besuchen.
When does the museum open?	Wann öffnet das Museum?
How much is the admission?	Wieviel kostet der Eintritt.
Do you have an English guide?	Haben Sie einen Englischführer?

Sightseeing

GETTING OUT

Do you have an audio guide?	Haben Sie einen Audioführer?
May I take photographs?	Darf ich fotografieren?
I do not use flashbulbs.	Ich benutze kein Blitzlicht.
I would like to visit the lake.	Ich möchte gern an den See fahren.
Can I take a bus there?	Kann ich einen Bus dorthin nehmen?
Which bus do I take?	Welchen Bus muss ich nehmen?
How long is the ride?	Wie lange dauert die Fahrt?

SHOPPING

 The malls of Germany are the so called *Fußgängerzonen* (pedestrian zones). These often include entire streets, many with a glass roof. All prices are actual prices. No additional charges or taxes are allowed by law. Most stores close in the early evening and don't open at all on Sundays.

I'm looking for a . . .	Ich suche nach einem . . .
bookstore.	Buchhandel.
camera store.	Fotogeschäft.
clothing store.	Bekleidungsgeschäft.
department store.	Kaufhaus.
flower shop.	Blumenladen.
hardware store.	Haushaltswarengeschäft/ Werkzeugladen.
health-food store.	Bioladen.
jewelry store.	Juwelier/Schmuckgeschäft.
leather-goods store.	Lederwarengeschäft.
liquor store.	Geschäft für alkoholische Getränke. (*available in every supermarket*)
newsstand.	Zeitungsstand.

record store.	Musikgeschäft/ Musikladen.
shoe store.	Schuhgeschäft.
shopping center.	Einkaufszentrum.
souvenir shop.	Souvenirladen.
stationer.	Schreibwarengeschäft.
tobacco store.	Tabakwarengeschäft.
toy store.	Spielwarengeschäft.
I would like to find a . . .	Ich suche nach einem . . .
jeweler.	Juwelier.
photographer.	Fotografen.
shoemaker.	Schuster.
tailor.	Schneider.
Can you help me?	Können Sie mir behilflich sein?
Can you show me . . .	Können Sie mir . . . zeigen?
I'm just browsing.	Ich möchte mich nur umsehen.
I'd like to buy . . .	Ich möchte . . . kaufen.
How much does it cost?	Wieviel kostet das?
How much is this in dollars?	Wieviel ist das in Dollar?
Can you write down the price?	Würden Sie den Preis aufschreiben?
Do you have a less/more expensive one?	Haben Sie etwas Preiswerteres/Teureres?
Where do I pay?	Wo kann ich zahlen?
Can you gift wrap this?	Können Sie das als Geschenk einpacken?
I'd like to return this.	Ich möchte das hier umtauschen.
Here is my receipt.	Hier ist meine Quittung.

Many reputable department stores in Germany also have large gourmet food departments where you can sample food or buy many international and American brand products as well. The quality is usually excellent.

4 GETTING AROUND

From your originating flight, a stop over to two, customs at your destination, taxis and rental cars at the airport, to getting to your hotel and having to speak in a foreign tongue—this can be a trying time. Then too, you may need to find a cash machine or a bank, and maybe find a post office or a local FedEx or UPS center. We're here to help.

Don't underestimate jet lag. The seasoned traveler knows how to best handle this. But, for the first-time business traveler this can be a surprise. The excitement of new places and new contacts may temporarily mask it, but jet lag is the response of the body to a change of the daily waking-sleeping routine. It manifests itself as tiredness and sometimes disorientation. Best advice is to try to get some sleep on your flight and try not to rush into a meeting just after you land.

In this chapter, we cover:

We hope you'll not need them, but just in case, we list the words you may need in an emergency.

CAN YOU HELP ME?

Excuse me.	**Entschuldigung.**
Could you help me?	**Können Sie mir helfen?**
Yes./No.	**Ja./**Nein.
I'm sorry.	**Tut mir leid.**
Thank you very much.	Vielen Dank.
Do you speak English?	**Sprechen Sie Englisch?**
Do you understand English?	**Verstehen Sie Englisch?**
Do you know where the American Embassy is?	**Wissen Sie, wo die amerikanische Botschaft ist?**
I don't speak much German.	Ich spreche nicht viel Deutsch.
I don't understand.	**Ich verstehe nicht.**
Repeat please.	**Würden Sie das bitte wiederholen?**
Please speak more slowly.	**Bitte sprechen Sie etwas langsamer.**
Could you write that down please?	**Würden Sie das bitte aufschreiben?**
Spell it please.	Buchstabieren Sie bitte.
Where is the business center?	Wo ist das Geschäftszentrum/ Business-Center?
Where are the telephones?	**Wo sind die Telefone?**
Where are the rest rooms?	**Wo sind die Toiletten?**
Where is the men's bathroom/lavatory?	Wo ist die Herrentoilette/das Herren-WC?
Where is the women's bathroom/lavatory?	Wo ist die Damentoilette/das Damen-WC?

AIRPLANES, AIRPORTS, AND CUSTOMS

"Durch den Zoll"

ZOLLBEAMTER: *Sind das Ihre Taschen?*

HERR JONAS: *Ja, diese beiden. Gibt es ein Problem?*

ZOLLBEAMTER: *Öffnen Sie sie.*

HERR JONAS: *Nur Anzüge und Unterwäsche. Und meine Harmonika. Ich spiele gern darauf im Hotelzimmer, wenn ich auf Reisen bin.*

ZOLLBEAMTER: *Sie können gehen.*

"Getting Through Customs"

CUSTOMS OFFICIAL: *Are these your bags?*

MR. JONES: *Yes, these two. Is there a problem?*

CUSTOMS OFFICIAL: *Open them.*

MR. JONES: *Just suits and underwear. Plus my harmonica. I like to play it in the hotel room when I travel.*

CUSTOMS OFFICIAL: *You may go.*

Key Words

Arrivals	die Ankunft
Baggage pick-up area	die Gepäckabholung/das Gepäckband
Customs	der Zoll
Departure	der Abflug (plane)/die Abfahrt (train, bus)
Domestic flights	die Inlandsflüge
Gate	der Flugsteig
International flights	internationale Flüge
Make a reservation (to)	eine Reservierung machen

Passport	*der Pass*
Take a taxi (to)	*ein Taxi nehmen*
Ticket	*das Ticket/die Flugkarte* (plane)/*die Fahrkarte* (train/bus)

Here is/are my . . .

documents.
identification card.
passport.
ticket.

I need to buy . . .
a business-class ticket.

an economy ticket.

a first-class ticket.

a round-trip ticket.

a single/one-way ticket.

I'd like to . . . my
reservation.
cancel
change
confirm

I need to change my
reservation.

I need to change my seat.

May I have a smoking/
non-smoking seat?

Hier ist mein . . . /Hier sind
meine . . .
Papiere.
Personalausweis.
Pass.
Ticket/Flugkarte/Fahrkarte.

Ich muß . . .
**ein Ticket für die Business-
Klasse kaufen.**
ein Ticket für die
Touristenklasse kaufen.
ein Ticket erster
Klasse kaufen.
ein Ticket hin und
zurück kaufen.
ein einfaches Ticket kaufen.

**Ich möchte gern meine
Reservierung . . .
stornieren.**
ändern.
bestätigen.

**Ich muss meine Reservierung
ändern.**

Ich muss meinen Sitzplatz
ändern.
Kann ich einen Sitzplatz im
Raucher-/Nichtraucherabteil
bekommen?

May I have an aisle/ window seat?	**Kann ich einen Platz am Gang/**Fensterplatz **bekommen?**
Is there a direct flight to Berlin?	Gibt es einen Direktflug nach Berlin?
Is there an earlier/later flight?	Gibt es einen früheren/ späteren Flug?

While many more people smoke in Germany than in the United States, smoking is mostly banned in public transportation. When in company, do not expect others to ask you for permission to smoke. Because smoking is much more common, failing to do so is not considered to be rude in Germany.

AT THE HOTEL

"Das richtige Zimmer"

FRAU JANKE: *Der Schlüssel zu meinem Zimmer passt nicht.*

ANGESTELLTER: *Das tut mit leid, gnädige Frau. Ich habe Ihnen den falschen Schlüssel gegeben. Ich muss Ihnen ein anderes Zimmer geben. Dieses Zimmer ist bereits vergeben.*

FRAU JANKE: *Können Sie mir denn ein Zimmer mit Blick geben?*

ANGESTELLTER: *Ja, ich denke dieses Zimmer wird Ihnen gefallen. Ich bitte um Verzeihung für diese Unannehmlichkeit.*

"Getting the Right Room"

MS. JANKE: *This key to my room won't work.*

CLERK: *I'm sorry madam, I gave you the wrong key. In fact, I have to give you a different room. That one is actually taken.*

MS. JANKE: *Could you then give me a room with a view?*
CLERK: *Yes, I think you will enjoy this room. Sorry for the unpleasantness.*

Key Words

Bag(s)/Luggage	die Tasche(n)/das Gepäck
Bath	das Bad
Confirmation	die Bestätigung
Credit card	die Kreditkarte
Hotel	das Hotel
Reservation	die Reservierung
Room	das Zimmer

I have a reservation in the name of Schulz.	**Ich habe eine Reservierung auf den Namen Schulz.**
Here is my confirmation.	**Hier ist meine Bestätigung.**
How much are your rooms?	**Wieviel kosten Ihre Zimmer?**
What is the price for a double room?	Was kostet ein Doppelzimmer?
Do you take credit cards?	**Nehmen Sie Kreditkarten?**
Which credit cards do you take?	Welche Kreditkarten nehmen Sie?
Do you have any rooms available?	Haben Sie Zimmer frei?
Could you recommend any other hotels?	**Können Sie ein anderes Hotel empfehlen?**
I'd like . . .	Ich möchte . . .
a room for one/two night(s).	ein Zimmer für eine Nacht/zwei Nächte.
a single/double room.	ein Einzelzimmer/ Doppelzimmer.

a room with a private bath.	ein Zimmer mit separatem Bad.
a room with a queen-/ king-size bed.	ein Zimmer mit französischem/extra großem Doppelbett.
a suite.	eine Suite.

I need . . .

a wake-up call.	**Ich möchte geweckt werden.**
a late check-out.	Iche möchte spät auschecken.
a fax machine.	**Ich brauche ein Faxgerät.**
a telephone.	Ich brauche ein Telefon.
an Internet connection.	Ich brauche Internet-Zugang.

Is there . . .   **Gibt es . . .**

a business center?	**ein Geschäftszentrum?**
an Internet connection in my room?	Zugang zum Internet in meinem Zimmer?
an exercise room?	einen Fitnessraum?
a gym?	ein Fitnesscenter?
a Jacuzzi?	einen Whirlpool?
a photocopier?	einen Kopierer?
a printer?	einen Drucker?
a restaurant in the hotel?	ein Restaurant im Hotel?
a swimming pool?	einen Swimmingpool?

Can a porter take my bags up to the room?	**Kann ein Page meine Taschen auf das Zimmer bringen?**
May I leave my bags?	**Kann ich meine Taschen hierlassen?**
Are there any messages for me?	**Gibt es irgendwelche Nachrichten für mich?**
May I see the room?	Darf ich das Zimmer ansehen?
We want adjacent rooms.	Wir möchten Anschlusszimmer.

131

You might have the following problems . . .

The room/bathroom needs cleaning.	Das Zimmer/Bad muss gesäubert werden.
I need more towels/ blankets.	Ich brauche mehr Handtücher/Decken.
The room is too small.	Das Zimmer ist zu klein.
I did not receive my newspaper.	Ich habe meine Zeitung nicht bekommen.
The room is too noisy.	Das Zimmer ist zu laut.
The door will not open.	Die Tür lässt sich nicht öffnen.
The door will not lock.	Die Tür lässt sich nicht abschließen.
The telephone does not work.	Das Telefon funktioniert nicht.
The heating/air-conditioning is not working.	Die Heizung/Klimaanlage funktioniert nicht.
Can you put the heat up?	Können Sie die Heizung höher stellen?
How do I make a telephone call?	Wie mache ich einen Telefonanruf?
How do I make a local/ international telephone call?	Wie führe ich ein Ortsgespräch/Ferngespräch?
I need room service.	Ich möchte Room Service.
I'd like to order dinner to my room.	Ich möchte Abendessen auf mein Zimmer bestellen.
I need laundry service.	Ich brauche einen Wäscheservice.
I need these shirts/suits cleaned overnight.	Ich muss diese Hemden/ Anzüge über Nacht reinigen lassen.
Can I have these clothes cleaned/laundered today?	Kann ich diese Kleidungsstücke heute reinigen/waschen lassen?
Can you have this stain removed?	Können Sie diesen Fleck entfernen?

How much does it cost to have this cleaned/laundered?	Wieviel kostet es, das hier reinigen/waschen zu lassen?
Can I extend my stay one/two day(s)?	Kann ich meinen Aufenthalt um einen Tag/zwei Tage verlängern?
Can I have a late check-out?	Kann ich spät auschecken?
Can I leave my bags at the reception desk after check out?	Kann ich mein Gepäck nach dem Auschecken an der Rezeption lassen?
I want to check out.	Ich möchte auschecken.
May I have my bill?	Kann ich meine Rechnung bekommen?
There is a problem with my bill.	Es gibt ein Problem mit meiner Rechnung.
What is this charge for?	Wofür ist dieser Betrag?
Is there an airport shuttle?	Gibt es einen Flughafenbus?
What time does it leave?	Wann fährt er ab?
What time is the next one?	Wann fährt der nächste?
I would like a taxi.	Ich hätte gern ein Taxi.

CAR RENTALS

Cars with an automatic transmission are becoming more popular in Germany, but the traditional stick shift is still the rule. Make sure that you indicate what type of transmission you want when reserving a car, otherwise you will get a stick shift.

"Einen Automatik mieten"
HERR SCHMAL: *Hat dieses Auto Automatik-Schaltung?*
ANGESTELLTER: *Nein. Brauchen Sie die?*

HERR SCHMAL: *Ja. Sie können auf meiner Bestätigung sehen, dass ich das ausdrücklich verlangt habe.*

ANGESTELLTER: *Ja, ich sehe das. Es gibt aber ein kleines Problem. Es dauert ungefähr eine Stunde bis wir einen zur Verfügung haben.*

HERR SCHMAL: *Ich warte. Ich weiß nicht, wie man ein Auto mit Gangschaltung fährt.*

"Getting an Automatic Shift"

MR. SCHMAL: *Does this car have an automatic shift?*

CLERK: *No. Did you need that?*

MR. SCHMAL: *Yes. You can see from my confirmation that I specifically requested it.*

CLERK: *Yes, I see that. However, there is a slight problem. We won't have one for about one hour.*

MR. SCHMAL: *I will wait. I don't know how to drive a stick shift.*

Key Words

Automatic shift	Automatik-Schaltung/der Automatik (refers to entire car)
Car	das Auto/der Wagen
Directions	die Anweisungen
Driver's license	der Führerschein
Gas	das Benzin
Gas station	die Tankstelle
Insurance	die Versicherung
Map	die Karte/die Straßenkarte
Stick shift	Gangschaltung

I need to rent a car.	Ich möchte/muss ein Auto mieten.
Here is my reservation number.	Hier ist meine Reservierungsnummer.
Here is my driver's license.	Hier ist mein Führerschein.
I need . . .	Ich möchte/brauche . . .
air-conditioning.	eine Klimaanlage.
an automatic shift.	einen Automatik.
a compact.	einen Kleinwagen.
a convertible	einen offenen Wagen.
an intermediate.	einen Mittelklassewagen.
a luxury.	einen Luxuswagen.
a mid-sized car.	einen mittelgroßen Wagen.
a stick shift.	einen Wagen mit Gangschaltung.
Is insurance included?	Ist die Versicherung eingeschlossen?
How much is the insurance?	Wieviel kostet die Versicherung?
I want full insurance.	Ich möchte die volle Versicherung.
How is the mileage charged?	Wieviel Kilometergeld berechnen Sie?
Is there unlimited mileage?	Gibt es unbegrenzte Kilometerzahl?
Is gas included?	Ist das Benzin eingeschlossen?
Do I need to fill the tank when I return?	Muss ich tanken, bevor ich den Wagen zurückbringe?
Is there a drop-off charge?	Berechnen Sie eine Rückgabegebühr?
Which credit cards do you take?	Welche Kreditkarten nehmen Sie?

May I pay by check?	Kann ich mit Scheck bezahlen?[13]
I need a map.	**Ich brauche eine Karte.**
I need directions.	**Ich brauche eine Wegbeschreibung.**
Can you help me find . . .	Können Sie mir helfen . . . finden?
How do I get to . . .	Wie komme ich . . .
the airport?	zum Flughafen?
a bank?	zu einer Bank?
a gas station?	zu einer Tankstelle?
the hotel?	zum Hotel?
a good restaurant?	zu einem guten Restaurant?
Is this the road to . . . ?	**Ist dies die Straße nach/ zu . . . ?**
Turn right/left.	**Biegen Sie rechts ab/links ab.**
Go straight ahead.	**Fahren Sie geradeaus.**
Turn around.	**Kehren Sie um.**
Go two traffic lights and turn right/left.	Biegen Sie nach der zweiten Ampel rechts/links ab.
Opposite	gegenüber
U-turn	die Wende
Next to	neben
Fill it up please.	**Volltanken, bitte.**
I need . . .	Ich brauche . . .
diesel.	Diesel.
regular.	Normalbenzin.
supreme.	Super.
unleaded.	Bleifrei

There is no unleaded gasoline in Germany. The four types available are diesel, normal, super, and extra-super. If you are not sure which one

---

[13]Regular bank checks are not accepted in Germany when paying directly.

is the right gasoline for your car, get super. It's the most common.

Could you check the tire pressure?	Können Sie den Reifendruck prüfen?
Could you check the water?	Können Sie den Wasserstand prüfen?
How much do I owe you?	Wieviel schulde ich Ihnen?
Where do I park?	Wo kann ich parken?
Is there parking nearby?	Gibt es Parkmöglichkeiten in der Nähe?
I am having a problem with my car.	Ich habe ein Problem mit meinem Auto.
It won't start.	Es springt nicht an.
The battery is dead.	Die Batterie ist leer.
I'm out of gas.	Ich habe kein Benzin mehr.
I have a flat tire.	Ich habe einen Platten.
The brakes won't work.	Die Bremsen funktionieren nicht.
The headlights don't work.	Die Scheinwerfer funktionieren nicht.
May I use the phone?	Darf ich das Telefon benutzen?
Could you help me?	Können Sie mir helfen?
My car has broken down.	Mein Auto ist kaputt.
Can you tow it?	Können Sie es abschleppen?
Can you repair it?	Können Sie es reparieren?
Do you have a . . .	Haben Sie . . .
flashlight?	eine Taschenlampe?
jack?	einen Wagenheber?
screwdriver?	einen Schraubenzieher?
tools?	Werkzeug?
wrench?	einen Schraubenschlüssel?
There's been an accident.	Es hat einen Unfall gegeben.

I have had an accident.	Ich habe einen Unfall gehabt.
People are hurt.	Es gibt Verletzte.
It is serious.	Es ist sehr schlimm.
It is not serious.	Es ist nicht sehr schlimm.
Can we exchange driver's license numbers?	Können wir die Personalien (personal information) austauschen?[14]
Can we exchange insurance cards?	Können wir unsere Versicherungsinformationen austauschen?

AT THE TRAIN STATION

Getting around in many countries involves trains. This comes as a surprise to the first time U.S. business traveler who is not accustomed to using trains in the United States. Often a quick trip to another city involves hopping on a train, which is usually quite punctual and pleasant.

While you can buy tickets at a ticket counter as well as on the train for most long-distance trains, you have to buy your ticket for a short-distance train, the subway, or a bus at the station. Remember to carry some change with you, since many stations have only ticket machines. The penalty for getting caught in a random ticket control without a ticket is quite high. People who get caught several times might even get a criminal record. You are usually better off buying multiple tickets, or tickets that are valid for a certain period of time, rather than getting a single ticket.

---

[14]Note that a driver's license does not have a unique number in Germany.

Key Words

Arrival time	die Ankunftszeit
Departure time	die Abfahrtszeit
Platform	der Bahnsteig
Reservation	die Reservierung
Sleeping car	der Schlafwagen
Ticket	die Fahrkarte
Ticket office	der Fahrkartenschalter
Time	die Zeit
Timetable	der Fahrplan

Where is the ticket office?	Wo ist der Fahrkartenschalter?
I want to go to . . .	Ich möchte nach . . .
How much does a ticket cost to . . . ?	Wieviel kostet eine Fahrkarte nach . . . ?
What gate does the train for . . . leave on?	Von welchem Bahnsteig fährt der Zug nach . . . ?
Do I need to change trains?	Muss ich umsteigen?
Is there a dining/buffet car?	Gibt es einen Speisewagen?
Am I on the right train?	Bin ich im richtigen Zug?
Is this an open seat?	Ist dieser Platz noch frei?
What stop is this?	Welcher Bahnhof ist dies?

BARBER SHOP AND BEAUTY PARLOR

In a beauty salon or a barber shop a tip of 10 percent is customary. Many employees of a barbershop or beauty salon have their own

139

Sparschwein (piggy bank) for their tips. Customers usually don't hand the tip to a hairdresser, but put it in their *Sparschwein*.

"Beim Frisör/Im Schönheitssalon"

FRAU JAKOBI: *Würden Sie mein Haar bitte ungefähr auf diese Länge schneiden?*
FRISÖR: *Das ist vielleicht ein wenig zu viel.*
FRAU JAKOBI: *Was ist mit dieser Länge?*
FRISÖR: *Ja. Ich denke das sieht besser aus.*

"At the Barber Shop/Beauty Shop"

MS. JAKOBI: *Could you cut my hair about this much?*
HAIRDRESSER: *I think that that might be too much.*
MS. JAKOBI: *How about this much?*
HAIRDRESSER: *Yes. I think that will look better.*

Key Words

Blow-dry	fönen
Haircut	der Haarschnitt
Manicure	die Maniküre
Nails	die Fingernägel
Shave	die Rasur
Shampoo	das Shampoo

Is there a barber shop/ beauty parlor nearby?	Gibt es einen Frisör/ Schönheitssalon in der Nähe?
Do I need an appointment?	Brauche ich einen Termin?
I need a haircut.	Ich brauche einen Haarschnitt.

I'd like to have a . . .	Ich möchte gern . . .
blow-dry.	mein Haar gefönt haben.
cut.	mein Haar schneiden lassen.
facial.	eine Kosmetikbehandlung für das Gesicht.
manicure.	eine Maniküre.
shampoo.	mein Haar waschen lassen.
I'd like a shave.	Ich möchte eine Rasur.
Could you trim my mustache/beard?	Können Sie meinen Schnurbart/Bart stutzen?

CASH MACHINES AND BANKING

Where is the nearest cash machine?	**Wo ist der nächste Geldautomat?**
Where is the nearest bank?	**Wo ist die nächste Bank?**
Is there a money exchange office near here?	**Gibt es eine Wechselstube in der Nähe?**
Do you change money?	**Wechseln Sie Geld?**
What is the exchange rate?	**Was ist der Wechselkurs?**
I'd like to change a hundred dollars.	**Ich möchte gern einhundert Dollar wechseln.**
I need your passport.	**Ich brauche Ihren Pass.**

POST OFFICE

Many privately operated postal services emerged after the deregulation of the Government owned *Post* throughout Germany. The largest international one today is UPS. FedEx is present, but not widely known. The business is highly competitive in Germany as it declined somewhat with e-mail and other electronic transfer possibilities.

Where is the post office/ FedEx office?	Wo ist das Postamt/Federal Express-Büro?
Do you have overnight service?	Haben Sie einen Lieferservice über Nacht?
I would like postage for this . . .	Ich möchte gern Porto für . . .
letter.	diesen Brief.
package.	dieses Paket.
postcard.	diese Postkarte.
When will the letter/ package arrive?	Wann wird der Brief/das Paket ankommen?
I'd like to send it . . .	Ich möchte ihn/sie/es . . .
insured.	versichern lassen.
overnight.	über Nacht schicken.
registered.	als Einschreiben.

IN AN EMERGENCY: DOCTORS, DENTISTS, HOSPITALS, OPTICIANS, AND PHARMACIES

Doctors and hospitals do not accept credit cards or checks. One of the reasons might simply be that hardly anyone pays in those facilities because everything goes through the national insurance system. However, some dentists might accept credit cards.

"In der Apotheke"[15]

HERR JAHN: *Ich habe eine schlimmen Husten. Können Sie etwas dafür empfehlen?*
APOTHEKERIN: *Möchten Sie einen Saft oder Lutschtabletten?*

---

[15]Every pharmacy (*Apotheke*) has a sign at the door or in the window stating which pharmacy close by is open for emergencies that night or weekend.

HERR JAHN: *Haben Sie Lutschtabletten mit Kirschgeschmack?*
APOTHEKERIN: *Nein, aber wir haben diese hier mit Honiggeschmack.*

"At the Pharmacy"
MR. JAHN: *I have a bad cough. Could you recommend something for it?*
PHARMACIST: *Do you want a syrup or lozenge?*
MR. JAHN: *Do you have cherry-flavored lozenges?*
PHARMACIST: *No, but we have these honey-flavored ones.*

Key Words

Cold	die Erkältung
Doctor	der Arzt/die Ärztin
Emergency	der Notfall
Eye Doctor	der Augenarzt/die Augenärztin
Eyeglasses	die Brille (always singular)
Flu	die Grippe
Headache	die Kopfschmerzen (always plural)
I don't feel well.	Ich fühle mich nicht wohl.
I got hurt.	Ich habe mich verletzt.
Nurse	der Krankenpfleger/die Krankenschwester
Optician	der Optiker/die Optikerin
Pharmacist	der Apotheker/die Apothekerin
Toothache	die Zahnschmerzen (always plural)

I want/need to go to . . .	**Ich möchte/muss . . .**
a dentist.	**zu einem Zahnarzt.**
a doctor.	zu einem Arzt.
an eye doctor.	zu einem Augenarzt.
a hospital.	in ein Krankenhaus.
an optician.	zu einem Optiker.
a pharmacy.	zu einer Apotheke.
I need to see a/an . . .	Ich muss einen . . .
allergist.	Facharzt für Allergien . . .
general practitioner.	praktischen Arzt . . .
gynecologist.	Gynäkologen . . .
internist.	Internisten . . .
	aufsuchen.
Please call an ambulance.	**Bitte rufen Sie einen Krankenwagen.**
Please call a doctor.	**Bitte rufen Sie einen Arzt.**
Please call the police.	**Bitte rufen Sie die Polizei.**
There has been an accident.	**Es gab einen Unfall.**
Someone is hurt.	**Jemand ist verletzt.**
Is there anyone here who speaks English?	**Gibt es hier jemand, der Englisch spricht?**
Can I have an appointment?	**Kann ich einen Termin bekommen?**
I'm not allergic to penicillin.	**Ich bin nicht allergisch gegen Penicillin.**
I'm allergic to penicillin.	**Ich bin gegen Penicillin allergisch.**
I don't feel well.	**Ich fühle mich nicht wohl.**
I don't know what I have.	**Ich weiß nicht was mir fehlt.**
I think I have a fever.	**Ich glaube ich habe Fieber.**
I have asthma.	**Ich habe Asthma.**
I have (a) . . .	Ich habe . . .
backache.	Rückenschmerzen.
cold.	eine Erkältung.

constipation.	Verstopfung.
cough.	Husten.
cut.	mich geschnitten.
diarrhea.	Durchfall.
earache.	Ohrenschmerzen.
hay fever.	Heuschnupfen.
headache.	Kopfschmerzen.
heart trouble.	Herzprobleme.
stomachache.	Magenschmerzen.
pain.	Schmerzen.

I feel dizzy/sick.	Mir ist schwindelig/übel.
I can't sleep.	Ich kann nicht schlafen.
Can you fill this prescription for me?	Können Sie mir dieses Rezept geben?

Do you have . . .	Haben Sie . . .
an antacid?	Magentabletten?
an antiseptic?	eine antiseptische Lösung?
aspirin?	Aspirin?
Band-Aids?	Pflaster?
contact-lens solution?	eine Lösung für Kontaktlinsen?
a disinfectant?	eine Desinfektionslösung?
eye drops?	Augentropfen?
sanitary napkins?	Monatbinden?
sleeping pills?	Schlaftabletten?
tampons?	Tampons?
a thermometer?	ein Thermometer?
throat lozenges?	Halstabletten?
vitamins?	Vitamine?

I'll wait for it.	Ich warte.

A prescription is almost never filled in German pharmacies. The patient is given the original sealed packages of medicine as they are prepacked by the pharmaceutical companies. Generic brands are almost nonexistent.

5 GETTING BUSINESSIZED

In this chapter we cover important business vocabulary that has not yet found a place in previous chapters, such as names for office objects, job titles, and terminology used in different departments of a company. (An extended glossary of industry-specific terms is provided in the back of the book.)

The chapter is organized as follows:

> **Finding Your Way Around the Office**
> **Office Objects**
> **Titles by Level**
> **Organization Charts**
> **Functional Areas of a Company**

Getting acclimated to the overseas office means getting comfortable so you can concentrate on being effective in your job.

So, let's start at the office as you're just settling in. . . .

FINDING YOUR WAY AROUND THE OFFICE

"Sich im Büro einleben"
HERR HOLM: *Sie können diesen Schreibtisch benutzen während Sie hier sind.*
FRAU WILMS: *Wie telefoniere ich nach außen?*
HERR HOLM: *Drücken Sie eine dieser Tasten für eine Leitung nach außen.*
FRAU WILMS: *Ich muss auch ein Fax schicken.*
HERR HOLM: *Gleich am Ende dieses Koridors hinter dem Kopierer.*

"Getting Acclimated to the Office"

MR. HOLM: *You can use this desk while you're here.*

MS. WILMS: *How do I dial out?*

MR. HOLM: *Press any one of these buttons to get an outside line.*

MS. WILMS: *I also need to send a fax.*

MR. HOLM: *Just down the hall past the copier.*

Key Words

Coffee	der Kaffee
Coffee machine	die Kaffeemaschine
Coat	der Mantel
Chair	der Stuhl/der Sessel (padded)
Computer	der Computer
Copier	der Kopierer
Cubicle	die Büroeinheit/das Cubicle
Desk	der Schreibtisch
Fax	das Fax
File	die Ablage/die Akte
Ladies' room	die Damentoilette
Letter	der Brief
Mail	die Post
Manual	die Anleitung
Men's room	die Herrentoilette
Office	das Büro
Pen	der Kugelschreiber
Pencil	der Bleistift
Phone	das Telefon
Printer	der Drucker
Rest room	die Toilette
Tea	der Tee

It is quite common in Germany, Austria, and Switzerland to have a second breakfast at the office. Most companies have an official breakfast break (about 15 to 30 minutes). In the afternoon there is the traditional coffee break. This, however, is becoming less common.

I'm here to see Mr. Müller.	Ich bin hier für einen Termin mit Herrn Müller.
Is this the office of Ms. Weigel?	Ist das hier Frau Weigels Büro?
Can you tell me how to get there?	Können Sie mir sagen, wie ich dorthin komme?
Yes, I can wait.	Ja, ich kann warten.
Where can I hang my coat?	Wo kann ich meinen Mantel aufhängen?
Is there a restroom?	Gibt es hier eine Toilette?
Where is the copier?	Wo ist der Kopierer?
Where can I get some . . . coffee? tea? water?	Wo kann ich . . . bekommen? Kaffee Tee Wasser
Where is the . . . cafeteria? lunch room? ladies' room? men's room?	Wo ist . . . die Cafeteria/die Kantine? der Speiseraum? die Damentoilette? die Herrentoilette?
Where are the . . . restrooms?	Wo sind die Toiletten?
How do I get an outside line?	Wie bekomme ich eine Leitung nach außen?
How can I make a local call?	Wie kann ich ein Ortsgespräch führen?

| How can I make a long-distance call? | Wie kann ich ein Ferngespräch führen? |
| How can I make an overseas call? | Wie kann ich ein Gespräch nach Übersee führen? |

Do you have a . . .	Haben Sie . . .
cafeteria?	eine Cafeteria/die Kantine?
conference room?	einen Konferenzraum?
copier?	einen Kopierer?
extra desk?	einen extra Schreibtisch?
office I can use?	ein Büro, das ich benutzen kann?
phone?	ein Telefon?
telephone directory?	ein Telefonbuch?

Could you show me/us the . . .	Können Sie mir/uns zeigen, wo . . .
elevator?	der Fahrstuhl ist?
exit?	der Ausgang ist?
rest room?	die Toilette ist?
staircase?	die Treppe ist?
way out?	der Weg nach draußen ist?

Where is the . . .	Wo ist . . .
accounting department?	die Buchhaltung?
mail room?	die Postabteilung/der Postraum?
personnel department?	die Personalabteilung?
shipping department?	der Versand?
warehouse?	das Lager?

Who is responsible for . . .	Wer ist für . . .
arranging my flight?	die Buchung meines Fluges . . .
fixing the copier?	die Reparatur des Kopierers . . .
running the copier?	den Betrieb des Kopierers . . .
sending mail?	das Abschicken der Post . . .
	verantwortlich?

"Ein Packet schicken"

HERR SCHMID: *Ich möchte dieses Paket in die Vereinigten Staaten schicken.*

ANGESTELLTER: *Wie bald möchten Sie, dass es dort ankommt?*

HERR SCHMID: *In zwei oder drei Tagen. Ist das ein Problem?*

ANGESTELLTER: *Nein, überhaupt nicht.*

"Shipping a Package"

MR. SCHMID: *I would like to ship this package to the United States.*

CLERK: *How soon do you want it to get there?*

MR. SCHMID: *In two or three days. Will that be a problem?*

CLERK: *No, not at all.*

OFFICE OBJECTS

Here's a list of office objects in alphabetical order:

Cabinets	Schränke
Bookcase	das Bücherregal
File cabinet	der Aktenschrank
Hanging cabinet	der Hängeschrank
Lateral file	die waagerechte Hängeakte
Letter/Legal size	DIN A4 (*European letter size; legal doesn't exist*)
Mobile file	die mobile Akte/der Aktenordner
Safe	der Safe
Steel cabinet	der Stahlschrank
Storage cabinet	der Vorratsschrank
Vertical file	die Hängeakte
Carts and Stands	Wagen und Ständer
Book cart	der Bücherrolltisch

Computer cart	der Computerrolltisch
Mail cart	der Rolltisch für die Postverteilung
Printer/fax stand	das Druckerregal/der Faxständer
Storage cart	der Rolltisch für Büromaterial

Chairs	Sessel/Stühle
Ergonomic chair	der ergonomische Sessel
Executive chair	der Chefsessel
Folding chair	der Klappstuhl
Leather chair	der Ledersessel
Manager chair	der Chefsessel
Side chair	der Ersatzstuhl
Stacking chair	der Stapelstuhl
Swivel chair	der Drehstuhl

And, what would we do without computers? When they are down we are down.

Computer Accessories	Computerzubehör
Adapter	der Adapter
Cable	das Kabel
Data cartridge	die Datenkassette
Diskette or floppy disk	die Diskette/die Floppy
Keyboard	die Tastatur/das Keyboard
Monitor	der Monitor/der Bildschirm
Mouse	die Maus
Mouse pad	die Mausmatte
Power cord	die Stromleitung
Surge protector	der Stromüberspannungsschutz
Wrist rest	die Handgelenkstütze
Zip® drive	das Ziplaufwerk/der Zipdrive

| Desks | Schreibtische |
| Computer desk | der Computertisch |

Steel desk	der Stahlschreibtisch
Wood desk	der Holzschreibtisch
Work center	der integrierte Arbeitsplatz

Desktop Material — Schreibtischplatten-material

Glass	das Glas
Leather	das Leder
Metal	das Metall
Plastic	der Kunststoff
Steel	der Stahl
Wood	das Holz

Furnishings — Weiteres Zubehör im Büro

Business card file	die Visitenkarten-Kartei
Book shelf	das Bücherregal
Bulletin board	das schwarze Brett
Calendar	der Kalender
Chalk board	die Tafel
Clock	die Uhr
Coat hook or rack	der Garderobenhaken/-ständer
Coffee table	der Kaffeetisch
Cork board	die Korkwand
Cup	die Tasse
Desk lamp	die Schreibtischlampe
Door stop or jam	der Türstopper
Easel	der Präsentationsständer/ die Staffelei
Floor lamp	die Stehlampe
Floor mat	die Fußbodenmatte
Frame	der Rahmen
Paper clip	die Büroklammer
Paper cutter	der Papierschneider/die Schneidemaschine
Picture	das Bild
Projection screen	die Leinwand
Push pin	die Heftzwecke/die Reißzwecke

Punch	der Locher
Rubber band	das Gummiband
Ruler	das Lineal
Scissors	die Schere
Stamp	der Stempel
Stamp moistener	das Stempelkissen
Stapler	der Hefter
Staple remover	der Klammernentferner
Tacks	die Heftzwecken
Tape dispenser	der Tesaständer (brand)
Telephone book	das Telefonbuch
Three-hole punch	der amerikanische Locher[16]
Wall board	die Wandtafel
Waste basket	der Papierkorb
Wall planner	der Wandplaner

Gotta Keep Organized

Organizers	Ordner
Appointment Book	der Terminkalender
Basket tray	die Ablage
Binder	die Mappe/der Ordner/der Hefter
Bookend	die Buchstütze
Business card holder	der Visitenkartenständer
Desk organizer	der Utensilienhalter
In/Out boxes	die Ablage für Eingangspost/ Ausgangspost
Hanging wall pockets	der Wandpapierhalter
Magazine rack	der Zeitschriftenständer
Pencil caddy	der Bleistifthalter
Rolodex® card file	der Rolodex/die Rotationskartei
Stacking letter tray	die stapelbare Briefablage

---

[16]A typical German hole punch makes only two holes centered towards the middle side of the paper, about three inches apart. If you need to file those papers back in America, it's better to wait. With the German punch you'll never get it right.

Tray	die Ablage
Vertical holder	der vertikale Papierhalter

Maybe someday we'll eliminate paperwork, but for now we still need to write things down. So, here are the words for it.

Paper and Forms	Papiere und Formulare
Bond	die Papierqualität/-art
Business card	die Visitenkarte
Business stationery	das Geschäftsbriefpapier
Clipboard	die Schreibunterlage
Columnar or accounting sheets	die Buchhaltungsbogen
Continuous computer paper	das perforierte Computerpapier
Computer paper	das Computerpapier
Construction paper	das Bauzeichenpapier
Copier paper	das Kopiererpapier
Drafting or architecture paper	das Zeichenpapier
Envelope	der Umschlag
File folder	der Aktenordner
Folder	die Mappe/der Hefter/der Ordner
Form	das Formular
Graph paper	das Milimeterpapier
Hanging file holder	der Halter für Hängeakten
Label	das Etikett
Large business envelope	der DIN-A4-Umschlag
Letterhead	der Briefkopf
Letter opener	der Brieföffner
Message pad	der Nachrichtennotizblock
Notebook	das Notizbuch
Note pad	der Notizblock
Post-it® notes	die Heftzettel

Report cover	die Berichtmappe
Reporter notebook	das Reporternotizbuch
Ruled writing pad	der linierte Schreibblock
Scratch pad	der Kritzelblock
Steno pad	der Stenoblock
Writing pad	der Schreibblock

When bringing American-sized documents to Germany, keep in mind that paper sizes differ slightly. DIN A4 (German Industry Norm) paper is different in length from the normal American letter size. Legal-size format does not exist.

Pens and Pencils	Stifte und Bleistifte
Ballpoint pen	der Kugelschreiber
Correction fluid	das flüssige Tip-Ex® (brand)
Eraser	das Radiergummi
Highlighter	der Highlighter
Ink pen	der Tintenstift
Lead	das Blei
Marker	der Textmarker
Mechanical pencil	der mechanische Bleistift
Pen	der Stift/der Schreiber
Pencil	der Bleistift
Pencil sharpener	der Anspitzer
Refills	die Nachfüllminen (for ballpoint pens)
Retractable pen	der Stift mit einfahrbarer Mine
Wood pencil	der hölzerne Bleistift
Writing pen	der Schreibstift

Printers/Faxes	Drucker/Faxgeräte
Cartridge	die Patrone/die Kassette/ die Kartusche
Fax paper	das Faxpapier
Inkjet	der Tintenstrahldrucker
Laser	der Laserdrucker

Replacement cartridge	die Ersatzpatrone
Ribbon	das Farbband
Toner cartridge	die Druckflüssigkeitspatrone
Typewriter ribbon	das Schreibmaschinenband

Tables	Tische
Computer table	der Computertisch
Conference table	der Konferenztisch
Drafting/artist table	der Zeichentisch
Folding table	der Klapptisch
Utility table	der Tisch für Büromaterial

Miscellany	Sonstiges
Battery	die Batterie
Broom	der Besen
Cleaning cloth	das Putztuch
Cleaning supplies	die Reinigungsmittel
Duct tape	das Klebeband
Duster	der Abstauber
Extension cord	die Verlängerungsschnur
Fan	der Ventilator
Flashlight	die Taschenlampe
Floor mat	die Bodenmatte
Glue	der Klebstoff

Just as in the States, there are many brand names that are used as generic names for a particular object in Germany. A few of those used in the office are: *Tesa* (Scotch® tape), *Tip-Ex* (Wite-out®), *Tempo* (Kleenex®), or *Uhu* (glue stick).

Light bulb	die Glühbirne
Lock	das Schloss
Masking tape	das Abklebeband
Postal meter	die Portomachine
Postal scale	die Postwaage
Scotch® tape	das Tesa® band
Shipping tape	das Verpackungsklebeband

Tape	das Klebeband
Trash bag	die Abfalltüte

TITLES BY LEVEL

A standardized system of titles has been developed within most U.S. firms. For instance, the term *vice president* means a significant level of management, usually also an officer. *Officer* often designates a level that can approve certain significant expenditures. However, sometimes even within the United States titles can differ. For instance, in most companies and organizations the term *manager* means a person who heads up a sub-area of responsibility, like the *manager of recruiting*. But, the person in charge of human resources is typically a vice president or director. However, in a few companies the term *manager* is the equivalent of the title *vice president* or *director*.

When you venture to other countries, titles can be quite dissimilar. For instance, in some countries the term *director* is often equivalent to *president* or *vice president*.

Chairman	der Vorsitzende/die Vorsitzende
President	der Geschäftsührer/die Geschäftsführerin
Vice President	der stellvertretende Geschäftsführer/die stellvertretende Geschäftsführerin
Director	der Direktor/die Direktorin
Manager	der Manager/die Managerin
Managing Director	der Betriebsleiter/die Betriebsleiterin
Supervisor	der Abteilungsleiter/die Abteilungsleiterin

Senior Analyst	der Hauptfinanzanalytiker/ die Hauptfinanzanalytikerin
Analyst	der Finanzanalytiker/die Finanzanalytikerin
Junior Analyst	der Finanzanalyseassistent/ die Finanzanalyseassistentin
Coordinator	der Koordinator/die Koordinatorin
Administrative Assistant	der Verwaltungsangestellte, die Verwaltungsangestellte
Secretary	der Sekretär/die Sekretärin
Receptionist	der Rezeptionist/die Rezeptionistin

"Büropolitik"

HERR SCHMID: *Haben Sie gesehen, wie Herr Dr. Waller versucht hat die Präsentation zu dominieren, als der Betriebsleiter ins Zimmer kam?*
HERR HOLM: *Ja. Er war ruhig bis dahin, aber dann versuchte er zu zeigen, daß er für den Bericht verantwortlich sei.*
HERR SCHMID: *Er hat einige Leute damit verärgert, sich als Hauptverantwortlichen für den Bericht darzustellen, wo er doch kaum daran gearbeitet hat.*
HERR HOLM: *Gibt es in den Vereinigten Staaten auch Leute, die so etwas machen?*

"Office Politics"

MR. SCHMID: *Did you see Dr. Waller trying to dominate the presentation when the managing director came into the room?*
MR. HOLM: *Yes. He was quiet up until then, but then he tried to show that he was responsible for the report.*

MR. SCHMID: *He made some people angry for taking all the credit for the report when he hardly worked on it.*
MR. HOLM: *Do you have people in the United States who do that, too?*

ORGANIZATION CHARTS

Key Words

Authority	die Vollmacht
Chart	das Schaubild
Dotted line	die punktierte Linie
Matrix	die Matrix
Organization	die Organisation/die Gesellschaft
Responsibility	die Verantwortlichkeit
Solid line	die ungebrochene Linie
Title	der Titel

Organization of a Company in the United States

Board of Directors
Vorstand

Chairman CEO
Vorstandsvorsitzender

President CEO
Geschäftsführer

Vice President Operations
Abteilungsleiter Produktion

Vice President Marketing
Abteilungsleiter Marketing

Vice President Finance and Administration
Abteilungsleiter Finanz und Verwaltung

Milwaukee Plant
Milwaukee Fabrik

New Products
Neue Produkte

Treasurer
Schatzmeister

Data Processing
Datenverarbeitung

China Plant
Fabrik in China

Sales
Verkauf

Controller
Finanzkontrolle

Purchasing
Einkauf

Public Relations
Public Relations

Accounting
Buchhaltung

Human Resources
Personalabteilung

Organization of a Company in Germany

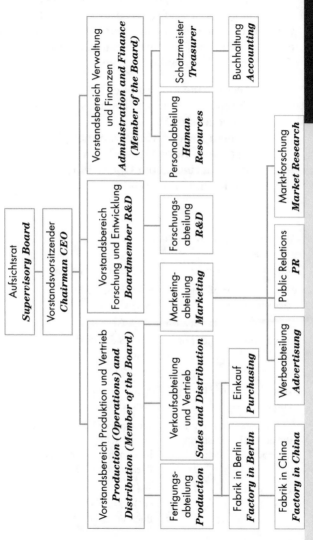

Aufsichtsrat
Supervisory Board

Vorstandsvorsitzender
Chairman CEO

Vorstandsbereich Produktion und Vertrieb
**Production (Operations) and
Distribution (Member of the Board)**

Vorstandsbereich
Forschung und Entwicklung R&D
Boardmember R&D

Vorstandsbereich Verwaltung
und Finanzen
**Administration and Finance
(Member of the Board)**

Fertigungs-
abteilung
Production

Verkaufsabteilung
und Vertrieb
Sales and Distribution

Marketing-
abteilung
Marketing

Forschungs-
abteilung
R&D

Personalabteilung
**Human
Resources**

Schatzmeister
Treasurer

Buchhaltung
Accounting

Fabrik in Berlin
Factory in Berlin

Einkauf
Purchasing

Fabrik in China
Factory in China

Werbeabteilung
Advertisung

Public Relations
PR

Markt-Forschung
Market Research

FUNCTIONAL AREAS OF A COMPANY

Looking for a word in your field of endeavor? You will probably find it below. These are the main areas within a company or organization. Many of these terms, of course, also apply to organizations outside of a company. The areas covered are:

Accounting and Finance
Computer Systems (Data Processing)
Human Resources (Personnel)
Legal and International Law
Manufacturing and Operations
Marketing and Sales

Accounting and Finance

What form do I use to submit my expenses?	Welches Formular muss ich für meine Spesen ausfüllen?
Where are your billing records kept?	Wo werden die Rechnungskopien aufbewahrt?
Are you on a calendar or fiscal year?	Gehen Sie nach dem Kalenderjahr oder dem Steuerjahr?
When do we close the books?	Wann werden die Bücher abgeschlossen?
Is your organization on the accrual or cash method?	Machen Sie in Ihrer Firma periodische Kostenabrechnung oder Barabrechnung?
Account	das Konto
Accountant	der Buchhalter/die Buchhalterin

Accrual method	Methode der Kostenkompensation für z.B. Spesen mit periodischer Abrechnung
Amortization	die Amortisierung
Assets	das Guthaben/Vermögen
Audit	die Rechnungsprüfung/die Buchprüfung
Balance sheet	die Bilanz
Bankruptcy	der Konkurs
Billing records	die Rechnungsunterlagen
Bills	die Rechnungen
Break even	der Ausgleich
Budget	das Budget/die Kostenplanung
Calendar year	das Kalenderjahr
Capital	das Kapital/das Vermögen
Capital budget	der Finanzierungsplan
Capital improvements	die Kapitalwerterhöhung
Cash	das Bargeld
Cash flow	die Liquidität
Cash method	direkte Spesenvergütung/ Kostenabrechnung in bar
Chart of accounts	das Kontenschaubild
Closing of the books	der Bilanzabschluss
Command	die Anweisung
Controller	der Revisor
Cost	die Kosten
Cost accounting	die Kostenbuchhaltung
Credit	der Kredit
Debit	die Belastung
Debt	die Schulden
Default	der Standardwert/der Verzug
Depreciation	die Abschreibung
Disbursement	die Auszahlung
Dividends	die Dividenden

Equity	das Eigenkapital/ das Aktienkapital
Fair market value	der angemessene Marktwert
Financial analyst	der Finanzanalytiker/die Finanzanalytikerin
Financial statement	die Finanzaufstellung/Bilanz
First In—First Out (FIFO)	Bearbeitung wie eingetroffen
Fiscal year	das Steuerjahr
General ledger	das Hauptbuch
Goodwill	der geschätzte Firmenwert
Gross income	das Bruttoeinkommen
Gross sales	der Bruttoumsatz
Income	das Einkommen
Income statement	die Einkommenserklärung
Interest	die Zinsen
Inventory	die Inventur
Invoice	die Rechnung
Journal	das Geschäftsbuch
Last In—First Out (LIFO)	Bearbeitung des zuletzt Eingetroffenen
Ledger	das Hauptbuch
Liabilities	die Verbindlichkeiten
Liquid asset	die flüssigen Mittel
Margin	die Marge/die Spanne
Market value	der Marktwert
Net earnings	der Nettogewinn
Net worth	das Nettovermögen
Operating expenses	die laufenden Betriebskosten
Overhead	die fixen Kosten
Payroll	die Lohn-und Gehaltsliste
Per diem	pro Tag das Tagegeld
Profit	der Gewinn
Profit and loss statement	die Gewinn-und Verlustrechnung

Requisition	die Requisition/die Entnahme
Return on investment	der Investitionsertrag/ die Rendite Revenue der Rohgewinn
Sales	der Verkauf/der Umsatz
Statement of cash flows	die Liquiditätserklärung
Stock	die Aktie
Straight-line depreciation	die lineare Abschreibung
Trial balance	die Rohbilanz
Voucher	der Beleg
Wages	die Gehaltszahlungen
Zero-based budgeting	die Kostenplanung auf Nullbasis

Computer Systems (Data Processing)
(See also *Telecommunications* in the *Glossary of Industry-Specific Terms*)

What is my password?	**Was ist mein Passwort?**[17]
How do I get a password?	**Wie bekomme ich ein Passwort?**
My printer won't work.	**Mein Drucker funktioniert nicht.**
Who can help me with my computer?	**Wer kann mir mit meinem Computer helfen?**
Access (to) the Internet	der Zugang zum Internet
Access code	der Zugangscode
Alt key	die Alt-Taste
Analog	analog
Application	das Anwendungsprogramm

---

[17]Many computer terms are English borrowings in German as in many other languages.

165

At sign (@)	das At-Zeichen (@)/der Klammeraffe
Attach a file (to) e-mail	eine Datei als Anlage zur E-Mail schicken
Attachment	das Attachment/der Anhang
Back slash	der umgekehrte Schrägstrich
Backspace key	die Rücktaste
Banner ad	der Werbe-Banner
BASIC language	die BASIC-Computersprache
Baud	das Baud/die Baud-Rate (die Übertragungsgeschwindigkeit des Modems)
Beta program	das Betaprogramm
Beta test	der Betatest
Boot (to)	herauffahren (booten)
Broadband	das Breitband
Browse (to)	browsen
Browser	der Browser
Bug	der Bug/der Fehler/die Wanze
Byte	das Byte
CD-ROM	die CD-Rom
CD-ROM drive	das CD-Rom-Laufwerk
Cell	die Zelle/die Matrixzelle
Central Processing Unit (CPU)	der CPU (*sometimes also*: die)
Chip	der Chip
Click (to)	klicken
Clip art	die Clip-Art
Clock speed	die Megahertzgeschwindigkeit (IBM)/die Clock-speed (Mac)
Close (to)	schließen
COBOL language	die COBOL-Sprache
Command	der Befehl
Communications port	der Kommunikationsport

Compatible	kompatibel
Compressed file	die komprimiate Datei
Control (Ctrl) key	die Control-Taste
Copy	die Kopie
Copy (to)	kopieren
CPU (Central Processing Unit)	der CPU
Crash	der Absturz
Cursor	der Cursor
Cut (to)	ausschneiden
Data	die Daten
Data base	die Datei/die Datenbasis
Debug (to)	entwanzen/debuggen
Delete (to)	löschen
Delete key	die Löschtaste
Desktop computer	der PC
Desktop publishing	das Desktop-Publishing
Dialog box	das Dialogfeld
Digital	digital
Disk	die Diskette
Disk drive	das Diskettenlaufwerk
Diskette	die Diskette
Document	das Dokument
Double-click (to)	doppelklicken
Download (to)	downloaden/herunterladen
Drag and drop (to)	Drag-and-drop
DRAM or SRAM	der dynamische Arbeitsspeicher/der statische Arbeitsspeicher
DVD	die DVD
E-commerce	der elektronische Handel
E-commerce companies	Firmen mit elektronischem Verkauf
Educational software	die Bildungssoftware
E-mail	die E-Mail
E-mail (to)	mailen
Engine	der Motor
Enter (to)	eingeben/entern

Enter key	die Enter-Taste
Entertainment software	die Unterhaltungssoftware
Error message	die Fehlernachricht
Escape (Esc) key	die Escape-Taste
Field	das Feld
File	die Datei
Flat screen	der Flachbildschirm
Folder	die Akte/die Aktenmappe
Font	der Schriftsatz
FORTRAN language	die FORTRAN-Sprache
Forward an e-mail (to)	eine E-Mail weiterleiten
Forward slash	der Schrägstrich
Gigabyte	das Gigabyte
Graphics	die Graphiken
Go online (to)	Online gehen
Hacker	der Hacker
Hard drive	das Festplattenlaufwerk
Hardware	die Hardware
Hertz	das Hertz
Host	der Host/der Webhost/der Server-Platz-Vermieter
Host (to)	Server-Platz vermieten
Hypertext	der Hypertext
IBM-compatible	IBM-kompatibel
Icon	das Ikon
Insert (to)	einfügen
Install (to)	installieren
Instruction	die Instruktion
Integrated circuit	der integrierte Schaltkreis
Internet	das Internet
Internet address	die Internetadresse
Internet advertising	die Internetwerbung
ISP (Internet Service Provider)	der Internetanbieter/der Online-Service

Key (to)	eingeben
Keyboard	die Tastatur/das Keyboard
Language	die Sprache
Laptop	der Laptop
Laser printer	der Laserdrucker
LCD screen	der LCD-Bildschirm
Left click (to)	links klicken
Load (to)	laden/speichern
Log on/off (to)	einloggen/ausloggen
Mail merge	das Mailmerge
Mainframe	der Großrechner
Maximize (to)	maximieren
Megahertz	das Megahertz
Memory	der Speicher
Menu	das Menü
Minimize (to)	minimieren
Microprocessor (Intel, Motorola)	der Mikroprozessor
Modem	das Modem
Monitor	der Monitor
Monitor (to)	verfolgen/observieren
Mouse	die Maus
Mouse pad	die Mausmatte
Nanosecond	die Nanosekunde
Network	das Netzwerk
Notebook computer	das Notebook
Online	online
Open (to)	öffnen
Operating system (Windows, Linux, Unix)	das Betriebssystem (Windows, Linux, Unix)
Palmtop computer	der Palmtop
Page	die Seite
Page down/up (to)	vorblättern/zurückblättern
Parallel port	der Parallelport
Password	das Passwort

169

Paste (to)	einfügen
PC (Personal Computer)	der PC
Plotter	der Kurvenschreiber
Portal	das Portal/das Cybertor
Press a button (to)	eine Taste drücken
Print (to)	drucken
Printer	der Drucker
Program	das Programm
Program (to)	programmieren
Programmable logic devices	programmierbare logische Apparate
Programmer	der Programmierer/die Programmiererin
Prompt	das Prompt/die Aufforderungsmeldung
Record	aufnehmen
Right click (to)	rechts klicken
Save (to)	speichern
Scan (to)	scannen
Scanner	der Scanner
Screen	der Bildschirm
Screen (to)	checken/überprüfen screenen (*telephone only*)
Scroll (to)	scrollen (vorscrollen/ zurückscrollen)
Search	die Suche
Search (to)	suchen
Search engine	die Suchmaschine
Serial port	die serielle Schmittstelle
Server	der Server
Shift key	die Umschalttaste
Software	die Software
Sort (to)	sortieren
Space bar	die Leertaste
Speaker	der Lautsprecher
Spell check (to)	Rechtschreibung prüfen
Spell checker	die Rechtschreibprüfung

Surf the Internet (to)	das Internet surfen
System	das System
Tab key	die Tabulatortaste
Technical support	der technische Kundendienst
Telecommuting	die Telearbeit
Teleconferencing	eine Telekonferenz abhalten
Use (to)	benutzen
User	der User
User-friendly	benutzerfreundlich
Virus	der Computervirus
Voice recognition	die Spracherkennung
Web	das Netz/das Web
Web browser	der Browser
Web page	die Webseite
Web site	der Web-Site (*often called*: Homepage)
Wireless	kabellos
Word processor	das Textverarbeitungsprogramm
World Wide Web (WWW)	das weltweite Netz (WWW)/das Internet
Zip® disk	die Zip®-Diskette
Zip® drive	der Zip®-Drive/das Zip-Laufwerk

Many of the acronyms and abbreviations used in America are used in Germany as well. A chat room (or "chat party") on the Net is also referred to as @-Party or Klammeraffen-Party (Clip-Monkey Party). ASAP, AFK (away from keyboard), B4N (bye for now), BBL (be back later), BTW (by the way), CU (see you), GA (go ahead), IC (I see) or WB (welcome back) are commonly used in German Internet communications.

Human Resources (Personnel)

Where do you keep the personnel files?	Wo bewahren Sie die Personalakten auf?
What do you keep in the personnel files?	Was kommt in die Personalakten?
What organization regulates the hiring and firing in your country?	Welche Organisation ist hier für die Regelungen bei der Einstellung oder Kündigung von Arbeitnehmern zuständig?
How much do you use the Internet for hiring in your country?	Welchen Stellenwert hat das Internet beim Einstellungsprozess in Ihrem Land?
How much turnover do you have at this plant?	Wie hoch ist die Kündigungsrate in dieser Fabrik?
What benefits do you offer?	Welche Sozialleistungen bieten Sie?
How much vacation do you give for a new hire?	Wieviel Urlaub geben Sie einem neuen Angestellten?
What is your normal retirement age?	Was ist Ihr normales Rentenalter?

Every employee of a German company automatically receives health insurance and dental benefits. The insurance costs are deducted from the paycheck, and half of the amount is contributed by the employer. Employees receive a minimum of four weeks vacation annually, which increases with years of employment. The insurance covers most of the salary in the case of sickness.

Absent	nicht anwesend
Advertise a position/job (to)	eine Stelle ausschreiben/eine Stellenanzeige aufgeben

Appraise job performance (to)	die Arbeitsleistung beurteilen
Actuary	der Versicherungs-mathematiker/die im
Background	die persönlichen Daten (of a person)
Beneficiary	der Nutznießer
Bonus	der Bonus
Career	das Berufsleben
Compensation	das Entgelt/die Berahlung
Counsel (to)	beraten
Counseling	die Beratung
Corporate culture	die Firmenkultur
Cross training	gegenseitige Schulung
Deferred compensation	die Nachzugskompensierung
Disability	die Arbeitsunfähigkeit
Dotted-line responsibility	die teilweise Verantwortlichkeit
Employee benefits	die Sozialleistungen
Employee turnover	die Kündigungsrate
Employment	die Arbeit/die Anstellung
Expatiate	sich verbreiten
Flextime	gleitende Arbeitszeit
Fringe benefits	die Vergünstigungen
Health insurance	die Krankenversicherung
Human relations	die Personalabteilung (no real equivalent)
Human resources	die Personalabteilung
Interview	das Vorstellungsgespräch
Interview (to)	ein Vorstellungsgespräch führen
Job	die Arbeitsstelle
Job description	die Stellenbeschreibung
Job listing / ad(vertisement)	die Stellenanzeige
Job skills	die (gefragten) Fähigkeiten

Life insurance	die Lebensversicherung
List a job (to)	eine Stelle ausschreiben
Manage (to)	managen/leiten
Management	das Management
Management training	das Managementtraining
Matrix management	das Matrix-Management
Merit increase	die Gehaltserhöhung Gasierend auf Leistung
Micromanage	das Mikro-Managen
Morale	die Arbeitsmoral
Motivation	die Motivation
Nepotism	der Nepotismus/die Vetternwirtschaft
On-the-job training	die Schulung am Arbeitsplatz
Organization	die Organisation
Organization chart	das Firmenschaubild/das Organigram
Paycheck	die Gehaltsabrechnung/der Lohnscheck
Pension	die Rente/die Pension
Performance appraisal	die Leistungsbeurteilung
Personnel	die Personalabteilung
Personnel file	die Personalakte
Position	die Stellung/die Position
Promote (to)	befördern
Promotion	die Beförderung
Recruiter	der Personalagent/die Personalagentin
Relocation	der Standortwechsel
Resume	der Lebenslauf
Retire (to)	in den Ruhestand treten
Retirement plan	die Rentenversicherung
Restructuring	die Restrukturierung
Salary	das Gehalt
Salary grade	die Gehaltsstufe
Salary survey	die Einkommensumfrage

Seniority	die Seniorität
Skills	die Fähigkeiten
Solid-line responsibility	die absolute Verantwortlichkeit
Stock options	die Aktienoptionen
Supervise (to)	leiten/überwachen
Supervisor	der Leiter/die Leiterin
Train (to)	trainieren/schulen
Training	das Training/die Schulung
Turnover	die Kündigungsrate
Unemployment	die Arbeitslosigkeit
Vacation	der Urlaub
Wages	das Gehalt/das Einkommen

Legal and International Law

What is the procedure to apply for a patent, copyright, or trademark in your country?	Was ist die Vorgehensweise, um ein Patent, ein Copyright oder ein Markenzeichen in Ihrem Land anzumelden?
Do you recognize a service mark in your country?	Werden in Ihrem Land Dienstleistungspunkte gegeben?
What is the procedure to register a prescription drug in your country?	Was ist die Vorgehensweise, um ein verschreibungspflichtiges Medikament in Ihrem Land registrieren zu lassen?
How much legal work do you do out-of-house?	Wieviele Rechtsangelegenheiten lassen Sie außer Haus erledigen?
Affidavit	die eidesstattliche Erklärung
Alibi	das Alibi
Appeal	der Einspruch
Appeal (to)	Berufung einlegen
Attorney	der Anwalt

Bail	die Kaution/die Freilassung gegen Kaution
Bankruptcy	der Konkurs
Bar	die Anwaltschaft
Barrister	der Barrister/der Anwalt
Bench	der Richterstuhl
Boilerplate	die Matritze/der Mustervertrag
Brief	die Rechtsunterlagen
Bylaws	die Satzungsbestimmungen
Cartel	das Kartell
Cease and desist order	die Schweigepflicht
Civil law	das Zivilrecht
Consideration	die Erwägung
Contract	der Vertrag
Copyright	das Copyright
Copyright (to)	das Copyright eintragen lassen
Corpus	das Korpus
Court	das Gericht
Covenant	der Schwur
Crime	das Verbrechen
Crime (to commit)	ein Verbrechen begehen
Cross-examination	das Kreuzverhör
Cross-examine (to)	ins Kreuzverhör nehmen
Damages	der Schaden
Defense	die Verteidigung
Defraud	der Betrug
Defraud (to)	betrügen/hintergehen
Discovery	die Entdeckung
Evidence	das Beweismaterial
Felony	der Kapitalverbrechen
Fiduciary	treuhänderisch
Find (to)	finden
Finding	das Urteil/der Urteilsspruch
Fraud	der Betrug
Fraud (to)	betrügen/beschwindeln

Indict (to)	Anklage erheben/anklagen
Indictment	die Anklageerhebung
In-house	hausintern
International law	das internationale Gesetz
Judge	der Richter
Judge (to)	urteilen
Judgement	das Urteil
Jury	die Geschworenen
Law	das Gesetz
Law firm	die Anwaltsfirma
Lawsuit	die Klage
Lawyer	der Anwalt
Legal	rechtlich/legal
Litigation	der Prozess/der Rechtsstreit
Malpractice	das Berufsvergehen/ das Amtsvergehen (*in public office*)
Motion	der Antrag
Negligence	die Vernachlässigung
Order (to)	anordnen
Patent	das Patent
Patent (to)	patentieren lassen
Plaintiff	der Kläger/die Klägerin (*company*)
Probate	die gerichtliche Testamentsbestätigung
Prosecute (to)	anklagen
Prosecutor	der Ankläger
Restrain (to)	zurückhalten/in die Schranken weisen
Restraining order	die gerichtliche Verbotsverfügung
Service mark	die Dienstleistungsmarke/der Leistungspunkt

Solicitor	der Justizbeamte
Sue (to)	klagen
Suit	die Klage
Tax	die Steuer
Tax (to)	besteuern
Tort	das Delikt
Trademark	das Warenzeichen

Manufacturing and Operations

Where are your main production plants?	Wo sind Ihre Hauptsproduktionsstätten?
How many shifts do you run?	Wieviele Schichten arbeiten Sie?
Is your plant unionized?	Ist die Fabrik gewerkschaftlich organisiert?
What is your through-put at this plant?	Wie hoch ist die Produktionsleistung in dieser Fabrik?
How many cars and trucks will you produce at this plant this year?	Wieviele PKWs und LKWs werden Sie dieses Jahr in dieser Fabrik herstellen?
Where does engineering fit into your organization?	Wie sieht es in Ihrer Firma mit der technischen Entwicklung/dem Ingenieurwesen aus?
What types of engineers do you employ?	Welche Art von Ingenieuren beschäftigen Sie?
How many engineers do you employ?	Wie viele Ingenieure beschäftigen Sie?

All larger German companies are required to have a workers' representation board (*Betriebsrat*). The members are employees of the company, and often belong to the union as well. However, the union is only involved if there are extreme disputes. Most issues are resolved in negotiations between the *Betriebsrat* and the management of a company. Unions function on a higher level by negotiating issues such as minimum pay, vacation, and other benefits.

Accident	der Unfall
Assembly line	das Fließband
Controls	die Kontrollinstrumente
Engineer	der Ingenieur/die Ingenieurin
Engineer (to)	konstruieren/entwickeln
Ear plugs	der Lärmschutz
Fabricate	das Fabrikat
Factory	die Fabrik
Factory floor	die Fabriketage
Floor	die Etage
Foreman	der Vorarbeiter/die Vorarbeiterin
Forge (to)	schmieden
Fork lift	der Gabelstapler
Gasket	die Dichtung
Goggles	die Schutzbrille
Inventory	der Lagerbestand/die Inventur
Just-in-time inventory	die JIT-Lagerhaltung
Just-in-time manufacture	die JIT-Produktionsplanung/ die JIT-Herstellung
Machinery	der Maschinenpark
Manufacture (to)	herstellen
Manufacturer	der Hersteller
Model	das Modell
Operate (to)	operieren
Operations	die Betriebsleitung/die Produktion

Plant	das Werk/die Fabrik
Plant manager	der Werksmanager/der Fabrikmanager
Prefabricate	die Vorfertigung
Procurement	die Beschaffung
Purchase (to)	einkaufen
Purchasing	der Einkauf
Quality	die Qualität
Quality control	die Qualitätskontrolle
Raw materials	das Rohmaterial
Railroad	die Eisenbahn/die Bahn
Safety	die Sicherheit
Safety goggles	die Sicherheitsbrille
Schedule	der Terminplan
Schedule (to)	einplanen
Scheduling	die Terminplanung
Shift (first, second, third)	die (Früh-, Tag-, Nacht-) schicht
Ship (to)	senden/verschicken
Shipping	der Versand
Specifications	die Spezifikationen
Supervisor	der Leiter/die Leiterin
Supplier	der Zulieferer
Tank	der Tank
Total Quality Management (TQM)	das TQM/die Gesamtqualitätsleitung
Union	die Gewerkschaft
Union contract	der Gewerkschaftsvertrag
Vat	der Los-Container (*assembly line only*)
Warehouse	das Lagerhaus
Worker(s)	der/die Arbeiter

Marketing and Sales

| What is your advertising budget for the year? | Wie hoch ist das Werbebudget für das Jahr? |

Which advertising agency do you use?	Welche Werbeagentur benutzen Sie?
Which media do you use, and why?	Welche Medien benutzen Sie und warum?
Who are your product (or service) competitors?	Wer ist Ihre Konkurrenz?
What is your market share?	Wie hoch ist Ihr Marktanteil?

"Kundenbeschwerden"

FRAU JOHANN: *Warum haben wir so viele Beschwerden von unseren Kunden?*

HERR SANDER: *Das ist der Grund, warum Sie eingestellt wurden.*

FRAU JOHANN: *Dann lassen Sie die Kundenvertreter eine Woche lang die verschiedenen Beschwerden auflisten.*

HERR SANDER: *Können Sie ein Formblatt entwerfen?*

FRAU JOHANN: *Ja, ich werde es heute Nachmittag fertig haben.*

"Customer Complaints"

MS. JOHANN: *Why are we getting so many complaints from our customers?*

MR. SANDER: *That's why we hired you.*

MS. JOHANN: *Then let's have the customer representatives keep a log of the various types of complaints for a full week.*

MR. SANDER: *Could you design the log?*

MS. JOHANN: *Yes, I'll have it ready this afternoon.*

The customer service of most companies in Germany, Austria, and Switzerland is generally quite efficient, courteous, and fast. When it comes to returns, you might, however, run into some resistance. Goods will be exchanged or repaired, but usually not taken back.

Account	die Kunde/die Kundin
Account executive	der Kundenbetreuer/die Kundenbetreuerin
Ad/Advertisement	die Anzeige/das Inserat (*magazines and newspapers only*)
Ad campaign	die Werbekampagne
Advertising	die Werbung
Advertising effectiveness	die Werbeeffektivität
Advertising manager	der Werbeleiter/die Werbeleiterin
Advertising objectives	die Werbeziele
Advertising rates	die Anzeigeraten
Agency	die Agentur
Agent	der Werbeagent/die Werbeagentin
Art director	der Art-Direktor/die Art-Direktin
Artwork	die künstlerische Gestaltung
Audience	das Publikum
Audience measurement	das Messen der Zuschauerrate (*TV*)
Audience profile	das Publikumsprofil
Bait and switch advertising	die Lockvogelwerbung[18]
Banner ad	die Bannerwerbung (*Internet only*)
Bar code	der Strichkode
Barriers to entry	die Zutrittsschranke/ die Zugangsbeschränkung
Billboard	die Reklametafel

---

[18]Most bait-and-switch advertising is against the law in Germany. A company is not allowed to undermine another product in their advertising, or present their product as superior to others. If a company claims in their advertising that their product is the best, they have to prove it beyond a doubt. They usually can't.

Billings	das Umsatzvolumen (*advertising only*)
Blow-in	die Werbeeinlage
Brochure	die Broschüre
Brand	die Marke
Brand loyalty	die Markentreue
Brand name	der Markenname
Broadcast media	die Übertragungsmedien
Buyer	der Einkäufer/die Einkäuferin
Campaign	die Kampagne
Captive market	der Eigenbedarfsmarkt
Catalog	der Katalog
Circular	das Rundschreiben/Zirkular
Circulation	die Auflage/der Umlauf
Classified advertising	die Rubrikwerbung
Closing date	der Einsendeschluss
Cold call	der Überraschungsanruf
Commercial	kommerziell
Commodity Product	das Grundstoffprodukt/die Bedarfsgüter
Competition	die Konkurrenz
Competitive advantage	der Konkurrenzvorteil
Consumer	der Konsument/der Verbraucher
Consumer research	die Verbraucherforschung
Copy	die Kopie
Corporate communications	die innerbetriebliche Kommunikation
Creative director	der Creative-Director
Creativity	die Kreativität
Culture	die Kultur
Customer	der Kunde/die Kundin
Customer complaints	die Kundenbeschwerden
Customer satisfaction	die Kundenzufriedenstellung
Customer service	der Kundendienst
Database	die Datenbank
Demand	die Nachfrage

Demographics	die demografischen Angaben
Direct mail	die Postwurfsendung
Discount	der Rabatt
Distribution	die Verteilung/die Auslieferung
Economic factors	die wirtschaftlichen Faktoren
Elastic demand	die elastische Nachfrage
Endorsement	die Persönlichkeitswerbung
Exposure	die Publicity
Expressed warranty	die ausdrückliche Garantie
Focus group	die Fokusgruppe
Forecast	die Voraussage
Frequency	die Häufigkeit
Fulfillment	die Zufriedenstellung
Galley proof	der Fahnenabzug
General sales manager	der Verkaufsleiter/die Verkaufsleiterin
Global marketing	das globale Marketing
Graphic design	das grafische Design
Hard sell	die aggressive Verkaufswerbung
Illustration	die Illustration
Image	das Image
Implied warranty	die eingeschlossene Garantie
Impulse buying	der Impulskauf
Incentive	der Anreiz
Inelastic demand	die unflexible Nachfrage
Infomercial	die Informationswerbesendung
Insert	die Zeitschrifteneinlage
Institutional marketing	das institutionelle Marketing
Inventory	die Inventur
Island display	das Verkaufsinseldisplay/die alleinstehende Werbeauslage
Jobber	der Mittelsmann/der Industriedirektverkäufer

Junk mail	Wurfsendungen
Kiosk	der Kiosk
Label	das Etikett
Layout	das Layout
Lead	der Leitartikel (*paper*)/der Spitzenreiter (*sales*)/der Vorschub (*printing*)
Licensing	die Lizenzierung
Lifestyle	der Lebensstil
List price	der Listenpreis
Logo	das Logo/das Firmenzeichen
Magazine	die Zeitschrift/die Illustrierte
Mail order	die Katalogbestellung
Mailing list	die Adressenliste
Margin	die Spanne
Markdown	der Nachlass
Market(s)	der Markt/die Märkte
Market (to)	vermarkten
Marketing	das Marketing
Marketing budget	das Marketingbudget
Marketing director	der Marketingdirektor
Marketing manager	der Marketingmanager
Marketing plan	der Marketingplan
Market niche	die Marktnische
Market penetration	der Markteinbruch
Market research	die Marktforschung
Market share	der Marktanteil
Mass marketing	die Massenvermarktung
Mass media	die Massenmedien
Media	die Medien
Media buyer	der Medienkäufer
Media research	die Medienforschung
Merchandise	die Ware
Merchandizing	die Warenauslage
Message	die Nachricht/die Werbeaussage

National account	der landesweite Kunde
Needs	die Bedürfnisse
New product development	die Produktentwicklung
News conference	die Nachrichtenkonferenz
Newspaper	die Zeitung
News release	die Nachrichtenveröffentlichung
Niche	die Nische
Niche marketing	das Nischenmarketing
Opinion research	die Meinungsumfrage
Order form	das Auftragsformular
Outdoor advertising	die Außenwerbung
Outdoor billboards	die Großflächenwerbung
Packaging	die Verpackung
PMS colors (Pantone Matching System)	die Pantone-Farbskala
Point-of-sale advertising	die Kassenwerbung
Premium	die Prämie
Price	der Preis
Price (to)	auspreisen
Pricing	die Auspreisung
Product(s)	das Produkt/die Produkte
Product design	das Produktdesign
Product liability	die Produkthaftung
Product life	die Lebensdauer des Produkts
Product launch	der Produktstart
Product mix	das Produktsortiment
Promotion	die Verkaufspromotion
Prospect	der Prospekt
Publicity	der Bekanntheitsgrad/die Publicity
Public relations	die Public-Relations-Abteilung
Publication	die Veröffentlichung
Qualified lead	vielversprechender, möglicher Spitzenreiter

Radio	das Radio
Rate(s)	die Rate(n)
Rate card	die Anzeigenpreisliste
Reach	die Reichweite
Readership	die Leserschaft
Rebate	der Rabatt
Recall	die Wiedererkennung einer Werbung
Repetition	die Wiederholung
Research	die Forschung
Research report	der Forschungsbericht
Response(s)	die Reaktion(en)
Returns and allowances	Umtausch und Kundenkulanz
Rollout	die Ausrollung/die Marktverbreiterung (*area increase*)
Sales	der Umsatz/der Verkauf
Sales analysis	die Umsatzanalyse
Sales contest	der Verkaufswettbewerb
Sales force	das Verkaufspersonal
Sales manager	der Verkaufsmanager
Salesperson	der Verkäufer/die Verkäuferin
Sales report	der Verkaufsbericht
Sales representative	der Verkaufsrepräsentant/der Vertreter
Segmentation	die Marktsegmentierung
Sell (to)	verkaufen
Selling	das Verkaufen
Services	die Dienstleistungen
Share of market	die Marktverteilung
Shelf life	die Lagerungsdauer
Slogan	der Slogan
Specialty product	das Spezialprodukt
Sponsor	der Schirmherr/der Sponsor
Sponsor (to)	sponsern
Spot (radio and TV)	der Werbespot
Storyboard	das Werbespot-Layout
Strategy	die Werbestrategie
Subliminal advertising	die sublime Werbung

Supplier	der Zulieferer
Supply and demand	Angebot und Nachfrage
Target audience	der gezielte Hörerkreis
Target marketing	das gezielte Marketing
Television	das Fernsehen
Test group	die Testgruppe
Test market	der Testmarkt
Trade magazine	die Handelsillustrierte
Trade show	die Handelsmesse
Trial offer	das Angebot mit Rücktrittsgarantie
Unit pricing	die Preisfestlegung pro Einheit
Universal Product Code system (UPCS)	das universale Produktcode-System
Vendor	der Händler/der Zulieferer
Wants	die Bedürfnisse
Warehouse	das Lagerhaus
Warranty	die Garantieurkunde
Web site	der Web-Site
Word-of-mouth advertising	Mund-zu-Mund-Werbung/Propaganda

6 REFERENCE

Here's a place to find words and phrases for everything we missed in other chapters. This chapter contains some critical information to keep you on schedule—so important in any organization—such as expressions used for telling time or words for numbers.

We'll start with words and phrases we hope you'll never have to use, but in an emergency they're critical.

> **Emergency Expressions**
> **Telling Time**
> **Days of the Week**
> **Months of the Year**
> **Seasons of the Year**
> **Ordinal Numbers**
> **Cardinal Numbers**
> **Basic Mathematical Terms**
> **Acronyms and Abbreviations**
> **Countries, Continents, and**
>   **Languages**

EMERGENCY EXPRESSIONS

Help!	Hilfe!
Fire!	Feuer!
Hurry!	Schnell!
Call an ambulance!	Rufen Sie einen Krankenwagen!
Call the police!	Rufen Sie die Polizei!
Call the fire department!	Rufen Sie die Feuerwehr!
Stop, thief!	Haltet den Dieb!
Stop him/her!	Halten Sie ihn/sie!

Someone/he/she/they stole my . . .	Jemand/Er/Sie hat meine . . .
bag!	Tasche gestohlen!
briefcase!	Aktentasche gestohlen!
wallet!	meine Brieftasche/Geldbörse gestohlen!
watch!	meine Uhr gestohlen!
Leave me alone!	Lassen Sie mich in Ruhe!
Can you help me please?	Können Sie mir bitte helfen?
Where's the police station?	Wo ist die Polizeistation?
I need a lawyer.	Ich brauche einen Anwalt.
Can I make a telephone call?	Kann ich einen Anruf machen?
Do you speak English?	Sprechen Sie Englisch?
Can you tell me where the U.S. embassy is?	Können Sie mir sagen, wo die amerikanische Botschaft ist?

TELLING TIME

In the United States, most offices use A.M. and P.M. after the number to distinguish between morning and afternoon hours, for instance 9:00 A.M. and 9:00 P.M. Elsewhere, however, the 24-hour system is often used in offices and for other official purposes. For instance, following 12 noon, the hours are 13, 14, . . . and so forth as opposed to 1, 2, . . . and so forth. An easy way to keep this straight is to subtract or add 12 to the hours you're accustomed to. For instance, if someone says 15:00 hours (spoken as 15 hundred hours), you know that it's really 3:00 P.M. Or, likewise, if it's 2:00 P.M. you add 12 to get 14:00 hours. The U.S. Army adopted this system to make sure there would be no misunderstanding of what time was meant. But for business there is little confusion: When we say we'll meet at 4, we know that it's P.M. not A.M.

What time is it?	Wieviel Uhr ist es?
It's 10:30 A.M.	Es ist zehn Uhr dreißig.
It's exactly 9:00 A.M.	Es ist genau neun Uhr.
Shortly after 10 a.m.	Kurz nach zehn.
Around noon.	Um die Mittagszeit.
What year is it?	Welches Jahr ist es?
It's the year 2002.	Es ist das Jahr zweitausendundzwei.
What time do we begin?	Um wieviel Uhr fangen wir an?
We begin at 10:30 sharp.	Wir fangen pünktlich um zehn Uhr dreißig an.
The meeting will start at . . .	Die Besprechung (Sitzung) beginnt um . . .
The meeting will end at . . .	Die Besprechung (Sitzung) endet um . . .
It's break time.	Es ist Zeit für die Pause.
We will have a coffee break at . . .	Um . . . werden wir eine Kaffeepause machen.
Lunch will be served at . . .	Das Mittagessen wird um . . . serviert.
Lunch will last . . .	Das Mittagessen dauert . . .
I'm early./It's early.	Ich bin frühzeitig hier./Es ist früh.
I'm on time./It's on time.	Ich bin pünktlich./Es ist pünktlich.
I'm late./It's late.	Ich bin spät./Es ist spät.
I'm too late./It's too late.	Ich bin zu spät./Es ist zu spät.
Is this clock right?	Geht diese Uhr richtig?
It's running slow/fast.	Sie geht nach/vor.
It's five minutes slow/fast.	Sie geht fünf Minuten nach/vor.
When will it start?	Wann fängt es an?
In . . .	In . . .
about two minutes.	zirka zwei Minuten.
five minutes.	fünf Minuten.

one hour.	einer Stunde.
a half hour.	einer halben Stunde.
a quarter hour.	einer Viertelstunde.
an hour-and-a-half.	anderthalb Stunden.
Tomorrow/the day after tomorrow/in three days.	**Morgen/**übermorgen/in drei Tagen.
Next week/month/year.	Nächste Woche/nächsten Monat/nächstes Jahr.
Soon.	**Bald.**

When did it happen?	**Wann ist es passiert?**
Five minutes ago.	**Vor fünf Minuten.**
A half hour ago.	Vor einer halben Stunde.
An hour ago.	Vor einer Stunde.
Yesterday/the day before yesterday.	Gestern/vorgestern.
Last month/year.	Letzten Monat/letztes Jahr.
Hours/days/months/ years ago.	Vor Stunden/vor Tagen/vor Monaten/vor Jahren.
In the middle of the night/day.	Mitten am Tag/mitten in der Nacht.
Recently.	Kürzlich.
A long time ago.	Vor Kurzem.

How long did it last?	**Wie lange hat es gedauert?**
(Very) long.	**(Sehr) lange.**
(Very) short.	**(Sehr) kurz.**
A half hour.	Eine halbe Stunde.
An hour.	Eine Stunde.
For hours.	Vier Stunden.
All day long.	Den ganzen Tag.
All night long.	Die ganze Nacht.
All month.	Den ganzen Monat.

For the Specific Time

It is . . .	**Es ist . . .**
one o'clock.	**ein Uhr.**
1 A.M.	ein Uhr früh.

1 P.M.	dreizehn Uhr (ein Uhr Mittag)
1:15	dreizehn Uhr fünfzehn (Viertel nach eins).
1:30/half past one.	dreizehn Uhr dreißig/halb zwei.
1:45/quarter to two.	dreizehn Uhr fünfundvierzig/Viertel vor zwei.
1:10/ten minutes after one.	dreizehn Uhr zehn/zehn Minuten nach eins.
1:50/ten to two.	dreizehn Uhr fünfzig/zehn vor zwei.

"Der richtige Zeitunterschied"

HERR HASE: *Wie groß ist der Zeitunterschied zu New York?*

FRAU KESSLER: *Es ist hier sechs Stunden später.*

HERR HASE: *In anderen Worten, wenn es hier vierzehn Uhr ist, dann ist es . . .*

FRAU KESSLER: *Acht Uhr morgens zu Hause in New York.*

"Getting the Time Zone Right"

MR. HASE: *How many hours' difference is it in New York?*

MS. KESSLER: *It is here six hours earlier.*

MR. HASE: *In other words, when it is two in the afternoon here, it is . . .*

MS. KESSLER: *Eight in the morning back home in New York.*

What time of day is it?	Welche Tageszeit ist es?
It's . . .	Es ist . . .
dawn.	Sonnenaufgang.
early morning.	früher Morgen.

morning.	**Morgen.**
mid-morning.	mittlerer Morgen.
late morning.	später Morgen.
noon.	**Mittag.**
early afternoon.	früher Nachmittag.
mid-afternoon.	mittlerer Nachmittag.
late afternoon.	**später Nachmittag.**
dusk.	Dämmerung.
early evening.	früher Abend.
evening.	**Abend.**
late evening.	Spätabend.
midnight.	**Mitternacht.**

DAYS OF THE WEEK

What day of the week is it?	Welchen Wochentag haben wir?
It's . . .	Es ist . . .
Monday.	**Montag.**
Tuesday.	**Dienstag.**
Wednesday.	**Mittwoch.**
Thursday.	**Donnerstag.**
Friday.	**Freitag.**
Saturday.	**Samstag.**
Sunday.	**Sonntag.**

Weekday	**der Wochentag**
Weeknight	**der Abend in der Woche**
Weekend	**das Wochenende**

Yesterday	**gestern**
The day before yesterday	**vorgestern**
Today	**heute**
Tomorrow	**morgen**
The day after tomorrow	**übermorgen**

Last week	**letzte Woche**
This week	**diese Woche**
Next week	**nächste Woche**

On Tuesday	am Dienstag
Next Thursday	nächsten Donnerstag
When does it take place?	**Wann findet es statt?**
Each Tuesday/Tuesdays	**Jeden Dienstag/Dienstags**
Once/twice/three times a week/month/year	**Einmal/zweimal/dreimal** die Woche/im Monat/**im Jahr.**

MONTHS OF THE YEAR

| What month is it? | **Welchen Monat haben wir?** |
| It's . . . | Es ist . . . |

January.	**Januar.**
February.	**Februar.**
March.	**März.**
April.	**April.**
May.	**Mai.**
June.	**Juni.**
July.	**Juli.**
August.	**August.**
September.	**September.**
October.	**Oktober.**
November.	**November.**
December.	**Dezember.**

Last month	**letzter Monat**
This month	**dieser Monat**
Next month	**nächster Monat**

| Two months ago | **vor zwei Monaten** |
| In a month | **in einem Monat** |

SEASONS OF THE YEAR

What season is it?	**Welche Jahreszeit ist es?**
It's . . .	Es ist . . .
Spring.	**Frühling.**
Summer.	**Sommer.**

| Fall. | Herbst. |
| Winter. | Winter. |

Last year	letztes Jahr
This year	dieses Jahr
Next year	nächstes Jahr

| Two years ago | vor zwei Jahren |
| In two years | in zwei Jahren |

ORDINAL NUMBERS

What position is it?	In welcher Reihenfolge steht es?
It's . . .	Es ist . . .
First (1st)	der erste[1] (1.)
Second (2nd)	der zweite (2.)
Third (3rd)	der dritte (3.)
Fourth (4th)	der vierte (4.)
Fifth (5th)	der fünfte (5.)
Sixth (6th)	der sechste (6.)
Seventh (7th)	der siebte (7.)
Eighth (8th)	der achte (8.)
Ninth (9th)	der neunte (9.)
Tenth (10th)	der zehnte (10.)
Twentieth (20th)	der zwanzigste (20.)

CARDINAL NUMBERS

0 null	9 neun
1 eins	10 zehn
2 zwei	11 elf
3 drei	12 zwölf
4 vier	13 dreizehn
5 fünf	14 vierzehn
6 sechs	15 fünfzehn
7 sieben	16 sechzehn
8 acht	17 siebzehn

---

[1]In German, ordinal numbers take adjectival endings. Please refer to the grammar summary on page 229 for more on adjectives.

18 achtzehn	29 neunundzwanzig
19 neunzehn	30 dreißig
20 zwanzig	40 vierzig
21 einundzwanzig	50 fünfzig
22 zweiundzwanzig	60 sechzig
23 dreiundzwanzig	70 siebzig
24 vierundzwanzig	80 achtzig
25 fünfundzwanzig	90 neunzig
26 sechsundzwanzig	100 einhundert/hundert
27 siebenundzwanzig	200 zweihundert
28 achtundzwanzig	210 zweihundert(und)zehn

$1,000^2$	eintausend
10,000	zehntausend
100,000	hunderttausend
1,000,000	eine Million
1,000,000,000	eine Milliarde

½	ein Halb
⅓	ein Drittel
¼	ein Viertel
⅕	ein Fünftel
⅒	ein Zehntel
1/100	ein Hundertstel

0.1	null Komma eins
0.2	null Komma zwei
0.5	null Komma fünf
0.25	null Komma fünfundzwanzig
0.75	null Komma fünfundsiebzig

BASIC MATHEMATICAL TERMS

Absolute value	der absolute Zahlenwert
Acute angle	der Spitzwinkel
Add (to)	addieren
Addition	die Addition

---

[2] In German, a period (.) is used in place of a comma (,), while a comma is used in place of a decimal point. Therefore, the English number 1,000 would be written as 1.000 in German, and the English number 0.25 would be written 0,25 in German.

Algebra	die Algebra
Algorithm	der Algorithmus
Amortize (to)	amortisieren
Angle	der Winkel
Approximation	die Annäherung
Area	die Fläche (*surface*)
Asymptote	die Asymptote
Average	der Durchschnitt
Axis (horizontal/vertical)	die Achse (horizontale/ vertikale)
Bell-shaped curve	die glockenförmige Kurve
Binary	binär
Bimodal distribution	zweigleisige Verteilung
Binomial	binomisch
Boolean algebra	boolesche Algebra
Breakeven analysis	die Gewinnschwellenanalyse
Calculate (to)	berechnen
Calculator	der Rechner
Calculus	die Differential- und Integralrechnung
Cardinal number	die Kardinalzahl
Chaos theory	die Chaostheorie
Chi square test	der Chi-Quadrat-Anpassungstest/der Test der wahrscheinlichen Dichte
Circumference	der Umfang
Coefficient	der Koeffizient
Compound interest	der Zinseszins
Concave	konkav
Count (to)	zählen
Cone	der Kegel
Congruent	kongruent
Constant	konstant
Convex	konvex
Correlation	die Beziehung
Cube	der Würfel
Cubed root	die kubische Wurzel/ die Wurzel hoch drei

Cylinder	der Zylinder
Decimal	dezimal
Delta	delta
Denominator	der Nenner
Dependent variable	die abhängige Variable
Depth	die Tiefe
Derivative	die Ableitung/die Funktion
Diameter	der Durchmesser
Difference	die Differenz
Differentiation	die Differenzierung
Digit	die Ziffer
Dispersion	die Streuung
Divide (to)	dividieren
Division	die Division/die Teilung
Ellipsis	die Ellipse
Elliptical	elliptisch
Equation	die Gleichung
Exponent	der Exponent
F distribution	die F-Verteilung
Factor	der Faktor
Factorial	die Fakultät
Formula	die Formel
Fraction	der Bruch
Future value	der Zukunftswert/der zukünftige Wert
Geometry	die Geometrie
Geometric figure	die geometrische Figur
Geometric progression	die geometrische Progression
Geometric shape	die geometrische Figur
Height	die Höhe
Histogram	das Histogramm
Hyperbola	die Hyperbel
Hypotenuse	die Hypotenuse
Hypothesis	die Hypothese
Imaginary number	die imaginäre Zahl
Independent variable	die unabhängige Variable
Inequalities	die Ungleichheiten

Infinity	die Unendlichkeit
Inflection point	der Wendepunkt
Integer	die Ganzzahl/die Vollzahl
Integral	das Integral
Integration	die Integration
Interest	die Zinsen
Interval	das Intervall
Inverse	die Inversion/die Umkehrung
Irrational number	die irrationale Zahl
Length	die Länge
Linear	linear
Linear programming	die lineare Programmierung
Logarithm	der Logarithmus
Matrix	die Matrix
Mean	der Mittelwert/der Durchschnitt
Median (value)	der Mittelwert
Multiple	das Vielfache/das Mehrfache
Multiplication	die Multiplikation
Multiply (to)	multiplizieren
Net present value	der Nettozeitwert
Nominal	nominal
Null hypothesis	die Nullhypothese
Numerator	der Zähler
Obtuse angle	der stumpfe Winkel
Octagon	das Oktagon
Optimization	die Optimierung
Ordinal number	die Ordinalzahl
Origin	der Ursprung
Outline	der Umriss
Parabola	die Parabel
Parameter	der Parameter
Parallel	parallel
Parallelogram	das Parallelogramm
Pascal's triangle	das paskalsche Dreieck
Pentagon	das Pentagon
Percent	das Prozent

Percentage	der Prozentsatz
Perpendicular	die Mittelsenkrechte
Pi	das Pi
Plain	die Fläche
Polygon	das Vieleck
Polynomial	polynominal
Power	die Potenz
Prism	das Prisma
Present value	der Zeitwert
Probability	die Wahrscheinlichkeit
Proportion	die Proportion
Pyramid	die Pyramide
Quadratic equation	die quadratische Gleichung
Quotient	der Quotient
R-squared	r-Quadrat
Radical sign	das Wurzelzeichen
Radius	der Radius
Random	zufällig/willkürlich
Random number	die Zufallszahl
Range	der Bereich
Rational number	die rationale Zahl
Ratio	das Verhältnis
Real	real
Reciprocal	umgekehrt/reziprok
Rectangular	rechteckig
Regression line	die rückläufige Linie
Rhomboid	die Romboide
Rhombus	die Rombe
Right angle	der rechte Winkel
Sample	die Probe
Scientific notation	der wissenschaftliche Vermerk
Sigma	das Sigma/die Standartabweichung
Significance	die Signifikanz/die Bedeutsamkeit
Six sigma	die sechs Sigmata/die sechs Standardabweichungen

Skewed distribution	die schiefe Verteilung
Sphere	die Kugel
Square	das Quadrat
Square of a number	die Quadratzahl
Square root	die Quadratwurzel
Standard deviation	die Standardabweichung/das Sigma
Statistics	die Statistik
Student's t-test	die statistische T-Verteilung
Subtract (to)	abziehen
Subtraction	die Subtraktion
Sum	die Summe
T-test	der statistische T-Verteilungstest
Tri-dimensional	dreidimensional
Variable	die Variable
Vector	der Vektor
Volume	das Volumen
Weight	das Gewicht
Weighted average	das Durchschnittsgewicht
Width	die Breite
Zero	die Null

ACRONYMS AND ABBREVIATIONS

The English column is listed alphabetically and contains the names of important American associations (with their acronyms) and abbreviations. The German translation or an equivalent is given in the right column. In addition, the left column also contains the translation of common or important German acronyms and abbreviations. The relevant acronyms or abbreviations in each column are in boldface type.

AAA American Automobile Association

ADAC Allgemeiner Deutscher Automobilclub (*similar association for Germany*)

AD&D Accidental Death and Dismemberment	Unfallversicherung im Todesfall oder bei völliger Arbeitsunfähigkeit
A.D.	n.Chr. nach Christi
ADP Automated Data Processing	Automatische Datenverarbeitung
aka also known as	auch bekannt als
AMEX American Stock Exchange	AMEX Amerikanische Börse
Among other (things)	u.a. unter anderem
And similar	u.ä. und ähnliches
APR Annual Percentage Rate	jährliche Zinsrate/jahrlicher Zinssatz
Arrival	Ank. Ankunft
ASAP as soon as possible	SBWM so bald wie möglich (*also:* ASAP)
ASCII American Standard Code for Information Interchange	ASCIA Amerikanischer Standardcode für Informationsaustausch
ATM Automated Teller Machine	Geldautomat
At the present time	z.Z. zur Zeit
Austrian Automobile, Motorcycle, and Touring	ÖAMTC Österreichischer Automobil-, Association Motorrad- und Touring-Club
Automobile Association of Switzerland	ACS Automobil-Club der Schweiz
B.C.	v. Chr. vor Christus
BLS Bureau of Labor Statistics	Amt für Arbeitsstatistik
bps bits per second	BpS Bits pro Sekunde

ca circa	**ca.** zirka
CAP Common Agricultural Policy	**GAP** Gemeinsame Agrarpolitik
Central European Time	**MEZ** Mitteleuropäische Zeit
CD Compact Disc	**CD** (Compact Disc)
CD-ROM Compact Disc, Read-Only Memory	**CD-ROM**
CEO Chief Executive Officer	Generaldirektor/ Geschäftsführer(in)
CERN Conseil Europeen pour la Recherche Nucleaire	**CERN** (*same*)
CFO Chief Financial Officer	Finanzdirektor/ Finanzleiter(in)
CIS Commonwealth of Independent States	Gemeinschaft Unabhängiger Staaten
CISC Complex Instruction Set Computer	(same, but not common)
c/o care of	**z. Hdn.** (zu Händen von) also: **c/o**
COBOL Common Business Oriented Language	**COBOL**
COD Cash On Delivery or Collect On Delivery	per Nachnahme
COLA Cost Of Living Adjustment	Teuerungszulage
COO Chief Operating Officer	Produktionsdirektor/ Betriebsleiter
CPA Certified Public Accountant	zertifizierter öffentlicher Buchhalter (Steuerberater).
CPI Consumer Price Index	Konsumenten-Preis-Index
cpi characters per inch	**cpi** Zeichen per Zoll

CPM Cost Per Thousand	**KPT** Kosten pro Tausend
cps characters per second	**cps** Zeichen pro Sekunde
CPU Central Processing Unit	**CPU** (*same*)
CRT Cathode Ray Tube	Kathodenröhre
Departure	**Abf** Abfahrt/Abflug
DMV Department of Motor Vehicles	**KFZ-Amt** Kraftfahrzeugsamt
DOS Disk Operating System	**DOS** (*same*)
DP Data Processing	**EDV** elektronische Datenverarbeitung
DSL Digital Subscriber Line	**ADSL** Asymmetrische digitale Teilnehmerleitung
DTP Desktop Publishing	**DTP** desktop publishing
EAFE Europe, Australia, Far East	**EAFE** (*same*)
EC European Community	**EC** European Community
EEC European Economic Community	**EEC** European Economic Community
EFT Electronic Funds Transfer	elektronische Geldüberweisung
EIB Export-Import Bank	**EIB** (*same*)
EMU European Economic and Monetary Union	**EMU** (*same*)
Error 404 (file not found)	Fehler 404 (Datei nicht gefunden)
etc. et cetera	**usw.** und so weiter
EU European Union	**EU** Europäische Union
FAQ Frequently Asked Questions	Häufig gestellte Fragen
FAS Free Alongside Ship	frei Kai

Fax Facsimile transmission **Fax** (*same*)

FDA Food and Drug Administration — Amerikanisches Amt für die Zulassung von Lebensmitteln und Medikamenten

Fed Federal Reserve System — die Bundesbank

FIFO First In, First Out — Bearbeitung nach Eingangsreihenfolge

FMV Fair Market Value — angemessener Marktwert

FOB Free On Board — Verladung frei

FORTRAN Formula Translation — **FORTRAN**

FTP File Transfer Protocol **FTP** (*same*)

FV Future Value — Zukunftswert

FYI For Your Information — zu Ihrer Information

G or GB gigabyte **GB** (*same*)

GATT General Agreement on Tarifs and Trade — Internationales Tarif- und Handelsabkommen (*slightly similar*)

GDP Gross Domestic Product — Bruttoinlandsprodukt

GNP Gross National Product — **BNP** Bruttonationalprodukt

GTC Good Till Canceled — gültig bis zum Wiederruf

GUI Graphical User Interface — **GUI** (*same*)

HDTV High Definition Television — **HDTV** (*same*)

HMO Health Maintenance Organization — **AOK** Allgemeine Ortskrankenkasse (*similar organization*)

HP Horsepower	**PS** Pferdestärke
HR Human Resources	**P.A.** Personalabteilung
HTML Hypertext Markup Language	**HTML** (*same*)
HTTP Hypertext Transport Protocol	**HTTP** (*same*)
Hz Hertz	**Hz** Hertz
IMF International Monetary Fund	**IWF** Internationaler Währungsfonds
Inc. Incorporated	**Fa.** Firma
incl. inclusive	**einschl.** einschließlich
I/O Input-Output	**I/O** (*only electronics/computer*)
IP Internet Protocol	**IP** Internet-Protokoll
IRC Internet Relay Chat	**IRC** Internet-Übertragungs-Chat
IRR Internal Rate of Return	interne Profitrate
ISBN International Standard Book Number	**ISBN** Internationale Standardbuchnummer
ISDN Integrated Services Digital Network	**ISDN** Internationale Services-Digital-Netzwerk
ISSN International Standard Serial Number	**ISSN** Internationale Standardseriennummer
ITC International Trade Commission	**ITC** Internationale Handelskommission
JIT Just-In-Time inventory or Just-In-Time manufacturing	**JIT**-Lagerhaltung/JIT-Produktion
K or KB Kilobyte	**K or KB** Kilobyte
LAN Local Area Network	**LAN** Lokales Netzwerk
LCD Liquid Crystal Display	**LCD** Liquid-Crystal-Display

LED Light-Emitting Diode	**LED** Lichtdiode
Limited partnership corporation	**KG** Kommanditgesellschaft
Ltd. Company with limited liability	**GmbH** Gesellschaft mit beschränkter Haftung
MB or Megs Megabyte	**MB** or **Megs** Megabytes
MBO Management By Objectives	zielorientiertes Management
MFN Most-Favored Nation	bevorzugte Nation
MHz Megahertz	**MHz** Megahertz
MICR Magnetic Ink Character Recognition	**MICR** (*same*)
MIPS Million Instructions Per Second	**MIPS** (*same*)
MIS Management Information Systems	**MIS** Management-Informations-Systeme
MLM Multi-Level Marketing	**MLM** Multi-Level-Marketing
NAFTA North American Free Trade Agreement	**NAFTA** Nordamerikanisches Freihandelsabkommen
NASA National Aeronautics and Space Administration	**NASA** Amerikanische Luft- und aumfahrtadministration
NASD National Association of Securities Dealers	**NASD** Amerikanischer Verband der Börsenmakler
NASDAQ National Association of Securities Dealers Automated Quotation	**NASDAQ** Amerikanischer Verband der Börsenmakler mit automatischer Quotierung
NAV Net Asset Value	der Nettobetriebswert

NOI Net Operating Income	das Nettobetriebseinkommen
NOL Net Operating Loss	der Nettobetriebsverlust
NPV Net Present Value	**NZW** Nettozeitwert
ns nanosecond	**ns** Nanosekunde
NYSE New York Stock Exchange	**NYSE** New Yorker Börse
OCR Optical Character Recognition	Optische Zeichenerkennung
OECD Organization for Economic Cooperation and Development	Organisation für wirtschaftliche Kooperation und Entwicklung
OEM Original Equipment Manufacturer	Originalhersteller
OJT On-the-Job Training	das Training am Arbeitsplatz
OPEC Organization of Petroleum Exporting Countries	**OPEC** (*same*)
OPM Other People's Money	**ALG** anderer Leute Geld (*uncommon*)
P&L Profit and Loss statement	die Gewinn- und Verlustrechnung
PC Personal Computer	**PC** (*only abbreviation used*)
PCS Personal Communications Services	persönliche Kommunikationsdienste
PDA Personal Digital Assistant	Persönlicher Minicomputer
P/E Price/Earnings ratio	Preis-Gewinn-Verhältnis
PERT Program Evaluation Review Technique	Technik zur nachträglichen Programmbeurteilung
PGIM Potential Gross Income Multiplier	potenzieller Bruttoumsatzmultiplikator

PIN Personal Identification Number	**PIN** persönliche Identifikationsnummer
PMS Pantone® Matching System	Pantone-Farbskala
POP Point-Of-Purchase display	Kassenverkaufsdisplay
PPP Purchasing Power Parity	Kaufkraftsparität
prefab Prefabricated house	Fertighaus
Public company (stock market)	**AG** Aktiengesellschaft
PV Present Value	**ZW** Zeitwert
R&D Research and Development	**F&E** Forschung und Entwicklung (also: **R&D**)
RAM Random Access Memory	**RAM** Random Access Memory
Registered Association	**e.V.** eingetragener Verein
RGB Red, Green, and Blue	**RGB** rot, grün und blau
ROI Return On Investment	**ROI** Investitionsgewinn
ROM Read-Only Memory	**ROM** (read only memory)
SIG Special-Interest Group	spezielle Interessengruppe
SKU Stock-Keeping Unit	Lagerhaltungseinheit
SLIP Serial Line Internet Protocol	SLIP
SMSA Standard Metropolitan Statistical Area	Urbanes standardmäßiges Statistikgebiet
SOP Standard Operating Procedure	standardisierte Betriebsrichtlinie
spec on speculation	auf angenommener Basis
Street	**Str.** Straße

210

T or TB terabyte	**T or TB** Terabyte
T&E Travel and Entertainment expense	Fahrtkosten und Unterhaltungsspesen
TIN Taxpayer Identification Number	die Steuernummer
Top Level Domain for Austria (**.as**)	**as** Internet-Spitzendomäne für Österreich
Top Level Domain for Germany (**.de**)	**de** Internet-Spitzendomäne für Deutschland
Top level Domain for Switzerland (**.ch**)	**ch** Internet-Spitzendomäne für die Schweiz
TQM Total Quality Management	**TQM** Gesamtqualitätsleitung
UPC Universal Product Code	**UPC** (universeller Poduktcode)
URL Uniform Resource Locator	**URL** (einheitlicher Ressourcenlokalisator)
VAT Value Added Tax	**MwSt** die Mehrwertsteuer
VGA Video Graphic Array	**VGA** Video-Graphik-Anordnung
VP Vice President	**VP** Vizepräsident(in)
WAIS Wide Area Information Server	Informationsserver mit großem Streugebiet
WWW World Wide Web	**WWW** WoldWideWeb
YTD Year-To-Date	laufendes Jahr

COUNTRIES, CONTINENTS, AND LANGUAGES
Countries

Argentina	Argentinien
Australia	Australien
Bolivia	Bolivien

Brazil	Brasilien
Canada	Kanada
Chile	Chile
China	China
Colombia	Kolumbien
Costa Rica	Costa Rica
Cuba	Kuba
Dominican Republic	Dominikanische Republik
Ecuador	Ecuador
Egypt	Ägypten
El Salvador	El Salvador
England	England
Finland	Finnland
France	Frankreich
Germany	Deutschland
Great Britain	Großbritanien
Greece	Griechenland
Guatemala	Guatemala
Haiti	Haiti
Holland	Holland
Honduras	Honduras
Hungary	Ungarn
Iceland	Island
Iran	Iran
Iraq	Irak
Ireland	Irland
Israel	Israel
Italy	Italien
Japan	Japan
Malaysia	Malaysia
Mexico	Mexiko
Morocco	Marokko
Nicaragua	Nicaragua
Norway	Norwegen
Panama	Panama
Paraguay	Paraguay
Peru	Peru
Poland	Polen

Portugal	Portugal
Puerto Rico	Puerto Rico
Romania	Rumänien
Russia	Russland
Saudi Arabia	Saudi Arabien
South Africa	Südafrika
Spain	Spanien
Sweden	Schweden
Switzerland	Schweiz (die)
Thailand	Thailand
Taiwan	Taiwan
Turkey	Türkei (die)
United States of America	Vereinigte Staaten von Amerika
Uruguay	Uruguay
Venezuela	Venezuela

Continents

Africa	Afrika
Antarctica	Antarktis (die)
Asia	Asien
Australia	Australien
Europe	Europa
North America	Nordamerika
South America	Südamerika

Languages

Arabic	arabisch
Bengali	bengali
Chinese (Cantonese)	kantonesisch
Chinese (Mandarin)	mandarin
English	englisch
Finnish	finnisch
French	französisch
Greek	griechisch
German	deutsch
Hebrew	hebräisch

Hungarian	ungarisch
Hindi	hindi
Italian	italienisch
Japanese	japanisch
Korean	koreanisch
Malay	malaysisch
Polish	polisch
Portuguese	portugiesisch
Russian	russisch
Spanish	spanisch
Swedish	schwedisch
Thai	thai
Turkish	türkisch
Ukrainian	ukrainisch

APPENDIX A: Measurements

Miles/Kilometers

1 kilometer (km) =				1 mile = 1.61 km				
0.62 miles				(1,61 km)				

Kilometers	1	5	10	15	20	50	75	100	150
Miles	0.62	3.1	6.2	9.3	12.4	31	46.5	62	93

Gallons/Liters

1 liter (l) =			1 gallon = 3.75 liters				
0.26 gallon			(3,75 l)				

Liters	10	15	20	30	40	50	60	70
Gallons	2.6	3.9	5.2	7.8	10.4	13	15.6	18.2

Women's Clothing Sizes

Coats, dresses, suits, skirts, slacks

U.S.	4	6	8	10	12	14	16
Europe	36	38	40	42	44	46	48

Blouses/Sweaters

U.S.	32/6	34/8	36/10	38/12	40/14	42/16
Europe	38/2	40/3	42/4	44/5	46/6	48/7

Shoes

U.S.	4	4½	5	5½	6	6½	7	7½	8	8½	9	9½	10	11
Europe	35	35	36	36	37	37	38	38	39	39	40	40	41	42

Men's Clothing Sizes

Suits/Coats

U.S.	34	36	38	40	42	44	46	48
Europe	44	46	48	50	52	54	56	58

Slacks

U.S.	30	31	32	33	34	35	36	37	38	39
Europe	38	39–40	41	42	43	44–45	46	47	48–49	50

Shirts

U.S.	14	$14^{1/2}$	15	$15^{1/2}$	16	$16^{1/2}$	17	$17^{1/2}$	18
Europe	36	37	38	39	40	41	42	43	44

Sweaters

U.S.	XS/36	S/38	M/40	L/42	XL/44
Europe	42/2	44/3	46–48/4	50/5	52–54/6

Shoes

U.S.	7	$7^{1/2}$	8	$8^{1/2}$	9	$9^{1/2}$	10	$10^{1/2}$	11
Europe	39	40	41	42	43	43	44	44	45

APPENDIX A

Measurements

Weights and Measures

Weight

Metric
1 gram (g) = 0.035 ounce
100 grams = 3.5 ounces
1 kilogram (kilo) = 2.2 pounds

U.S.
1 ounce = 28.35 grams
1 pound = 454 grams
100 pounds = 45.4 kilos

Liquid

Metric
1 liter (l) = 4.226 cups
1 l = 2.113 pints
1 l = 1.056 quarts
1 l = 0.264 gallon

U.S.
1 cup = 0.236 liter
1 pint = 0.473 l
1 quart = 0.947 l
1 gallon = 3.785 l

Temperature Conversions

To Convert
Celsius to Fahrenheit

$(9/5)C° + 32 = F°$
1. Divide by 5
2. Multiply by 9
3. Add 32

To Convert Fahrenheit
to Celsius

$(F° - 32)5/9 = C°$
1. Subtract 32
2. Divide by 9
3. Multiply by 5

Celsius	–17.8	0	10	15.6	23.9	30	37	100
Fahrenheit	0	32	50	60	75	86	98.6	212

y of Switzerland
thedral Ave NW
gton, D.C. 20008
2) 745–7900
2) 387–2564

RICAN CONSULATES:

any:

ssy to the United States Berlin
ädtische Kirchstr. 4–5
Berlin
al Republic of Germany
(030) 8305–0

assy of the United States Berlin
ular Section
allee 170
5 Berlin
eral Republic of Germany
rican Citizen Services:
(030) 832–9233
: (030) 8305–1215

. Consulate General Munich
niginstraße 5
39 München
deral Republic of Germany
l.: (089) 2888–0
x: (089) 280–9998

Austria:

merican Embassy Vienna
onsular Section
artenbaupromenade 2
–1010 Wien
el.: (01) 31339–0
ax: (01) 512 58 35

APPENDIX B:
Useful Addresses, Telephone Numbers, and Web Sites

EMERGENCY TELEPHONE NUMBERS:

	Germany	Austria	Switzerland
Ambulance	112	144	118
Fire	112	122	118
Police	110	133	117
Information	01188	011811	01188

COUNTRY CODE/INFORMATION:

Germany: 49 (plus city code)
Austria: 43 (plus city code)
Switzerland: 41 (plus city code)

Do not dial the 0 of the city code if you call from outside the country.

EMBASSIES/CONSULATES:

German Consulates/Embassies in the United States:

German Embassy
4645 Reservoir Rd.
Washington, DC 20007–1998
Tel.: (202) 298–4000
Fax: (202) 298–4249 or (202) 333–2653

German Consulate General
871 United Nations Plaza
New York, NY 10017
Tel.: (212) 610–9700
Fax: (212) 610–9702/3/4/5

German Consulate General
1960 Jackson Street

San Francisco, CA 94109
Tel.: (415) 775–1061
Fax: (415) 775–0187
E-mail: gksf@pacbell.net

German Consulate General
1330 Post Oak Blvd., Suite 1850
Houston, TX 77056
Tel.: (713) 627–7770
Fax: (713) 627–0506
E-mail: info@germanconsulatehouston.org

German Consulate General
6222 Wilshire Blvd., Suite 500
Los Angeles, CA 90048
Tel.: (323) 930–2703
Fax: (323) 930–2805
E-mail: losangeles@germanconsulate.org

Austrian Consulates/Embassies in the United States:

Austrian Embassy
3524 International Court, NW
Washington, DC 20008–3027
Tel.: (202) 895–6700
Fax: (202) 895–6750
Consular Section
Tel.: (202) 895–6767
Fax: (202) 895–6773
E-mail: obwascon@sysnet.net

Austrian Consulate, Chicago
Wrigley Building, Suite 707
400 N. Michigan Avenue
Chicago, IL 60611
Tel.: (312) 222–1515
Fax: (312) 222–4113
E-mail: AustriaCG@aol.com

Austrian Consulate, Los Angeles
11859 Wilshire Blvd., Suite 501
Los Angeles, CA 90025
Tel.: (310) 444–9310
Fax: (310) 477–9897
E-mail: ausconsla@aol.com

Austrian Consulate, New York
31 East 69th Street
New York, NY 10021
Tel.: (212) 737–6400
Fax: (212) 772–8926
E-mail: austroko@interport.net

Swiss Consulates/Embassies in the United

Consulate General of Switzerland
11766 Wilshire Blvd., Suite 1400
Los Angeles, CA 90025
Tel.: (310) 575–1145
Fax: (310) 575–1982
E-mail: vertretung@los.rep.admin.ch

Consulate General of Switzerland
633 Third Avenue, 30th Floor
New York, NY 10017-6706
Tel.: (212) 599–5700 or (888) 847–4266
Fax: (212) 599–4266
E-mail: Consular Affairs: vertretung@nyc.r
                Commerce: trade@nyc.rep.admin.c

Consulate General of Switzerland
1000 Louisiana, Suite 5670
Houston, TX 77002
Tel.: (713) 650–0000
Fax: (713) 650–1321
E-mail: vertretung@hou.rep.admin.ch

In Switzerland:

Embassy of the United States Bern
Jubiläumsstraße 93, 3001 Bern
Important Telephone Numbers:
Embassy Bern: (031) 357–7011
24-hour Emergency Number: (031) 357–7218
Embassy Fax: (031) 357–7344

CHAMBERS OF COMMERCE:

For Germany:

German American Chamber of Commerce
40 W 57th St., 31st Floor
New York, NY 10029
Web site: www.gaccny.com
E-mail: info@gaccny.com

German American Chamber of Commerce
401 North Michigan Ave., Suite 2525
Chicago, IL 60611-4212
Tel.: (312) 644–2662

German American Chamber of Commerce
5220 Pacific Concourse Drive, Suite 280
Los Angeles, CA 90045
Tel.: (310) 297–7979
Fax: (310) 297–7966
Web site: gaccwest@earthlink.net

For Austria:

U.S. Austrian Chamber of Commerce
165 W 46th St., Suite 112
New York, NY 10036
Tel.: (212) 819–0117

For Switzerland:

Swiss-American Chamber of Commerce
608 Fifth Ave., Suite 309

New York, NY 10020
Tel.: (212) 246–7789
E-mail: swissny@mindspring.com

Swiss-American Chamber of Commerce
P.O. Box 26007
San Francisco, CA 04126
Tel.: (415) 433–6601

MAJOR AIRLINES:
All telephone numbers are toll-free and provide flight information as well as flight reservations.

In the US:	Lufthansa/Condor	(800) 645–3880
	Condor	(800) 524–6975
	Swissair	(800) 221–4750
	American Airlines	(800) 433–7300
	Delta	(800) 241–4141
In Germany:	Lufthansa	0180 380 38 03
	Condor	0180 380 38 03
	Delta	0180 333 78 88
In Switzerland:	Swissair	0848 800 600
	(Business Travel)	
In Austria:	Austrian Airlines	0180 300 05 20
	Aus Air Trans	0180 300 05 20
	Lufthansa	0800 900 800

INTERESTING SITES ON THE INTERNET:
Major search engines for German, Austrian, and Swiss sites are Yahoo, Fireball, Altavista, Hotbot, Lycos, and Excite. The top-level domain for Germany is .de, for Austria .at, and for Switzerland .ch. Many large online services and portals have a mirror site, i.e., MSN (Microsoft-Network).

Yahoo is a good way to start out looking for sites in Germany: **www.de.yahoo.com**.

A list of industry sites in Germany is provided at **web.msn.de/r?70&538-22043-673-4057**.

A list of industry sites in Switzerland is at **www. branchenbuch.ch**.

Austrian Yellow Pages (*Die Gelben Seiten des Internet*) are found at **www.oesterreichonline.at**.

An online telephone book including Yellow Pages (*die Gelben Seiten*) and e-mail addresses can be found at **www.t-online.de** for Germany, or **www.t-online.at** for Austria. Here you have the advantage of choosing other languages for your search.

If you want to find out about the German stock exchange or other financial information in German, one of the many possibilities is **www.t-online.de/finanzen**.

A German-American business guide in English and German is at **www.gaccny.com/en-US/Resources/index. html**.

You can access a free dictionary with 300,000 entries through **dict.leo.org**. Translation services as well as many free specialty dictionaries can be accessed through **www.provide.net/~kfulton/Dicts.html**.

The site for the major German weekly magazine *Der Spiegel* can be found at **www.spiegel.de**.

To check on weather, theaters, concerts, airline and train schedules, and any other events in major German cities go to **www.msn.de/meinestadt**.

Amazon has a German site as well. So if you need a German book, DVD, or video, go to **www.amazon.de**.

APPENDIX C:
National and Religious Holidays

HOLIDAYS IN GERMANY:

New Year's Day	January 1
Good Friday	Varies by year (not all states)
Easter Monday	Varies by year
Labor Day	May 1
Ascension Day	Varies by year
Whit Monday	Varies by year
National Unity Day	October 3
Christmas Day	December 25
Boxing Day	December 26

HOLIDAYS IN AUSTRIA:

New Year's Day	January 1
Epiphany	January 6
Easter Monday	Varies by year
Labor Day	May 1
Ascension Day	Varies by year
Whit Monday	Varies by year
Corpus Christi	Varies by year
Assumption of the Virgin	August 15
National Holiday	October 26
All Saints' Day	November 1
Immaculate Conception	December 8
Christmas Day	December 25
Boxing Day	December 26

HOLIDAYS IN SWITZERLAND:

New Year's Day	January 1
January 2	January 2 (not all cantons)
Good Friday	Varies by year
Easter Monday	Varies by year

National and Religious Holidays

Ascension Day	Varies by year
Whit Monday	Varies by year
National Day	August 1
Christmas Day	December 25
Boxing Day	December 26

APPENDIX D:
Grammar Summary
and Verb Charts

1. THE DEFINITE ARTICLE

	MASCULINE	FEMININE	NEUTER	PLURAL
Nom.	der	die	das	die
Acc.	den	die	das	die
Dat.	dem	der	dem	den
Gen.	des	der	des	der

2. DER-WORDS: DIESER, JENER, WELCHER, JEDER, ALLE, MANCHE, SOLCHE

	MASCULINE	FEMININE	NEUTER	PLURAL
Nom.	dieser	diese	dieses	diese
Acc.	diesen	diese	dieses	diese
Dat.	diesem	dieser	diesem	diesen
Gen.	dieses	dieser	dieses	dieser

3. THE INDEFINITE ARTICLE

	MASCULINE	FEMININE	NEUTER
Nom.	ein	eine	ein
Acc.	einen	eine	ein
Dat.	einem	einer	einem
Gen.	eines	einer	eines

4. EIN-WORDS: *KEIN, MEIN, DEIN, SEIN, IHR, UNSER, EUER, IHR, IHR*

	MASCULINE	FEMININE	NEUTER	PLURAL
Nom.	*mein*	*meine*	*mein*	*meine*
Acc.	*meinen*	*meine*	*mein*	*meine*
Dat.	*meinem*	*meiner*	*meinem*	*meinen*
Gen.	*meines*	*meiner*	*meines*	*meiner*

5. MASCULINE N-NOUNS

	SINGULAR	PLURAL
Nom.	*der Patient*	*die Patienten*
Acc.	*den Patienten*	*die Patienten*
Dat.	*dem Patienten*	*den Patienten*
Gen.	*des Patienten*	*der Patienten*

6. PRECEDED ADJECTIVES

	MASCULINE	FEMININE	NEUTER
Nom.	*der junge Mann*	*die alte Stadt*	*das graue Dach*
	ein junger Mann	*eine alte Stadt*	*ein graues Dach*

PLURAL

die guten Weine
keine guten Weine

	MASCULINE	FEMININE	NEUTER
Acc.	*den jungen Mann*	*die alte Stadt*	*das graue Dach*
	einen jungen Mann	*eine alte Stadt*	*ein graues Dach*

PLURAL

die guten Weine
keine guten Weine

Dat.	*dem jungen*	*der alten*	*dem grauen*
	Mann	*Stadt*	*Dach*
	einem jungen	*einer alten*	*einem grauen*
	Mann	*Stadt*	*Dach*

PLURAL

den guten Weinen
keinen guten Weinen

Gen.	*des jungen*	*der alten*	*des grauen*
	Mannes	*Stadt*	*Daches*
	eines jungen	*einer alten*	*eines grauen*
	Mannes	*Stadt*	*Daches*

PLURAL

der guten Weine
keiner guten Weine

7. UNPRECEDED ADJECTIVES

	MASCULINE	FEMININE	NEUTER	PLURAL
Nom.	*guter Kuchen*	*gute Torte*	*gutes Brot*	*gute Torten*
Acc.	*guten Kuchen*	*gute Torte*	*gutes Brot*	*gute Torten*
Dat.	*gutem Kuchen*	*guter Torte*	*gutem Brot*	*guten Torten*
Gen.	*guten Kuchens*	*guter Torte*	*guten Brotes*	*guter Torten*

8. PERSONAL PRONOUNS

SINGULAR

Nom.	*ich*	*du*	*er*	*sie*	*es*
Acc.	*mich*	*dich*	*ihn*	*sie*	*es*
Dat.	*mir*	*dir*	*ihm*	*ihr*	*ihm*

Nom.	wir	ihr	sie	Sie
Acc.	uns	euch	sie	Sie
Dat.	uns	euch	ihnen	Ihnen

9. INTERROGATIVE PRONOUNS

	MASC./FEM.	NEUTER
Nom.	wer	was
Acc.	wen	was
Dat.	wem	—
Gen.	wessen	wessen

10. THE DEMONSTRATIVE PRONOUNS

	MASCULINE	FEMININE	NEUTER	PLURAL
Nom.	der	die	das	die
Acc.	den	die	das	die
Dat.	dem	der	dem	denen

11. RELATIVE PRONOUNS

	MASCULINE	FEMININE	NEUTER	PLURAL
Nom.	der	die	das	die
Acc.	den	die	das	die
Dat.	dem	der	dem	denen
Gen.	dessen	deren	dessen	deren

12. VERBS IN THE INDICATIVE

PRESENT

I ask, I am asking, I do ask

ich	frage	wir	fragen
du	fragst	ihr	fragt
er/sie/es	fragt	sie	fragen
		Sie	fragen

PRESENT PERFECT

I have asked, I asked, I did ask

ich	habe gefragt	wir	haben gefragt
du	hast gefragt	ihr	habt gefragt
er/sie/es	hat gefragt	sie	haben gefragt
		Sie	haben gefragt

I have come, I came, I did come

ich	bin gekommen	wir	sind gekommen
du	bist gekommen	ihr	seid gekommen
er/sie/es	ist gekommen	sie	sind gekommen
		Sie	sind gekommen

SIMPLE PAST

I asked, I was asking

ich	fragte	wir	fragten
du	fragtest	ihr	fragtet
er/sie/es	fragte	sie	fragten
		Sie	fragten

I came, I was coming

ich	kam	wir	kamen
du	kamst	ihr	kamt
er/sie/es	kam	sie	kamen
		Sie	kamen

PAST PERFECT

I had asked

ich	hatte gefragt	wir	hatten gefragt
du	hattest gefragt	ihr	hattet gefragt
er/sie/es	hatte gefragt	sie	hatten gefragt
		Sie	hatten gefragt

I had come

ich	war gekommen	wir	waren gekommen
du	warst gekommen	ihr	wart gekommen
er/sie/es	war gekommen	sie	waren gekommen
		Sie	waren gekommen

FUTURE

I will ask

ich	werde fragen	wir	werden fragen
du	wirst fragen	ihr	werdet fragen
er/sie/es	wird fragen	sie	werden fragen
		Sie	werden fragen

13. VERBS IN THE SUBJUNCTIVE

PRESENT-TIME GENERAL SUBJUNCTIVE (SUBJUNCTIVE II)

I would ask

ich	fragte	wir	fragten
du	fragtest	ihr	fragtet
er/sie/es	fragte	sie	fragten
		Sie	fragten

I would come

ich	käme	wir	kämen
du	kämest	ihr	kämet
er/sie/es	käme	sie	kämen
		Sie	kämen

PAST-TIME GENERAL SUBJUNCTIVE (SUBJUNCTIVE II)

I would have asked

ich	*hätte gefragt*	*wir*	*hätten gefragt*
du	*hättest gefragt*	*ihr*	*hättet gefragt*
er/sie/es	*hätte gefragt*	*sie*	*hätten gefragt*
		Sie	*hätten gefragt*

I would have come

ich	*wäre gekommen*	*wir*	*wären gekommen*
du	*wärest gekommen*	*ihr*	*wäret gekommen*
er/sie/es	*wäre gekommen*	*sie*	*wären gekommen*
		Sie	*wären gekommen*

PRESENT-TIME SPECIAL SUBJUNCTIVE (SUBJUNCTIVE I)

I would ask

ich	*frage*	*wir*	*fragen*
du	*fragest*	*ihr*	*fraget*
er/sie/es	*frage*	*sie*	*fragen*
		Sie	*fragen*

I would come

ich	*komme*	*wir*	*kommen*
du	*kommest*	*ihr*	*kommet*
er/sie/es	*komme*	*sie*	*kommen*
		Sie	*kommen*

PAST-TIME SPECIAL SUBJUNCTIVE (SUBJUNCTIVE I)

I asked (indirect speech)

ich	habe gefragt	wir	haben gefragt
du	habest gefragt	ihr	habet gefragt
er/sie/es	habe gefragt	sie	haben gefragt
		Sie	haben gefragt

I came (indirect speech)

ich	sei gekommen	wir	seien gekommen
du	seiest gekommen	ihr	seiet gekommen
er/sie/es	sei gekommen	sie	seien gekommen
		Sie	seien gekommen

FUTURE-TIME SPECIAL SUBJUNCTIVE (SUBJUNCTIVE I)

I will ask (indirect speech)

ich	werde fragen	wir	werden fragen
du	werdest fragen	ihr	werdet fragen
er/sie/es	werde fragen	sie	werden fragen
		Sie	werden fragen

14. PASSIVE VOICE

PRESENT

I am asked

ich	werde gefragt	wir	werden gefragt
du	wirst gefragt	ihr	werdet gefragt
er/sie/es	wird gefragt	sie	werden gefragt
		Sie	werden gefragt

SIMPLE PAST

I was asked, I have been asked

ich	wurde gefragt	wir	wurden gefragt
du	wurdest gefragt	ihr	wurdet gefragt
er/sie/es	wurde gefragt	sie	wurden gefragt
		Sie	wurden gefragt

PRESENT PERFECT

I was asked, I have been asked

ich	bin gefragt worden	wir	sind gefragt worden
du	bist gefragt worden	ihr	seid gefragt worden
er/sie/es	ist gefragt worden	sie	sind gefragt worden
		Sie	sind gefragt worden

PAST PERFECT

I had been asked

ich	war gefragt worden	wir	waren gefragt worden
du	warst gefragt worden	ihr	wart gefragt worden
er/sie/es	war gefragt worden	sie	waren gefragt worden

15. PRINCIPAL PARTS OF STRONG VERBS, IRREGULAR WEAK VERBS, AND MODALS

INFINITIVE	PRESENT	SIMPLE PAST	PAST PARTICIPLE
anfangen to begin	*fängt an*	*fing an*	*angefangen*
backen to bake	*bäckt*	*buk (backte)*	*gebacken*
beginnen to begin		*begann*	*begonnen*

INFINITIVE	PRESENT	SIMPLE PAST	PAST PARTICIPLE
bekommen to receive		*bekam*	*bekommen*
beweisen to prove		*bewies*	*bewiesen*
bieten to offer		*bot*	*geboten*
bleiben to remain		*blieb*	*ist geblieben*
brechen to break	*bricht*	*brach*	*gebrochen*
bringen to bring		*brachte*	*gebracht*
denken to think		*dachte*	*gedacht*
dürfen to be allowed to	*darf*	*durfte*	*gedurft*
einladen to invite	*lädt ein*	*lud ein*	*eingeladen*
empfehlen to recommend	*empfiehlt*	*empfahl*	*empfohlen*
essen to eat	*ißt*	*aß*	*gegessen*
fahren to drive	*fährt*	*fuhr*	*ist gefahren*
fallen to fall	*fällt*	*fiel*	*ist gefallen*
finden to find		*fand*	*gefunden*

INFINITIVE	PRESENT	SIMPLE PAST	PAST PARTICIPLE
fliegen to fly		*flog*	*ist geflogen*
frieren to freeze		*fror*	*gefroren*
geben to give	*gibt*	*gab*	*gegeben*
gefallen to please	*gefällt*	*gefiel*	*gefallen*
gehen to go		*ging*	*ist gegangen*
genießen to enjoy		*genoss*	*genossen*
gewinnen to win		*gewann*	*gewonnen*
greifen to seize		*griff*	*gegriffen*
haben to have	*hat*	*hatte*	*gehabt*
halten to hold; to stop	*hält*	*hielt*	*gehalten*
hängen to hang, be hanging		*hing*	*gehangen*
heißen to be called, named		*hieß*	*geheißen*
helfen to help	*hilft*	*half*	*geholfen*

INFINITIVE	PRESENT	SIMPLE PAST	PAST PARTICIPLE
kennen to know		*kannte*	*gekannt*
kommen to come		*kam*	*ist gekommen*
können to be able to, can	*kann*	*konnte*	*gekonnt*
lassen to let, leave behind	*läßt*	*ließ*	*gelassen*
laufen to run, walk	*läuft*	*lief*	*ist gelaufen*
leiden to suffer		*litt*	*gelitten*
leihen to lend, to borrow		*lieh*	*geliehen*
lesen to read	*liest*	*las*	*gelesen*
liegen to lie (down)		*lag*	*gelegen*
mögen to like (to)	*mag*	*mochte*	*gemocht*
müssen to have to, must	*muss*	*musste*	*gemusst*
nehmen to take	*nimmt*	*nahm*	*genommen*
nennen to name, call		*nannte*	*genannt*

INFINITIVE	PRESENT	SIMPLE PAST	PAST PARTICIPLE
reiben to rub		*rieb*	*gerieben*
rennen to run		*rannte*	*ist gerannt*
rufen to call		*rief*	*gerufen*
scheinen to shine, seem		*schien*	*geschienen*
schlafen to sleep	*schläft*	*schlief*	*geschlafen*
schlagen to hit	*schlägt*	*schlug*	*geschlagen*
schließen to close		*schloss*	*geschlossen*
schneiden to cut		*schnitt*	*geschnitten*
schreiben to write		*schrieb*	*geschrieben*
schreien to scream		*schrie*	*geschrie(e)n*
schwimmen to swim		*schwamm*	*ist geschwommen*
sehen to see	*sieht*	*sah*	*gesehen*
sein to be	*ist*	*war*	*ist gewesen*
sitzen to sit		*saß*	*gesessen*

INFINITIVE	PRESENT	SIMPLE PAST	PAST PARTICIPLE
sollen should, to be supposed to	*soll*	*sollte*	*gesollt*
sprechen to speak	*spricht*	*sprach*	*gesprochen*
springen to jump		*sprang*	*ist gesprungen*
stehen to stand		*stand*	*gestanden*
steigen to climb		*stieg*	*ist gestiegen*
streiten to fight		*stritt*	*gestritten*
tragen to carry; to wear	*trägt*	*trug*	*getragen*
treffen to meet	*trifft*	*traf*	*getroffen*
treten to tread, kick	*tritt*	*trat*	*getreten*
trinken to drink		*trank*	*getrunken*
tun to do		*tat*	*getan*
verbieten to forbid		*verbot*	*verboten*
verbinden to connect		*verband*	*verbunden*
verlieren to lose		*verlor*	*verloren*

INFINITIVE	PRESENT	SIMPLE PAST	PAST PARTICIPLE
wachsen to grow	*wächst*	*wuchs*	*ist gewachsen*
waschen to wash	*wäscht*	*wusch*	*gewaschen*
werden to become; to get	*wird*	*wurde*	*ist geworden*
wissen to know	*weiß*	*wusste*	*gewusst*
wollen to want, wish, intend to	*will*	*wollte*	*gewollt*
ziehen to pull		*zog*	*gezogen*

GLOSSARY OF INDUSTRY-SPECIFIC TERMS

Here are various areas of commerce, government, and non-governmental activities. Each has its particular terminology, and we've offered some of the more common terms. The industries covered are:*

Advertising and Public Relations	*Werbung und Public Relations*
Agriculture	*Landwirtschaft*
Architecture and Construction	*Architektur und Bauindustrie*
Automotive	*Kraftfahrzeugtechnik*
Banking and Finance	*Bank- und Finanzwesen*
Computer and Systems	*Computer und Systeme*
Engineering	*Ingenieurwesen*
Entertainment, Journalism, and Media	*Unterhaltung, Journalismus und Medien*
Fashion	*Mode*
Government and Government Agencies	*Regierung und Behörden*
Insurance	*Versicherung*
Management Consulting	*Unternehmensberatung*
Mining and Petroleum	*Bergbau und Ölindustrie*
Non-Governmental	*Regierungsunabhängige Institutionen*
Perfume and Fragrance	*Parfüm und Duftstoffe*

*All nouns referring to persons in this glossary are stated in their masculine form. The feminine form of most nouns is formed by adding the suffix *-in* at the end. For example, *der Architekt* is the masculine form, and *die Architektin* is the feminine form. The feminine article is *die*.

Pharmaceutical, Medical, and Dental	*Pharmazie, Medizin, und Zahnmedizin*
Publishing	*Verlagswesen*
Real Estate	*Immobilien*
Shipping and Distribution	*Spedition und Lieferwesen*
Telecommunications	*Telekommunikation*
Textile	*Textilien*
Toys	*Spielwaren*
Watches, Scales, and Precision Instruments	*Uhren, Waagen und Präzisionsgeräte*
Wine	*Wein*

ADVERTISING AND PUBLIC RELATIONS
(See *Marketing and Sales under Functional Areas of a Company in* Chapter 5)

Account executive	*der Kundenberater*
Ad	*die Anzeige/das Inserat*
Ad agency	*die Werbeagentur*
Ad style	*der Anzeigenstil*
Ad time	*die Werbeschaltung/die Werbedauer*
Advertise (to)	*werben*
Advertisement	*die Anzeige/das Inserat/der Werbesot* (TV ad, radio ad)
Advertising	*die Werbung*
Advertising agency	*die Werbeagentur*
Advertising budget	*der Werbeetat*
Advertising campaign	*die Werbekampagne*
Advertising message	*die Werbeaussage*
Advertising papers	*die Werbeträger*
Advertising space	*die Werbespalte*

Advertising strategy	*die Werbestrategie*
Advertising vehicle	*das Werbeauto*
Air (to) / broadcast (to)	*ausstrahlen/senden*
Audience	*das Publikum*
Baseline	*die Grundlinie*
Block of commercials	*der Werbespotblock*
Brand-name promotion	*die Markenwerbung*
Broadcast times	*die Ausstrahlungszeiten/Sendezeiten*
Brochure	*die Broschüre*
Campaign	*die Kampagne*
Catalog	*der Katalog*
Commercial	*kommerziell*
Commodity	*der Bedarfsartikel/die Ware*
Competition	*die Konkurrenz*
Consumer research	*die Verbraucherumfrage*
Cooperative advertising	*die Gemeinschaftswerbung*
Cost per thousand	*die Kosten pro Tausend/KPT*
Coupon	*der Coupon*
Cover	*die Umschlag/Titelseite*
Daily press	*die Tagespresse*
Depth of coverage	*die Informationsintensivität*
Direct marketing	*das Direktmarketing*
Early adopter	*der Frühanwender/frühe Verbraucher*
Effectiveness	*die Effektivität*
Endorsement	*Unterstützung*
Focus group	*die Fokusgruppe*
Free shopper's papers	*kostenlose Käuferzeitungen*

Infomercial	*die Informationswerbung/die Informationswerbesendung (das Infomercial)*
In house	*hausintern*
Insert	*die Werbeeinlage*
In-store campaign	*die Ladenwerbung/ Werbekampagne innerhalb des Geschäfts*
Introductory campaign	*die Einführungskampagne*
Jingle	*der Werbesong/der gesungene Slogan*
Layout	*das Layout*
Leaflet	*der Werbezettel/der Reklamezettel*
Listenership	*die Hörerschaft*
Listening rate	*die Hörerrate*
Logo	*das Logo/das Firmenzeichen*
Madison Avenue	*die amerikanische Werbeindustrie schlechthin*
Mail/Letter campaign	*die Wurfsendung*
Market	*der Markt*
Market (to)	*auf den Markt bringen*
Marketing	*das Marketing*
Market research	*die Marktforschung*
Mass marketing	*die Massenwerbung*
Media	*die Medien*
Media agent	*der Medienagent*
Media plan	*die Medienschaltung* (only for time)
Merchandise	*die Verkaufswaren*

Merchandise (to)	*zum Verkauf präsentieren*
Merchandising	*die Verkaufspräsentation*
Misleading advertising	*die irreführende Werbung*
Niche	*die Marktnische*
Opener	*der Einführungsslogan/das A in AIDA* (uncommon)
Packaging	*die Verpackung*
Periodical	*die Zeitschrift*
Point-of-sale advertising	*die Kassenwerbung/die Werbung am Ort des Verkaufs*
Positioning	*die Auslage*
Poster advertising	*die Plakatwerbung*
Premium	*die Prämie*
Presentation	*die Präsentation*
Press officer	*der Presseleiter*
Press release	*die Pressemitteilung*
Prime time	*die Hauptsendezeit*
Product	*das Produkt*
Product information	*die Produktinformation*
Product life cycle	*die Lebensdauer der Ware*
Professional publication	*die Fachzeitschrift*
Promote (to)	*fördern*
Promotion	*die Promotion/die Verkaufsförderung*
Public relations	*die Public Relations/ die Öffentlichkeitsarbeit/die Imagepflege*
Publicity	*der Bekanntheitsgrad*

Radio spot and TV ad	*der Werbespot im Radio und im Fernsehen*
Readership	*die Leserschaft*
Sales	*der Verkauf*
Sales promotion	*die Absatzförderung*
Sample	*das Muster*
Sample products	*die Musterprodukte*
Selection	*die Auswahl*
Share	*der Anteil/der Marktanteil* (market share)
Slogan	*der Slogan*
Space	*der Platz/die Spalte*
Special offer	*das Sonderangebot*
Sponsor	*der Schirmherr/der Sponsor*
Sponsor (to)	*fördern/protegieren/ sponsern*
Sponsorship	*die Förderung*
Story board	*das Layout des Fernsehwerbespots*
Survey	*die Umfrage*
Target (to)	*abzielen*
Target group	*die Zielgruppe*
Target market	*der Zielmarkt*
Telemarketing	*das Telemarketing*
Test market	*der Testmarkt*
Trade show	*die Messe*
Trial	*der Versuch*
White space	*der Leerplatz/die Leerstellen*
Word-of-mouth advertising	*Mund zu Mund Werbung*

AGRICULTURE

Acre	*der Morgen*
Agronomy	*die Agrarwissenschaft*
Area	*das Gebiet*
Arid	*die Dürre/dürr*
Chemicals	*die Chemikalien*
Cotton	*die Baumwolle* (not produced in Germany)
Crop(s)	*die Saat*
Cropland	*das Saatland*
Cultivate (to)	*kultivieren/anbauen*
Cultivation	*die Kultivierung/der Anbau*
Drought	*die Trockenzeit*
Export	*der Export*
Farm	*der Bauernhof*
Farm (to)	*bewirtschaften*
Farmer	*der Landwirt/der Bauer*
Farm income	*das Hofeinkommen*
Farming	*die Landwirtschaft*
Feedstock	*das Viehfutter*
Fertilize (to)	*düngen*
Fertilizer(s)	*der Dünger*
Grow (to)	*anbauen*
Harvest	*die Ernte*
Harvest (to)	*ernten*
Herbicide	*das Herbizid*
Husbandry	*der Ackerbau/die Landwirtschaft*
Insecticide	*das Insektizid*
Irrigate (to)	*bewässern*

Irrigation	*die Bewässerung*
Irrigation system	*das Bewässerungs-system*
Land	*das Land*
Livestock	*die Viehzucht*
Machinery	*die land wirtschaftlichen Maschinen*
Pesticides	*die Pestizide*
Plant	*die Pflanze*
Plant (to)	*pflanzen/anbauen*
Planting	*die Bepflanzung*
Plow (to)	*pflügen*
Potatoes	*die Kartoffeln*
Price	*der Preis*
Price supports	*die Preisstabilisierung*
Produce (to)	*produzieren*
Production	*die Produktion*
Rice	*der Reis*
Seed (to)	*sähen*
Seeds	*die Saat*
Seed stock	*das Saatgut*
Soil	*der Boden*
Soil conservation	*die Bodenkon-servierung*
Store	*der Speicher* (agriculture only)
Subsidy	*die Subvention/der staatliche Zuschuss*
Surplus	*der Überschuss*
Tariff	*der Tarif* (also: *der Agrarzoll*)
Till (to)	*pflügen*

Tobacco	*der Tabak*
Vegetables	*das Gemüse*
Wheat	*der Weizen*
Yield	*der Gewinn/die Ausschüttung/die Ernte*

ARCHITECTURE AND CONSTRUCTION

Aluminum	*das Aluminium*
Architect	*der Architekt*
Art	*die Kunst*
Asphalt	*der Asphalt*
Blueprint	*das Blueprint/die Zeichnung*
Brick	*der Backstein*
Bricklayer	*der Maurer*
Build (to)	*bauen*
Builder	*die Baufirma* (company)
Building	*das Gebäude*
Building materials	*das Baumaterial*
Carpenter (master/ apprentice)	*der Tischler (der Meister/der Auszubildende)*
Cement	*der/das Zement*
Cement (to)	*zementieren*
Chart (to)	*(ein) zeichnen*
Cinder blocks	*der Schlackestein*
Computer design	*das Computerdesign*
Concrete	*der Beton*
Construct (to)	*bauen*
Construction	*der Bau*
Cool (to)	*kühlen*

Demolish (to)	*abreißen*
Design	*das Design/der Entwurf*
Design (to)	*entwerfen*
Designer	*der Designer*
Destroy (to)	*abreißen/zerstören*
Develop (to)	*erschließen*
Developer	*die Baugesellschaft*
Dig (to)	*graben*
Draft	*der Entwurf*
Draft (to)	*entwerfen*
Drafting	*technisches Zeichnen*
Draw (to)	*zeichnen*
Drawing	*die Zeichnung*
Elevator	*der Fahrstuhl*
Engineer	*der Ingenieur*
Excavate (to)	*ausheben*
Excavation	*die Aushebung/der Aushub*
Fix (to)	*befestigen/fixieren*
Fixture	*die Ausstattung*
Glass	*Glas*
Frosted	*Milchglas/bereiftes Glas*
Insulated	*Thermalglas*
Plexiglas™	*Plexiglas*
See-through	*transparentes Glas*
Safety	*Sicherheitsglas*
Gravel	*der Schotter*
Heat	*die Hitze*
Heat (to)	*erhitzen*
Heating and ventilation	*die Heizung und die Ventilation*

Implement (to)	*implementieren/ anwenden*
Iron	*das Eisen*
Ironworks	*die Eisenarbeiten/ Schmiedearbeiten*
Joiner	*der Schreiner/der Tischler*
Joint	*die Verbindung/das Gelenk*
Joist	*der Balken*
Land	*das Land*
Lay (to)	*legen*
Light	*das Licht*
Lighting	*die Beleuchtung*
Material	*das Material*
Measure (to)	*messen*
Metal	*das Metal*
Model	*das Modell*
Mortar	*der Mörtel*
Office layout	*der Büroplan* (also: *Layout*)
Paint	*die Farbe*
Paint (to)	*streichen*
Painter	*der Maler*
Parking	*das Parken/der Parkplatz*
Plan (to)	*planen*
Plans	*die Pläne*
Plasterer	*der Verputzer/der Stukkateur*
Plastic	*der Kunststoff/das Plastik*
Plumber	*der Klempner*

Refurbish (to)	*erneuern/aufpolieren*
Renovate (to)	*renovieren*
Repair (to)	*reparieren*
Replace (to)	*ersetzen*
Rock	*das Gestein/das Felsgestein/der Stein*
Steel	*der Stahl*
Stone	*der Stein*
Structure	*die Struktur*
Survey	*die Ausmessung/Vermessung*
Survey (to)	*ausmessen/vermessen*
Surveyor	*der Landmesser*
Tile	*die Kachel*
Tile (to)	*kacheln*
Weather (to)	*verwittern*
Welder	*das Schweißgerät*
Window	*das Fenster*
Wire (to)	*verkabeln*
Wood	*Holz*
Ebony	*das Ebenholz*
Cedar	*das Zedernholz*
Mahogany	*das Mahagoni*
Oak	*die Eiche/das Eichenholz*
Pine	*das Kiefernholz*
Redwood	*das Rotholz*

AUTOMOTIVE

ABS brakes	*die ABS-Bremse*
Air bag	*der Airbag*
Air cleaner	*der Luftreinigungsfilter*
Air filter	*der Luftfilter*
Air vent	*die Lüftungsklappe*

Antilock brakes	*die Bremse mit Anti-Blockier-System*
Ashtray	*der Aschenbecher*
Assembly line	*das Fließband*
Automatic shift	*die Automatik/die automatische Schaltung*
Automobile	*das Kraftfahrzeug/das Auto*
Auto show	*die Automobilmesse/die Automobilausstellung*
Axle	*die Achse*
Backlog	*der Rückstand/der Überhang*
Bearing	*die Lagerung/das Achslager*
Belt	*der Gurt*
Blinker	*der Blinker*
Body	*die Karosserie*
Body panel	*die Karosserieplatte/die Bodenplatte*
Body shop	*die Autospenglerei* (not common)/*die Autowerkstatt* (garage)
Brake	*die Bremse*
Brake (to)	*bremsen*
Brake cylinder	*der Bremszylinder*
Bucket seats	*der Kontursitz/der Formsitz*
Bumper	*die Stoßstange*
Bushing	*die Lagerung*
Buy (to)	*kaufen/erstehen*
Camshaft	*die Nockenwelle*
Car	*das Auto/der Wagen*
Carburetor	*der Vergaser*
Car dealer	*der Autoverkäufer*
Car maintenance	*die Autowartung*

Carpet	*der Teppich*
Catalytic converter	*der Katalysator*
CD player	*der CD-Spieler*
Chassis	*das Fahrgestell*
Child seat	*der Kindersitz*
Chrome	*der Chrom*
Cigarette lighter	*der Zigarettenanzünder*
Climate control	*die Klimaregelung*
Clock	*die Uhr*
Cockpit	*der Führerraum*
Competition	*die Konkurrenz*
Component	*die Komponente/das Einzelteil*
Component stage	*der Zustand des Autoteils*
Computer chip	*der Computerchip*
Connecting rod	*die Pleuelstange*
Console	*die Konsole*
Consolidation	*die Konsolidierung*
Convertible	*das Kabriolett*
Coolant	*die Kühlflüssigkeit*
Cooling system	*das Kühlsystem/ das Kühlungssystem*
Cooling and heating system	*das Kühl- und Heizsystem*
Corporate average fuel economy (CAFE)	*Durchschnittliche Wirtschaftlichkeit im Benzinverbrauch der Firma*
Cost competitiveness	*die Kostenwettbewerbsfähigkeit*
Crankshaft	*die Kurbelwelle*
Cream puff	*die rollende Luxusbadewanne/das Sofa auf Rädern* (literally: *Windbeutel*)

Cross member	*die Querstrebe*
Cruise control	*der Temporegler*
Cup holder	*der Becherhalter*
Customer support	*der Kundendienst*
Custom made	*individuell gefertigt*
Cylinder	*der Zylinder*
Cylinder head	*de Zylinderkopf*
Cylinder lining	*der Zylinderbelag*
Dash board	*das Amaturenbrett*
Dealer	*der Händler*
Defog (to)	*(Scheiben) entnebeln*
Defogger	*die Gebläseanlage*
Design	*das Design*
Designer	*der Designer*
Diesel	*der Diesel* (car)/*das Diesel* (gasoline)
Differential	*das Ausgleichsgetriebe*
Dimmer switch	*der Dimmschalter*
Displacement	*der Hubraum*
Distributor	*der Verteiler*
Door	*die Autotür*
Door handle	*der Türknopf*
Door lock	*das Türschloss*
Door panel	*die Türverkleidung*
Drive (to)	*fahren*
Driver's seat	*der Fahrersitz*
Drive train	*die Kardanwelle*
Electrical harness	*der elektrische Kabelbaum*
Electrical system	*das elektrische System*
Electronic system	*das elektronische System*
Emergency flasher	*der Notfallblinker*
Emission system	*die Auspuffanlage*
Engine	*der Motor*

Engine block	*der Motorblock*
Engine cradle	*das Motorenlager*
Engineer	*der Ingenieur*
Engineering	*die technische Konstruktion*
Environmental Protection Agency (EPA)	*das Amt für Umweltschutz*
Exhaust	*die Abgase/der Auspuff*
Exhaust manifold	*die Auspuffkrümmung/das Auspuffrohr*
Exhaust system	*das Auspuffsystem*
Experimental design	*das Entwurfsdesign*
Exterior	*das Wagenäußere*
Fabricate (to)	*herstellen*
Fabrication	*die Herstellung*
Fan	*der Ventilator*
Fiberglass	*das Fiberglas*
Fill (to)	*füllen*
Finish	*der Lack*
Four-door	*viertürig*
Frame	*der Autorahmen*
Fuel	*der Kraftstoff*
Fuel gage	*der Kraftstoffmesser/ der Benzinanzeiger*
Fuel pump	*die Benzinpumpe*
Fuel tank	*der Tank*
Fuse	*die Sicherung*
Fuse box	*die Sicherungsdose*
Garage	*die Werkstatt/die Garage* (parking)
Gasket	*die Dichtung*
Gas	*das Benzin*
Gas cap	*der Tankdeckel*
Gas tank	*der Benzintank*

Gauge	der Messer/die Anzeige
Gear	das Getriebe
Gear shift	die Getriebeschaltung
Glove compartment	das Handschuhfach
Headlight	der Scheinwerfer
Head rest	die Kopfstütze
Heating system	die Heizung
High beam	das Aufblendlicht
Hood	die Kühlerhaube/ die Motorhaube
Hood ornament	die Kühlerhaubenfigur
Hubcap	die Radkappe
Indicator lights	die Lichtkontrollanzeige
Instrument panel	das Amaturenbrett
Intake manifold	der Ansaugstutzen
Interior	die Innenausstattung
Inventory	die Inventur/der Bestand
Jack	der Wagenheber
Jobber	der Mittelsmann/der Industrieverkäufer
Key	der Schlüssel
Labor	das Labor
Leather	das Leder
Lemon	das Montagsauto (literally: a car produced on Monday)
Lights	die Beleuchtung/die Lampen
Light truck	der Kleinlastwagen
Light vehicle	der Kleinwagen
Lock	das Schloss

Lock (to)	*abschließen*
Lot	*der Parkplatz*
Machine shop	*die Maschinen-abteilung*
Machining	*die Maschinenbear-beitung*
Maintenance	*die Wartung*
Make (to)	*machen/tun*
Manual	*die Bedienungsan-leitung*
Miles per hour/ kilometers per hour	*die Meile pro Stunde/ der Stundenkilometer*
Miles per gallon/ kilometers per gallon	*Liter pro Kilometer*[19]
Mint condition	*in ausgezeichnetem Zustand*
Mirror	*der Spiegel*
Model	*das Modell*
New model	*das neue Modell*
Noise	*das Geräusch*
Odometer	*der Kilometerzähler*
Oil gauge	*der Ölstandmesser*
Oil pressure	*der Öldruck*
Open (to)	*öffnen*
Overhead cam	*die Obernocke*
Paint	*die Farbe*
Park (to)	*parken*
Parking	*der Parkplatz/das Parkhaus*
Parking brake	*die Handbremse*
Part	*das Autoteil*

---

[19]Gallon per kilometer is not used in Germany.

Parts distribution	*die Autoteilausliefer- ung*
Parts manufacturer	*der Hersteller von Autoteilen*
Passenger car	*der Personenkraftwa- gen/der PKW*
Passenger's seat	*der Beifahrersitz*
Pedal	*das Pedal*
Pickup truck	*der Kleinlastwagen* (also: *der Truck*)
Piston	*der Kolben*
Piston ring	*der Kolbenring*
Platform	*die Plattform*
Power brakes	*das elektrische Bremssystem*
Power windows	*die automatischen Fenster*
Price	*der Preis*
Price tag	*das Preisschild*
Radio	*das Radio*
Rear suspension	*die hintere Aufhängung*
Rearview mirror	*der Rückspiegel*
Repair shop	*die Werkstatt*
Replacement part	*das Ersatzteil*
Reverse (to)	*umdrehen*
Robot	*der Roboter/der Automat*
Rocker arm	*der Kipphebel*
Run (to)	*laufen*
Seal	*die Dichtung*
Seat	*der Sitz*
Seat belt	*der Sicherheitsgurt*
Sedan	*die Limousine*

Service	*der Service*
Service station	*die Werkstatt*
Shift (to)	*schalten*
Shop (to)	*kaufen*
Showroom	*das Autogeschäft*
Side mirror	*der Seitenspiegel*
Signal	*das Signal/das Zeichen*
Signal (to)	*anzeigen*
Sound system	*das Soundsystem/das Lautsprechersystem*
Spare tire	*der Ersatzreifen*
Spark plug	*die Zündkerze*
Speedometer	*der Geschwindigkeitsmesser*
Sports car	*der Sportwagen*
Stall (to)	*(den Motor) abwürgen*
Stamping	*das Stanzteil*
Start (to)	*starten*
Starter	*der Anlasser*
Start up	*anspringen*
Station wagon	*der Kombi*
Steer (to)	*lenken*
Steering wheel	*das Lenkrad*
Stick shift	*die manuelle Kupplung*
Strut	*die Strebe/die Verstrebung*
Sun roof	*das Schiebedach*
Supplier	*der Zulieferer*
Suspension	*die Aufhängung*
SUV (sports utility vehicle)	*der Sportkombi* (also: *SUV*)
Switch	*der Schalter*
System	*das System*
Tachometer	*das/der Tachometer*
Tire	*der Reifen*
Tool	*das Werkzeug*

Tool kit	*der Werkzeugkasten*
Torque	*das Drehmoment*
Transmission	*das Getriebe*
Truck	*der Kleinlastwagen/der Truck*
Trunk	*der Kofferraum*
Turn (to)	*umdrehen/wenden*
Turn into (to)	*biegen in*
Turn signal	*der Blinker*
Twin cap	*die Doppelvergaserkappe*
Two-door	*zweitürig*
Union	*der Verband/der Automobilclub*
Valve	*das Ventil*
Van	*der Kleinlastwagen*
Vanity mirror	*der Schminkspiegel*
Vehicle	*das Fahrzeug*
Vent	*die Luftklappe*
Vibration	*die Vibration*
Wagon	*der Kombiwagen*
Warning light	*das Warnlicht*
Wheel	*das Rad*
Window	*das Fenster*
Windshield	*die Windschutzscheibe*
Wipers	*die Scheibenwischer*

BANKING AND FINANCE

Account	*das Konto*
Accrue (to)	*anwachsen (Zinsen)*
Acquire (to)	*akquirieren/erwerben*
Acquisition	*die Akquisition*
Asset	*der Vermögenswert/das Guthaben*

Assets under management	das Vermögen unter Verwaltung
Automatic teller machine (ATM)	der Bankautomat/der Geldautomat
Back office	das der Öffentlichkeit nicht zugängliche Büro
Bailout	der Rückzug (von Investitionen)
Bond	die Anleihe
Bond market	der Anleihenmarkt
Borrow (to)	leihen
Borrowing	das Leihen
Bottom line	der springende Punkt/ das Wesentliche
Branch	die Zweigstelle
Branch manager	der Zweigstellenleiter
Capital	das Kapital
Cash	das Bargeld
Cash (to)	einlösen/auszahlen lassen
Cashier	der Kassierer
Central bank	die Zentralbank
Certificate of Deposit (CD)	die Bankeinlage
Check	der Scheck
Checking account	das Girokonto
Close (to)	schließen
Commercial bank	die Geschäftsbank
Commercial banking	das geschäftliche Bankwesen
Commission	die Komission
Commodity	die Kommodität
Corporate bond	der Firmenanteil
Correspondent banking	das Korrespon- denzbankwesen

Cost of funds	*die Anleihekosten*
Credit	*der Kredit*
Credit card	*die Kreditkarte*
Credit limit	*das Kreditlimit*
Credit line	*die maximale Kredithöhe*
Currency	*die Währung*
Day trader	*der Tagesspekulant/der Börsenmakler ohne Inventur am Tagesende*
Debt (short-term, long-term)	*die Verschuldung (kurzfristig, langfristig)*
Deficit	*das Defizit*
Deflation	*die Deflation*
Delinquency rate	*die Verzugsrate/die Rate des Zahlungsverzugs*
Deposit	*die Einzahlung*
Deposit (to)	*einzahlen*
Derivatives	*das derivative Produkt*
Down payment	*die Anzahlung*
Due date	*das Fälligkeitsdatum*
Earnings	*das Einkommen*
Economy	*die Wirtschaft*
Efficiency ratio	*die Effizienzrate*
Exchange rate	*der Wechselkurs*
Fee	*die Gebühr*
Financial adviser	*der Finanzberater*
Fiscal policy	*die Finanzpolitik*
Foreign exchange	*das Währungsgeschäft*
Futures contract	*die Kassa-Futures-Arbitrage*

Go long/short (to)	*langfristig/ kurzfristig*
Hedge	*das Hedgegeschäft/das Absicherungsgeschäft*
Hedge (to)	*absichern*
Hedge fund	*der Hedgefund*
Hedging	*das Hedgegeschäft*
Inflation	*die Inflation*
Institutional investor	*der intitutionelle Investor*
Interest	*die Zinsen*
Interest rate (fixed, floating)	*der Zinssatz (fest, angleichend)*
Invest (to)	*investieren*
Investment	*die Investition*
Investment bank	*die Investitionsbank*
Investment banking	*das Investitions- bankwesen*
Investment services	*die Investitionsdien- stleistungen/-services*
Letter of credit (L/C)	*der Kreditbrief/das Akkreditiv*
Liability	*die Haftung*
Liquid	*liquide*
Liquidate (to)	*liquidieren*
Lend (to)	*leihen*
Loan (short-term, long-term, secured)	*die Anleihe/der Kredit (kurzfristig, lang- fristig, versichert)*
Loan (to)	*Kredit geben/Anleihe geben*
Loan officer	*der Kreditleiter*
Loan volume	*die Kreditsumme*
Loss	*der Verlust*

Merchant bank	*die Handelsbank*
Merchant banking	*das Handelsbankwesen*
Merge (to)	*(sich) zusammen-schließen*
Merger	*der Zusammenschluss*
Monetary policy	*die Währungspolitik*
Money	*das Geld*
Mortgage	*die Hypothek*
Mortgage (to)	*eine Hypothek aufnehmen*
Mutual fund	*der Investitionsfond*
Net	*netto*
Net interest margin	*die Nettozinsspanne*
Non-revolving credit	*der Fälligkeitskredit*
Open (to) an account	*ein Konto eröffnen*
Open (to) letter of credit	*ein Akkreditiv eröffnen*
Overdraft	*(das Konto) überziehen*
Overdrawn	*(das Konto ist) überzogen*
Pay (to)	*zahlen*
Payment	*die Zahlungsrate*
Percent	*das Prozent*
Portfolio	*das Portefeuille*
Portfolio manager	*der Portefeuille-Manager*
Price	*der Preis*
Price (to)	*auspreisen*
Price/Earnings (P/E) ratio	*das Preis-Einkommens-Verhältnis*
Private banking	*das Privatbankwesen*
Profit	*der Profit/der Gewinn*
Profit (to)	*profitieren/gewinnen*
Profit margin	*die Profitspanne*

Recession	*die Rezession*
Repayment	*die Rückzahlung*
Retail banking	*das Einzelhandels-bankwesen*
Revolving credit	*der sich erneuernde Kredit/der Kredit ohne festgelegte Fälligkeit*
Safe-deposit box	*das Bankschließfach*
Save (to)	*sparen*
Savings account	*das Sparkonto*
Securitization	*die Kreditsicherung*
Security/Securities	*die Sicherheit(en)*
Share price	*der Aktienpreis*
Spread	*die Streuung*
Stock market	*die Börse*
Stockholder	*der Aktionär*
Stocks	*die Aktien*
Surplus	*der Überschuss*
Syndicate	*das Konsortium/das Kartell*
Syndicated loan	*der Gesellschafterkredit*
Takeover	*die Übernahme*
Tax	*die Steuer*
Tax (to)	*besteuern*
Teller	*der Bankangestellte*
Trade (to)	*handeln*
Trader	*der Händler/der Makler*
Transact (to)	*abwickeln/abschließen*
Transaction	*die Transaktion*
Transaction costs	*die Transaktionskosten*
Transfer (to)	*übertragen/umbuchen*
Traveler's checks	*der Reisescheck*
Treasury bonds	*der Schatzbrief*

Trust	*der Trust*
Trust (to)	*anvertrauen*
Trust officer	*der Treuhands-bevollmächtigte*
Underwrite (to)	*unterschreiben/ garantieren*
Underwriter	*der Zeichnungs-berechtigte/der Versicherer*
Wholesale banking	*das Großbankwesen*
Wire	*die Überweisung*
Wire (to)	*überweisen*
Withdraw (to)	*abheben*
Withdrawal	*die Abhebung*

ENGINEERING

Calculus	*die Differential- und Integralrechnung*
Chemical	*chemisch*
Civil	*zivil*
Design	*das Design/der Entwurf*
Develop (to)	*entwickeln/ erschließen*
Engineer	*der Ingenieur*
Instrument	*das Instrument*
Mathematics	*die Mathematik*
Mechanical	*mechanisch*
Nuclear	*nuklear*
Science	*die Wissenschaft*
Structural	*strukturell*
Technology	*die Technologie*
Test	*der Versuch/der Test*

ENTERTAINMENT, JOURNALISM, AND MEDIA

(See also *Publishing*, *Advertising* and *Public Relations*)

Actor	*der Schauspieler*
Artist	*der Künstler*
Choreographer	*der Choreograph*
Cinema	*das Kino*
Column	*die Zeitungsspalte*
Columnist	*der Kolumnist*
Commentary	*der Kommentar*
Contact	*der Kontakt*
Correspondent	*der Korrespondent*
Dancer	*der Tänzer*
Director	*der Direktor*
Edit (to)	*redigieren*
Edition	*die Ausgabe*
Editor	*der Redakteur/die Redakteurin*
Editorial	*redaktionell*
Editor-in-Chief	*der Chefredakteur*
Feature story	*die Hauptstory*
Headline	*die Schlagzeile*
Interpreter	*der Interpretierer/der Übersetzer*
Journalism	*der Journalismus*
Journalist	*der Journalist*
Music	*die Musik*
Musician	*der Musiker*
News (story)	*die Nachrichten/der Nachrichtentagespunkt*
Perform (to)	*auftreten*
Performance	*die Vorstellung/der Auftritt*

Photographer	*der Fotograf*
Post-production	*Aufgaben, die nach der Fertigstellung der Produktion geleistet werden müssen*
Producer	*der Produzent* (film, TV, radio) *der Regisseur* (theater)
Production	*die Produktion* (film)/ *die Inszenierung* (theater)
Radio	*das Radio*
Recording	*die Aufnahme*
Rehearsal	*die Probe*
Report (to)	*berichten/reportieren*
Reporter	*der Reporter/der Nachrichtensprecher*
Review	*die Kritik*
Score	*die Punktzahl*
Script	*das Script/das Drehbuch/das Manuskript*
Technician	*der Techniker*
Television	*das Fernsehen*
Translator	*der Übersetzer*
Writer	*der Autor*

FASHION
(See also *Textile*)

Accessories	*die Modeassessoires*
Accessorize	*Akzente setzen/ ausstatten/ beschmücken*
Appearance	*die Erscheinung/ das Auftreten*
Beauty	*die Schönheit*

Bell-bottoms	*die ausgestellten Hosen/ das weitgeschnittene Hosenbein*
Belt	*der Gürtel*
Bias cut	*der Diagonalschnitt/ der Schnitt schräg zur Stofffaser*
Blazer	*der Blazer*
Blouse	*die Bluse*
Boots	*die Stiefel/die Boots* (hiking)
Boutique	*die Boutique*
Bow tie	*die Fliege*
Bra	*der BH*
Bust	*die Büste*
Cap	*die Kappe*
Collar	*der Kragen*
Collection	*die Kollektion*
Corset	*das Korsett*
Couturier	*der Modedesigner*
Cover (to)	*bedecken/überspannen*
Cravat	*die Krawatte*
Design	*das Design*
Design (to)	*entwerfen*
Designer	*der Designer*
Dinner jacket	*das Abendjackett*
Double-breasted suit	*der zweireihige Anzug*
Dress	*das Kleid*
Dressing room	*der Ankleideraum*
Ear muff	*der Ohrenwärmer/die Ohrenmuffe*
Etiquette	*die Etikette*
Fabric	*der Stoff*

Fake fur	*der künstliche Pelz*
Fashion	*die Mode*
Fashion show	*die Modenschau*
Fur	*der Pelz*
Garment	*das Kleidungsstück*
Girdle	*der Strumpfgürtel*
Gloves	*die Handschuhe*
Hat	*der Hut*
Haute couture	*die Haute Couture*
Haute couturier	*der Maßschneider*
Heel	*der Hacken*
Hem	*der Saum*
Hem (to)	*säumen*
Hemline	*die Saumnaht*
Image	*das Image*
Jacket	*das Jackett*
Lapel	*der Aufschlag*
Length	*die Länge*
Lingerie	*die Damenunter-wäsche*
Metallics	*das metallische Gewebe*
Midiskirt	*der Midirock*
Miniskirt	*der Minirock*
Model	*das Mannequin*
Model (to)	*vorführen*
Muff	*der Muff*
Necktie	*die Krawatte/der Schlipps*
Nightgown	*das Nachthemd/ Negligee*
Non-crease	*knitterfrei*
Overcoat	*der Mantel*

Pad	*das Polster/die Wattierung*
Padded	*wattiert*
Pajamas	*der Schlafanzug*
Pants	*die Hose*
Plastics	*die Kunststoffmodeteile*
Platform shoes	*die Platformschuhe*
Pleat	*die Bügelfalte*
Proportion	*die Proportion*
Raincoat	*der Regenmantel*
Ready-to-wear	*von der Stange*
Relaxed	*ungezwungen*
Robe	*die Robe*
Runway	*der Laufsteg*
Sash	*die Schärpe*
Scarf	*der Schal*
Seam (finished, unfinished)	*die Naht (umgeschlagen, unbearbeitet)*
Season	*die Saison*
Separates	*die Zweiteiler/mehrteilig*
Shawl	*die Stola/der Umhang*
Sheath	*das Futteral*
Shirt	*das Hemd*
Shoes	*die Schuhe*
Shoulder pads	*die Schulterpolster*
Show	*die Show*
Show (to)	*zeigen/vorführen*
Showroom	*der Showroom*
Skirt	*der Rock*
Sleeve	*der Ärmel*
Socks	*die Socken*
Stiletto heel	*der hochhackige Schuh*

Stitch (to)	*nähen/sticken*
Stitching	*das Nähen/die Absteppung*
Stockings	*die Strümpfe*
Straight-leg	*nahtlos*
Style	*der Stil*
Suit	*der Anzug*
Sweater	*der Pullover*
Tailor	*der Schneider*
Tailor (to)	*schneidern*
Tailored	*geschneidert*
Tailoring	*das Schneidern*
Tank top	*der Tank-Top*
Three-piece suit	*der dreiteilige Anzug*
Tie	*die Krawatte/der Schlips*
Trousers	*die Hose*
T-shirt	*das T-Shirt*
Undergarment	*die Unterbekleidung*
Underwear	*die Unterwäsche*
Vest	*die Weste*
Waist	*die Hüfte*
Wardrobe	*die Garderobe*
Wedge (heel)	*der Keilabsatz/der Schuh mit Keilabsatz*

GOVERNMENT AND GOVERNMENT AGENCIES

Administration	*die Verwaltung*
Agency(ies)	*die Agentur(en)/die Behörde(n)*
Arts	*die Künste*

Association	*der Verband/die Gesellschaft*
Citizen	*der Einwohner*
Citizenship	*die Staatsange-hörigkeit*
College	*das Kolleg/die Hochschule*
Commission	*die Komission*
Committee	*das Komitee/der Ausschuss*
Community	*die Gemeinde*
Cultural	*kulturell*
Delegation	*die Delegation*
Department	*die Abteilung*
Development	*die Entwicklung*
Economic	*die Wirtschaft*
Education	*das Bildungswesen*
Environment	*die Umwelt*
Form	*das Formular*
Government	*die Regierung*
Governmental	*regierungszugehörig/ regierungsabhängig*
Grant	*die finanzielle Unterstützung/ Subvention/ Forschungssumme*
Highway	*die Autobahn/die Schnellstraße*
Housing	*das Wohnungswesen*
Industrial part	*das Industriegebiet*

Information	*die Information*
Institute	*das Institut*
International	*international*
Legislation	*das Gesetz/die Gesetzgebung*
Long range	*weitreichend*
Military	*das Militär/die Armee*
Negotiate (to)	*verhandeln*
Negotiation	*die Verhandlung*
Non-government agency	*nicht-regierungs-abhängiges Amt*
Non-profit	*allgemeinnützig*
Office	*das Büro/das Amt/die Behörde*
Park	*der Park*
Plan	*der Plan*
Plan (to)	*planen*
Planner	*der Planer*
Policy	*die Police*
Political	*politisch*
Politics	*die Politik*
Population	*die Bevölkerung*
Procedure	*der Vorgang/die Richtlinie*
Proposal	*der Vorschlag/das Angebot*
Public	*öffentlich*
Public service	*öffentlicher Dienst*
Recommendation	*die Empfehlung*
Region	*das Gebiet*

Regional	*regional*
Regional office	*das Regionalbüro*
Regulation	*die offizielle Regelung*
Regulatory agency	*die ausführende Behörde*
Report	*der Bericht*
Representative	*der Repräsentant*
Research	*die Forschung*
Resources	*die Ressourcen*
Road	*die Straße*
Rural	*ländlich*
Service	*der Dienst*
Social	*sozial*
Society	*die Gesellschaft*
Suburb	*die Vorstadt*
Transportation	*der Transport/das Transportwesen*
University	*die Universität*
Urban	*städtisch/urban*

INSURANCE

Actuary	*der Versicherungsvertreter*
Agent	*der Agent*
Annuity	*die Jahresrente*
Broker	*der Makler*
Casualty	*der Unfall/das Unfallopfer*
Claim	*der Versicherungsanspruch*
Commission	*die Kommission/die Provision*
Coverage	*der Versicherungsschutz*
Death benefit	*die Entschädigung im Todesfall*

Deductible	*die Eigenverant-wortlichkeit im Schadensfall/die absetzbare Summe* (taxes)
Endowment	*die Dotierung/die auszahlbare Summe im Überlebensfall*
Face value	*der Nominalwert*
Health	*die Gesundheit*
Insure (to)	*versichern*
Life	*das Leben*
Life expectancy	*die Lebenserwartung*
Mortality	*die Todesrate*
Peril	*das Risiko*
Policy	*die Police*
Policy owner	*der Besitzer der Police*
Premium	*die Versicherung-sprämie*
Property	*das Eigentum*
Reinsurance	*die Rückversicherung*
Reserve	*die Reserve*
Risk	*das Risiko*
Risk management	*das Risikomanage-ment*
Term	*die Zeitspanne*
Underwriter	*der Versicherungs-träger*
Universal	*universell*
Variable annuity	*die veränderliche Jahresrente*
Viatical settlement	*die vorzeitige Ausgleichszahlung im terminalen rankheits-fall*
Whole life	*auf Lebenszeit*

MANAGEMENT CONSULTING

Account	*das Konto*
Accounting executive	*der Kundenbetreuer*
Bill	*die Rechnung*
Bill (to)	*berechnen*
Entrepreneur	*der Unternehmer*
Expert	*der Experte*
Fee	*die Gebühr*
Implement (to)	*implementieren/ anwenden*
Implementation	*die Implementierung/ die Anwendung*
Manage (to)	*leiten/führen*
Management	*das Management*
Organize (to)	*organisieren*
Organization	*die Organisation/die Gesellschaft*
Organizational development	*die Organisationsen- twicklung*
Presentation	*die Präsentation*
Project	*das Projekt*
Proposal	*das Angebot*
Recommend (to)	*empfehlen*
Recommendation	*die Empfehlung*
Report	*der Bericht*
Report (to)	*berichten*
Specialize (to)	*(sich) spezialisieren*
Specialist	*der Spezialist*
Team build (to)	*ein Team aufbauen*
Team building	*das Team Building*

Time sheet	*der Arbeitszeiterfassungsbogen*
Train (to)	*trainieren/schulen*
Training	*das Training/die Schulung*
Value	*der Wert*
Value added	*der Wertzuwachs*

MINING AND PETROLEUM

Blasting	*die Sprengung*
Chemical	*die Chemikalie*
Coal	*die Kohle*
Conveyor	*das Förderband/die Förderanlage*
Cooling	*die Kühlung*
Copper	*das Kupfer*
Crosscut	*der Querstollen*
Crush (to)	*fördern/abbauen*
Crusher	*der Bergarbeiter/der Stollenarbeiter*
Crystal	*der Kristall*
Deposit	*die Ablagerung*
Diamond	*der Diamant*
Dig (to)	*graben*
Digging	*das Schürfen/der Schürfort*
Dredge (to)	*ausbaggern*
Dredging	*das Baggern*
Drilling	*das Bohren/die Bohrung*
Earth	*die Erde*
Engineer	*der Ingenieur*
Engineering	*das Ingenieurwesen*

Excavating	die Aushebung/der Aushub
Extraction	die Entfernung
Gas	das Gas
Gem	der Edelstein
Geologist	der Geologe
Gold	das Gold
Hydraulic	hydraulisch
Iron	das Eisen
Lead	das Blei
Metal	das Metall
Metallurgist	der Metallurge
Mine	die Mine/der Stollen
Mine (to)	abbauen/fördern
Mineral	die Mineralie
Natural gas	das Naturgas
Natural resources	die natürlichen Rohstoffquellen
Oil	das Öl
Open-pit	der Tagebau
Ore	das Erz
Outcrop	das Zutageliegen das Mineralvorkommen (zu Tage)
Pit	die Grube
Platform	die Platform/die Bohrinsel
Power	die Kraft
Processing	der Prozess
Pump	die Pumpe
Pump (to)	pumpen
Pumping	das Pumpen

Quarry	*der Steinbruch*
Quarry (to)	*Steine brechen/ abbauen*
Refine (to)	*raffinieren*
Refinery	*die Raffinerie*
Resources	*die Quellen*
Safety	*die Sicherheit*
Shaft	*der Schacht*
Silver	*das Silber*
Sluice	*die Schleuse*
Sluicing	*das Verschleusen*
Smelting	*das Schmelzen*
Strip mining	*der Tagebergbau*
Surface	*die Oberfläche*
Tin	*das Zinn* (also: *das Blech*)
Ton	*die Tonne*
Truck	*der Lastwagen*
Tunnel	*der Tunnel*
Tunnel (to)	*einen Tunnel bauen/ untertunneln*
Tunneling	*der Tunnelbau*
Vein	*die Ader* (in German more specified, i.e. *Goldader)*
Uranium	*das Uran*
Water	*das Wasser*
Waste	*der Abfallstoff*
Well	*der Schacht/das Bohrloch/der Brunnen*
Zinc	*das Zink*

NON-GOVERNMENTAL

Academic	*akademisch*
Analyst	*der Analytiker*
Associate	*der Kollege/der Mitarbeiter/der Gesellschafter* (co-investor)
Association	*der Verband/der Verein/die Gesellschaft*
Center	*das Zentrum/das Center*
Charity	*die Wohlfahrt*
College	*das College/die Hochschule/die Akademie*
Consult (to)	*konsultieren*
Consulting	*die Beratung*
Contract	*der Vertrag*
Contract (to)	*unter Vertrag stellen*
Coordinate	*koordinieren*
Council	*das Gremium, der Rat*
Database	*die Datenbasis/die Datei*
Develop (to)	*entwickeln*
Development	*die Entwicklung*
Directory	*das Verzeichnis/die Liste*
Donation	*die Spende*
Educate (to)	*ausbilden*
Education	*die Bildung*
Educational	*bildungsmäßig*
Enterprise	*das Unternehmen*
Fellowship	*die Mitgliedschaft*
Fine art	*die bildende Kunst*

Foundation	*die Stiftung*
Fundraiser	*der Spendensammler*
Fund raising	*die Spendensuche/ Spendensammeln*
Gift	*das Geschenk*
Grant	*die zur Verfügung gestellte Summe/die Subvention/die Unterstützung*
Information	*die Information*
Institute	*das Institut*
Institute (to)	*institutionieren*
Institution	*die Institution*
Interest group	*die Interessengruppe*
International	*international*
Issue (to)	*ausstellen*
Laboratory	*das Labor*
Library	*die Bibliothek*
Lobbying	*mittels organisierter Interessengruppen politischen Einfluss nehmen* (also: *lobbying*)
Museum	*das Museum*
Nonprofit group/not-for-profit group	*die allgemeinnützige Gruppe/Organization*
Organization	*die Organisation/die Gesellschaft*
Philanthropy	*die Philantrophie*
Professional association	*der Berufsverband*
Program	*das Programm*
Publish (to)	*veröffentlichen*

Raise funds (to)	*Geldmittel sammeln*
Report	*der Bericht*
Report (to)	*verantwortlich sein (jemandem gegenüber)*
Research	*die Forschung*
Research (to)	*forschen*
School	*die Schule*
Society	*die Gesellschaft*
Statistic	*die Statistik*
Strategy	*die Strategie*
Study	*die Studie*
Survey	*die Umfrage*
Survey (to)	*eine Umfrage machen*
University	*die Universität*

PERFUME AND FRAGRANCE

Aerosol	*das Aerosol*
Aftershave	*das Rasierwasser*
Air freshener	*das Antigeruchsspray*
Alcohol	*der Alkohol*
Aloe	*die Aloe*
Aroma	*das Aroma*
Base note	*die Grundduftnote*
Bath	*das Bad*
Bath oil	*das Badeöl*
Blush	*das Blush/das Rouge*
Citrus	*der Zitrusduft*
Cologne	*das Parfüm*
Compact	*die Puderdose*
Cosmetic(s)	*die Kosmetik/die Kosmetika*
Cream(s)	*die Creme(s)*
Deodorant	*das Deo*

Essential oils	*die ätherischen Öle*
Eye liner	*der Augenstift/der Eyeliner*
Eye shadow	*der Lidschatten*
Floral	*pflanzlich*
Fragrance	*der Duftstoff*
Fresh	*frisch*
Freshener	*das Erfrischungsspray*
Herbal	*pflanzlich*
Lemon	*die Zitrone*
Lipstick	*der Lippenstift*
Mascara	*die Maskara/ Wimperntusche*
Middle note	*die mittlere Duftnote*
Nose	*die Nase*
Oil	*das Öl*
Ointment	*die Salbe*
Olfactory	*vom Geruch her/den Geruch betreffend*
Orange	*der Orangenduft* (fragrance)
Oriental	*fern-östlich*
Perfume	*das Parfüm*
Powder	*der Puder*
Powdery	*puderartig*
Rouge	*das Rouge*
Salt	*das Salz*
Scent	*die Duftnote/der Duft*
Smell	*der Geruch*
Spicy	*würzig*
Soap	*die Seife*
Toiletries	*die Toilettenartikel*
Top note	*die obere Duftnote*

PHARMACEUTICAL, MEDICAL, AND DENTAL

Anesthesic	*das Betäubungsmittel*
Antibiotics	*die Antibiotika*
Approval	*die Genehmigung*
Approve (to)	*genehmigen*
Capsule	*die Kapsel*
Check-up	*die Überprüfung*
Clean (to)	*reinigen*
Cleaning	*die Reinigung*
Chemistry	*die Chemie*
Clinical trial	*der klinische Versuch*
Disease	*die Krankheit*
Double-blind data	*beidseitig verpflichtende Daten*
Drug	*die Droge/die Arznei/ das Medikament*
Drug trial (Phase I, Phase II, Phase III)	*der Arzneimitteltest (1. Phase, 2. Phase, 3. Phase)*
Exam	*die Untersuchung*
Examine (to)	*untersuchen*
Filling	*die Füllung*
Generic drugs	*die generischen Medikamente*
Hospital(s)	*das Krankenhaus/die Krankenhäuser*
Laboratory	*das Laboratorium*
Manufacture (to)	*herstellen*
Magnetic Resonance Imaging (MRI)	*das MRI*
Over-the-counter	*nicht rezeptpflichtig*

Patent	*das Patent*
Patent (to)	*patentieren*
Patented drug	*patentierte Arznei*
Patient	*der Patient*
Pharmaceutical company	*die pharmazeutische Firma*
Pharmacist	*der Apotheker/die Apothekerin*
Pharmacologist	*der Pharmazeut/die Pharmazeutin*
Pharmacy	*die Apotheke*
Pill	*die Tablette/die Pille* (contraceptive)
Placebo	*der Plazebo*
Poison	*das Gift*
Prescribe (to)	*verschreiben*
Prescription	*das Rezept*
Prescription drug	*das verschrei-bungspflichtige Medikament*
Proprietary drug	*das geschützte Medikament*
Rash (skin)	*der Ausschlag*
Release (to)	*freigeben*
Research	*die Forschung*
Root canal	*der Wurzelkanal*
Tablet	*die Tablette*
Test	*der Test*
Test (to)	*testen*
Testing	*das Testen*
Toxicology	*die Toxologie*
Treatment	*die Behandlung*
Veterinary drug	*das Tiermedikament*
Vitamins	*die Vitamine*
X ray	*die Röntgenaufnahme*

PUBLISHING

Acknowledgements	*die Danksagung*
Advance	*der Vorabdruck* (pre-print)/*der Vorschuss* (pre-payment)
Advanced sales	*der Vorverkauf*
Appendix	*der Anhang*
Art	*die künstlerische Gestaltung*
Asterisk	*das Sternchen/der Stern*
Author	*der Autor*
Author's corrections	*die Autorenkorrekturen*
Back ad	*die rückseitige Werbeanzeige bei Zeitschriften*
Backlist	*die Liste der Veröffentlichungen*
Best-seller	*der Bestseller*
Binding	*die Heftung*
Blockbuster	*der Knüller*
Blurb	*der Flopp/Kurzkommentar über ein Buch auf der Rückseite eines Buch*
Blow-in card	*die Einlagekarte/die eingelegte Werbekarte*
Body	*der Hautpttext/der Bodytext*
Bold type	*das Fettgedruckte/fettgedruckt*
Book	*das Buch*
Book jacket	*der Buchumschlag/der Außenumschlag*

Book store	*der Bücherladen/der Buchladen*
Border	*der Rand*
Box	*die Box/der Kasten*
Broadsheet newspaper	*die Planobogen-Zeitung*
Bullet points	*das Aufzählungszeichen*
Byline	*die Namenszeile des Autoren*
Caps (capital letters)	*die Großbuchstaben*
Caption	*die Überschrift*
Chapter	*das Kapitel*
Circulation	*die Auflage*
Color	*die Farbe*
Color photo	*das Farbfoto*
Contents	*der Inhalt*
Contrast	*der Kontrast*
Copy editor	*der Copy-Redakteur*
Copyright	*die Kopierrechte/das Copyright*
Cover	*der Umschlag*
Cropping	*der Buchschnitt*
Dagger	*das amerikanische Zeichen für "verstorben"*
Deadline	*der Stichtag/die Deadline*
Dots per inch	*die Punkte pro Zoll (dpi)*
Double dagger	*das Doppelkreuz*
Double-page spread	*die Doppelseite*
Edit (to)	*redigieren*
Editing	*die Redaktion*

Editor	*der Redakteur/die Redakteurin*
Electronic publishing	*das elektronische Verlagswesen*
End papers	*das Vorsatzpapier*
Fact check	*die Faktenüberprüfung*
Flush left/flush right	*rechtsbündig machen/ linksbündig machen*
Font	*der Schriftsatz*
Footnote	*die Fußnote*
Front-list	*das Verzeichnis der zukünftigen Veröffentlichungen*
Galley	*die Druckfahne*
Galley proof	*der Fahnenabzug*
Glossary	*das Stichwortverzeichnis/das Glossar*
Glossy	*glänzend*
Graphic	*die Graphik*
Hard cover	*das Buch im Festumschlag/das gebundene Buch*
Illustration	*die Illustration/die Bebilderung*
Imprint	*die Imprägnierung*
Index	*der Index*
International paper sizes	*die internationalen Papiergrößen*
Introduction	*die Einleitung*
International Standard Book Number (ISBN)	*die Internationale Standardbuchnummer (ISBN)*
International Standard Serial Number (ISSN)	*die Internationale Standardseriennummer (ISSN)*

Italics	*die kursiv schrift/ kursiv*
Jacket	*der Faltumschlag*
Justify	*justieren*
Landscape	*das Querformat*
Layout	*das Layout*
Legend	*die Legende*
Logo	*das Logo/das Firmenzeichen*
Loose-leaf	*das Ringbuchformat/ ungebunden*
Lowercase	*die Kleinbuchstaben/ klein geschrieben*
Magazine	*die Zeitschrift*
Manuscript	*das Manuskript*
Margins	*die Rahmenlinien*
Masthead	*das Impressum*
Mockup	*das Muster/der Prototyp*
Newspaper	*die Zeitung*
Newsstand	*der Zeitungsstand*
Page(s)	*die Seite(n)*
Page number	*die Seitenzahl*
Page proofs	*die Seitenüberprüfung*
Pagination	*die Seiten- Nummerierung*
Paperback	*das Taschenbuch*
Paragraph	*der Absatz*
Paragraph mark	*die Absatzmarkierung*
Percentage	*der Prozentsatz*
Pica	*das Pica (12 Zeichen per Zoll)*
Point	*der Punkt*
Portrait	*das Hochformat*

Printing	*der Druck*
Prologue	*die Einleitung/der Prolog*
Proof	*das Prüfen*
Proofread (to)	*Korrektur lesen*
Proofreader	*der Korrektor/der Korrekturleser*
Publisher	*der Verleger*
Publishing	*das Verlagswesen*
Pulp	*der Zellstoff*
Reference	*die Anmerkungen*
Reference marks	*die Anmerkungsmarkierung*
Remaindering	*die Remittendenentsorgung*
Reporter	*der Reporter*
Resolution	*die Resolution*
Royalty	*das Autorenhonorar*
Section mark	*die Sektionsmarkierung*
Sentence	*der Satz*
Soft cover	*der Weichumschlag*
Subscript/superscript	*tiefgestellt/hochgestellt (Schriftsatz)*
Subscription	*das Abonnement*
Tabloid	*die Boulevardzeitung/das Revolverblatt*
Template	*die Druckschablone*
Text	*der Text*
Title	*der Titel*
Trade book	*das im Handel erhältliche Buch*
Trim	*der Schnitt*
Typeface	*der Schriftsatz*

Watermark	*das Wasserzeichen*
Word wrap	*der (automatische) Zeilenumbruch*
Writer	*der Schriftsteller*

REAL ESTATE

Agent	*der Makler*
Agreement	*die Übereinkunft*
Air rights	*die Luftrechte*
Amortization	*die Amortisierung*
Annual percentage rate	*der jährliche Prozentsatz*
Apartment	*die Wohnung*
Appraisal	*die Schätzung*
Appraise (to)	*schätzen/bewerten*
Assessment	*die Bewertung*
Assign (to)	*die Zuordnung*
Assume	*annehmen*
Assumption	*die Annahme/die Zuversicht*
Attached	*beigefügt*
Attachment	*die Anlage*
Auction	*die Auktion*
Balloon mortgage	*die Hypothek mit hoher Resttilgung*
Bankruptcy	*der Konkurs*
Bearing wall	*die tragende Wand*
Bid (to)	*bieten*
Binder	*die Bindungsklausel*
Breach of contract	*der Vertragsbruch*
Bridge loan	*der Überbrückungskredit*
Broker	*der Makler*
Building	*das Gebäude*
Building codes	*die Bauregulierung*

Building permit	die Baugenehmigung
Buy (to)	kaufen
Buy-down	der Kauf von Immobilien mit (meist zeitlich begrenztem) niedrigem Zinssatz
Capitalization	die Kapitalisierung
Capital gains	der Kapitalgewinn bei Verleauf eines Hauses
Cash flow	die Flüssigkeit
Caveat emptor	Vorsicht beim Kauf is geboten!
Closing	der Vertragsabschluss
Closing costs	die Abschlusskosten
Collateral	die Sicherheiten
Commitment	die Verbindlichkeit/die Verpflichtung
Condemnation	die Schließung wegen Unzumutbarkeit
Condominium (condo)	die Eigentumswohnung
Contract	der Vertrag
Convey (to)	umwandeln
Conveyance	die Umwandlung
Cooperative (co-op)	die Eigentumswohnung in einer Mietergemeinschaft
Credit report	die Schufaauskunft
Debt-to-income ratio	das Schulden-Einkommensverhältnis
Deed	die Urkunde
Default (to)	verzögern/Verpflichtung nicht einhalten
Depreciation	die Abschreibung
Diversified	diversifiziert

Down-payment	*die Anzahlung*
Earnest money	*die Anzahlungs-summe/die Pfandsumme*
Easement	*die Grunddienst-barkeit* (here: *das Durchfahrtsrecht eines Anliegeis*)
Eminent domain	*der Hauptwohnsitz*
Equity	*das Eigenkapital*
Escrow	*die Treuhandhinter-legung*
Foreclosure	*die Verfallserklärung*
First mortgage	*die erste Hypothek*
Flood insurance	*die Überschwem-mungsversicherung*
Free and clear	*ohne Hypothek*
Freehold	*der schuldenfreie Grundbesitz*
General contractor	*das Bauunternehmen*
Hazard insurance	*die Gefahrenver-sicherung*
Hotel	*das Hotel*
Indemnity	*der Schadensersatz*
Industrial	*industriell*
Industrial park	*das Industriegebiet*
Insurance	*die Versicherung*
Interest	*die Zinsen*
Jumbo loan or mortgage	*der Großkredit oder die Hypothek*
Land	*das Land*
Landscaping	*die Landschaftsgesta-ltung*

Lease	*der Leasingvertrag/der Pachtvertrag*
Lease (to)	*pachten*
Lessee/Lessor	*der Pächter/der Verpächter*
Let	*die Vermietung/ vermieten*
Lien	*das Pfandrecht*
Manufactured housing	*das Wohnungswesen in Fertighäusern oder vorgefertigten Wohnparzellen*
Mortgage	*die Hypothek*
Note	*der Eintragungsvermerk*
Occupancy	*das Bewohnen*
Office	*das Büro*
Option	*die Option*
Owner	*der Eigentümer*
Partition	*die Unterteilung*
Points	*Punkte*
Power-of-attorney	*die Vollmacht*
Prefabricated construction	*die vorgefertigte Konstruktion*
Prepayment penalty	*die Stornogebühr*
Principal	*das Kapital/die Kapitalsumme*
Private mortgage insurance	*die private Hypothekenversicherung*
Probate	*die Erbschaft, der Nachlan*
Promissory note	*der Soldwechsel, der Schuldschein*

Property	*das Grundstück*
Public sale	*der öffentliche Verkauf*
Real estate	*die Immobilien*
Real estate investment trusts (REITS)	*die Bausparkasse*
Realtor	*der Immobilienmakler*
Refinance (to)	*neu finanzieren*
Rent	*die Miete*
Rent (to)	*mieten*
Rental	*Miet-*
Renter	*der Mieter*
Rescind (to)	*wiederrufen / zurücktreten*
Residential	*auf den Wohnsitz bezogen*
Riparian rights	*die Uferanliegerrechte*
Second mortgage	*die zweite Hypothek*
Self-storage	*die Selbstverwahrung*
Sell (to)	*verkaufen*
Settle (to)	*sich niederlassen*
Shopping mall	*das Einkaufszentrum*
Sublet (to)	*untervermieten*
Tenant	*der Mieter*
Tenure	
Title	*das Eigentumsrecht, das Grundeigentum*
Title insurance	*die Grundbesitzversicherung*
Title search	*die Grundbuchüberprüfung*
Trust	*die Treuhandgesellschaft*
Utilities	*die Nebenkosten*

Vacant	*leer*
Warranty deed	*die Garantieerklärung*
Zoning	*die Bebauun-gerichtlimien, der Bebaüngs-plan*

SHIPPING AND DISTRIBUTION

Agent	*der Agent*
Air freight	*die Luftfracht*
Airport	*der Flughafen*
Anchor	*der Anker*
Barge	*die Barkasse*
Bill	*die Rechnung*
Bill (to)	*in Rechnung stellen*
Bill of lading (B/L)	*das Konnossement*
Boat	*das Boot/das Schiff*
Box	*die Box/der Kasten*
Broker	*der Speditionsmakler*
Bulk carrier	*der Großspediteur*
By air	*mit Luftfracht*
By land	*über Land*
By sea	*auf dem Seeweg*
Cargo	*die Fracht*
Carload	*die LKW-Ladung*
Carrier	*der Spediteur*
Certificate	*das Zertifikat*
Charter	*der Charter*
Charter (to)	*chartern*
CIF (Costs, Insurance, and Freight)	*einschließlich Versicherung und Fracht*
Combine (to)	*verbinden, kombinieren*
Consign (to)	*übersenden*

Consignor	*der Absender*
Container	*der Container*
Containerization	*die Verfrachtung mittels Container*
Container ship	*das Containerschiff*
Corrugated box	*der Wellpappekarton*
Cost	*die Kosten*
Crate	*der Ladeverschlag*
Crew	*die Mannschaft*
Customs	*der Zoll*
Deliver (to)	*liefern*
Delivery	*die Lieferung*
Delivery note	*die Lieferungsmitteilung*
Delivery time	*die Lieferzeit*
Depot	*das Depot/das Lager*
Destination	*der Zielort*
Dispatch	*die Abfertigung*
Dispatch (to)	*abfertigen*
Dock	*der Hafen*
Dock (to)	*anlegen*
Double hulls	*der Öltanker (mit doppelwandigem Laderaum)*
Duty	*die Zollgebühr*
Estimate	*die Schätzung/der Kostenvoranschlag*
Estimate (to)	*schätzen*
Ferry	*die Fähre*
Fleet	*die Flotte*
Fork lift	*der Gabelstapler*
Forward	*die Weitergabe*
Forwarding	*die Weitergabe*
Fragile	*leicht zerbrechlich*

Free on Board (FOB)	einschließlich Verladekosten
Freight	die Fracht
Freight carrier	der Frachter
Freight costs	die Frachtkosten
Freighter	das Frachtschiff
Freight weights	das Frachtgewicht
Full containerload	die volle Containerladung
Goods	die Ware
Guaranteed arrival date	der garantierte Ankunftstermin
Hazardous materials	die gefährlichen Stoffe
Hire (to)	einstellen
Hub	der Knotenpunkt
Insurance	die Versicherung
Insure (to)	versichern
Island	die Insel
Isothermal container	der isothermische Container
Landing day	der Anlegetag
Liner	das Linienschiff/der Liner
Load	die Ladung
Load (to)	laden
Load capacity	die Ladekapazität
Loading	das Laden
Loader	der Verlader
Loan	der Kredit
Locks	die Schlösser
Lots	die Parzellen
Manager	der Manager
Manifest	das Ladungsverzeichnis

Merchant ship	das Handelsschiff
Message center	das Nachrichtenzen-
	trum
Oil tanker	der Öltanker
Off load (to)	entladen
On load (to)	beladen
Order	der Auftrag
Order (to)	bestellen/beauftragen
Overdraft	die Überziehung
Package	das Paket
Package (to)	packen
Packaging	die Verpackung
Packing	das Einpacken
Pallet	die Palette
Partial carload	die Teilladung beim
	LKW
Partial containerload	die Teilcontainer-
	ladung
Pick up (to)	abholen
Port	der Hafen
Profit	der Gewinn
Railroad	die Eisenbahn
Rails	die Schienen
Rail yard	der Güterbahnhof
Refrigerate (to)	kühlen
Refrigerated tank	der Kühltank
Refrigeration	die Kühlung
Reloading	die Wiederbeladung
Rent (to)	mieten
Route	die Route
Route (to)	die Route festlegen/
	leiten

Scrapping	*die Verschrottung*
Sea	*das Meer*
Sea lane	*der Seeweg*
Service	*der Service*
Ship	*das Schiff*
Ship (to)	*verschiffen/versenden*
Shipper	*die Verschiffungsfirma/ die Spedition*
Station	*der Bahnhof*
Storage	*das Lager*
Super tanker	*der Supertanker*
Surface	*die Oberfläche*
Tank	*der Tank*
Tanker	*der Tanker*
Taxes	*die Steuern*
Tie-down (to)	*festlegen/sich binden an* (contract)
Tonnage	*die Ladefähigkeit*
Track (to)	*den Lieferweg verfolgen*
Tracks (railroad)	*die Gleise*
Traffic	*der Verkehr*
Traffic coordinator	*der Verkehrskoordinator*
Train	*der Zug*
Transloading	*das Transloading/das Zwischenladen*
Transport	*der Transport*
Transport (to)	*transportieren*
Transport company	*die Spedition*
Transporting	*das Transportieren*
Transporter	*der Spediteur*
Truck	*der Lastwagen*
Truck (to)	*mit dem LKW befördern*

Trucking	*die LKW-Beförderung*
Van	*der Kleinlastwagen*
Union	*die Gewerkschaft*
Union representative	*der Vertreter der Gewerkschaft*
Unload (to)	*entladen*
Warehouse	*das Lager*
Yard	*der Hof*

TELECOMMUNICATIONS

(See also *Computer Systems* under *Functional Areas of a Company* in Chapter 5)

Analog	*analog*
Bandwidth	*die Bandbreite*
Baud	*das Baud/die Datenübertragungsgeschwindigkeit*
Cable	*das Kabel*
Capacity	*die Kapazität*
Cellular	*kabellos*
Cellular phone	*das Handy*
Data	*die Daten*
Data transmission	*die Datenübertragung*
Dedicated line	*die spezielle Leitung*
Digital	*digital*
Downlink	*die Verbindung*
DSL line	*die digitale Teilnehmeranschlussleitung (ADSL)*
E-commerce	*der elektronische Handel*
E-mail	*die/das E-Mail*

Fax/Facsimile	*das Fax/das Faximile*
Fiber optical line	*die Glasfaserka-belverbindung*
Hertz	*das Hertz*
High speed	*ultraschnell*
Identification number (ID number)	*die Identifikation-snummer*
Internet	*das Internet*
Intranet	*das Intranet/das Hausnetz*
Internet Service Providers (ISPs)	*der Online-Dienst*
Keyboard	*das Keyboard/die Tastatur*
Keypad	*das Keypad*
Local Area Network (LAN)	*das lokale Netzwerk*
Line	*die Leitung*
Link	*die Verbindung/der Link*
Liquid-crystal display	*das Liquid-Crystal-Display*
Local call	*das Ortsgespräch*
Long distance call	*das Ferngespräch*
Megahertz	*das Megahertz*
Menu	*das Menü*
Mobile phone	*das mobile Telefon/das Handy*
Modem	*das Modem*
Network	*das Netzwerk, das Netz*
Palmtop	*der Palmtop*
Password	*das Passwort/das Sicherheitskennwort*

Personal digital assistant (PDA)	*der PDA/der Newton/ der Palmtop*
Phone line	*die Telefonleitung*
Resolution	*die Resulotion/die Bildschärfe*
Satellite	*der Satellit*
Security	*die Sicherheit*
Server	*der Server*
Telecommunications	*die Telekommunika- tion*
Telegram	*das Telegramm*
Telephone	*das Telefon*
Transmit (to)	*übertragen*
Transmission	*die Übertragung*
Uplink	*die Verbrückung/die Studioverbindung*
Video conferencing	*die Videokonferenz*
Voice and data transmission	*die Sprach- und Datenübertragung*
Voice mail	*die Voice-Mail/das Sprachspeichersystem*
Web	*das Netz*
Web page	*die Webseite*
Web site	*der Web-Site*
Wireless	*kabellos*
World Wide Web (WWW)	*das WorldWideWeb (WWW)*

TEXTILES

Acidity	*der Säureanteil*
Acrylic	*das Acryl*
Alkalinity	*die Alkalinität*
Apparel	*die Kleidung*

Artist	der Künstler/der Designer
Bonded types	die verblendeten Stoffe
Braids	die Verflechtung
Braided	verflochten
Brocade	der Brokatstoff
Cloth	das Tuch
Clothing	die Kleidung
Color	die Farbe
Composite fabrics	der gemischte Stoff
Conventional method	die herkömmliche Methode
Converter	der Veredler
Cotton	die Baumwolle
Crimp	das Kräuselgarn
Cutting	das Schneiden
Cutting room	der Schneideraum
Damask	der Damast
Defect	der Fehler
Design	das Design
Dry-cleaning	das chemische Reinigen
Dye	die Färbung/das Färbemittel
Dye (to)	färben
Dyeing	das Färben
Elasticity	die Elastzität
Elongation	die Dehnung
Embroidered	bestickt
Engineer	der Ingenieur
Fabric	der Stoff
Fastness (of finishes and colors)	die Festigkeit/die Farbechtheit

Felt	*der Filzstoff*
Fiber	*die Faser*
Fiber masses	*die Faserung*
Fineness	*die Feinheit*
Finished cloth	*das fertige Tuch*
Flame-resistant	*feuerbeständig*
Flax	*der Flachs*
Flexibility	*die Flexibilität*
Floral	*mit Blumenmotiv*
Garment	*das Kleidungsstück*
Geometric	*geometrisch*
Hand finishing	*die Handfertigung*
Insulation	*die Wärmedämmung/ die Isolierung*
Interlacing	*die Vernahtung/die Verflechtung*
Jute	*der Jutestoff*
Knit (to)	*stricken*
Knitted	*gestrickt*
Knitting	*das Stricken*
Lace	*die Spitze/die Litze*
Laundering	*das Waschen*
Layer	*die Schicht*
Length	*die Länge*
Licensing	*die Lizenzierung*
Linen	*das Leinen*
Loom	*der Webstuhl*
Machinery	*der Maschinenpark*
Man-made fiber	*die künstliche Faser*
Manufacture	*Herstellung*
Manufacturing operations	*der Herstellung- sprozess*

Moisture absorption	*die Feuchtigkeitsaufnahme*
Natural fiber	*die Naturfaser*
Needle	*die Nadel*
Needle woven	*handgewebt*
Net	*das Netz*
Newer construction methods	*neue Herstellungsmethoden*
Nylon	*das Nylon*
Ornament	*das Ornament*
Patterns	*das Muster*
Polyester	*das Polyester*
Polyester filament	*der Polyesterfaden*
Porosity	*die Porösität*
Printed	*bedruckt*
Printing	*der Druck*
Processing	*die Verarbeitung*
Production	*die Herstellung*
Quality control	*die Qualitätskontrolle*
Quality label	*das Qualitätskennzeichen*
Rayon	*die Viskose/die Kunstseide*
Reaction to heat, sunlight, chemicals	*die Reaktion auf Wärme, Sonnenlicht, Chemikalien*
Resistance to creases	*die Knitterfreiheit*
Resistance to pests	*die Mottenresistenz*
Rug	*der Teppich*
Sew (to)	*nähen*
Sewing	*das Nähen*
Silk	*die Seide*

Silk-screen (to)	*der Siebdruck*
Spandex	*das Spandex*
Specialization	*die Spezialisierung*
Spinning	*das Spinnen*
Stable-fiber	*die Stabilfaser*
Strength	*die Haltbarkeit*
Structure	*die Struktur*
Synthetic fabric	*der synthetische Stoff*
Synthetic fibers	*die synthetischen Fasern*
Tapestry	*der Wandbehang*
Technician	*der Techniker*
Testing	*das Testen*
Texture	*das Gewebe/die Textur*
Thread	*der Zwirn/das Garn*
Trademark	*die Schutzmarke/das Warenzeichen*
Traditional	*traditionell*
Treat (to)	*behandeln*
Uniform thickness	*die einheitliche Stärke*
Velvet	*der Samt*
Volume of production	*die Produktionsmenge*
Water-repellent	*wasserabweisend*
Weave	*das Gewebte*
Weave (to)	*weben*
Weave and yarn structure	*die Web- und Garnstruktur*
Weaving	*das Weben*
Weight per unit area	*das Gewicht pro Einheitsfläche*
Width	*die Breite*
Wool	*die Wolle*
Worsted	*das Kammgarn*
Woven	*gewebt*

Textiles

INDUSTRY-SPECIFIC TERMS

Yarn	*das Garn*
Yard	*zirka ⁹⁄₁₀ Meter*

TOYS

Action figure	*die Aktionsfigur*
Activity set	*das Aktivspielzeug*
Age compression	*die Altersverkürzung/ der Kinder-wachsen-schneller-auf-Faktor*
Airplane	*das Flugzeug*
Animal	*das Tier*
Articulation	*die Sprach- und Mundbewegungsfähigkeit von Spielzeugpuppen*
Art supplies	*der Kunstbedarf*
Ball	*der Ball*
Battery	*die Batterie*
Blocks	*die Klötze*
Board game	*das Brettspiel*
Boat	*das Boot/das Schiff*
Brand-name toy	*das Markenspielzeug*
Building blocks	*die Bauklötze*
Building toy	*das Konstruktionsspielzeug*
Car	*das Auto*
Character	*die Charakterfigur*
Chemistry set	*der Chemiebaukasten*
Children	*die Kinder*
Clay	*der Ton/das Knetgummi*
Computer game	*das Computerspiel*
Creator	*der Designer/der Entwickler*
Doll	*die Puppe*

Education software	*die Bildungssoftware*
Frisbee	*das Frisbie/der Frisbee*
Fun	*der Spaß*
Fun (to have)	*Spaß haben*
Game	*das Spiel*
Glue	*der Klebstoff*
Hobby kit	*der Hobbykasten*
Hobby horse	*das Steckenpferd*
Hoop	*der Reif/der Spielreifen*
Infant toy	*das Säuglingsspiel-zeug/Kleinkinder-spielzeug*
Kaleidoscope	*das Kaleidoskop*
Kit	*das Sortiment/der Baukasten*
Kite	*der Drachen*
Letter	*der Buchstabe*
Marbles	*die Murmeln*
Microscope	*das Mikroskop*
Mobile	*mobil*
Model	*das Modell*
Musical toy	*das Musikspielzeug*
Novelty	*die Neuheit*
Part	*das Teil*
Picture book	*das Bilderbuch*
Pegboard	*die Stecktafel*
Plastic	*das Plastik*
Play	*das Spiel*
Play (to)	*spielen*
Playing	*das Spielen*
Playing cards	*das Kartenspiel*

Plush toys	*die Plüschspielwaren/ das wattierte Spielzeug*
Preschool activity toy	*das Aktivspielzeug fürs Vorschulalter*
Puppet	*die Puppe* (also: *doll*)/ *die Kasperpuppe*
Puzzle	*das Puzzlespiel*
Railroad	*die elektrische Eisenbahn*
Rattle	*die Rassel*
Re-issue	*die Neuauflage*
Riding toy	*das fahrbare Spielzeug*
Rocket	*die Rakete*
Rubber	*das Gummi*
Science set	*der Experimentierkasten*
Soldier	*der Soldat*
Sports equipment	*die Sportausrüstung*
Stuffed animal	*das Plüschtier*
Stuffed toy	*das Plüschspielzeug*
Teddy bear	*der Teddybär*
Top	*der Kreisel*
Trading cards	*die Tauschkarten*
Train	*die Eisenbahn*
Vehicle	*das Fahrzeug*
Video game	*das Videospiel*
Wagon	*der Wagon*
Wood	*das Holz*
Woodburning set	*der Holzeinbrennungs-Set*
Yo-yo	*das Jojo*

WATCHES, SCALES, AND PRECISION INSTRUMENTS

Analog	*analog*
Apparatus	*der Apparat*
Balance	*die Ballance*
Battery/Batteries	*die Batterie/die Batterien*
Brass	*das Messing*
Chain	*die Kette*
Chronograph	*der Chronograph*
Clock	*die Uhr*
Coil	*die Windung/die Spirale*
Digital	*digital*
Display	*die Auslage*
Friction	*die Reibung*
Gear	*das Zahnrad*
Gold	*das Gold*
Instrument	*das Instrument*
Integrated circuit	*der integrierte Schaltkreis*
Jewels	*der Schmuck*
Laboratory	*das Labor*
Laser	*der Laser*
Mainspring	*die Hauptfeder*
Measurements	*die Maße*
Mechanism	*der Mechanismus*
Miniature	*die Miniatur*
Miniaturization	*die Miniaturisierung*
Motion	*die Bewegung*
Movements	*die Bewegungen*

Optical	optisch
Oscillate (to)	oszillieren/pendeln/ schwingen
Oscillation	die Oszillierung
Pin	der Pinn/der Stift
Pivot	der Drehzapfen
Polished	poliert
Precision	die Präzision
Scale	die Skala, die Waage
Self-winding	selbst aufziehend
Shaft	der Schaft
Silver	das Silber
Spring	die Feder
Spring-driven	mit Federbetrieb
Steel	der Stahl
Stop watch	die Stoppuhr
Time	die Zeit
Time (to)	stoppen
Timepiece	das Zeitinstrument
Torque	das Drehmoment
Transistors	die Transistoren
Watch	die Uhr
Weights	die Uhrengewichte
Wheel	das Zahnrad
Wristwatch	die Armbanduhr

WINE

Acidity	der Säuregehalt
Age (to)	lagern
Aging	die Lagerung
Alcohol	der Alkohol
Aroma	das Aroma

Barrel	*das Fass*
Bordeaux	*der Bordeaux*
Bottle	*die Flasche*
Bottle (to)	*verkellern*
Bottled	*verkellert*
Brandy	*der Weinbrand*
Bubbles	*die Bläschen*
Burgundy	*der Burgunder*
Cabernet sauvignon	*der Cabernet Sauvignon*
Casks	*die Fässer*
Cellar	*der Weinkeller*
Champagne	*der Champagner*
"Character" of the wine	*der Weincharakter*
Chardonnay	*der Chardonnay*
Chianti	*der Chianti*
Clarifying	*die Klärung*
Climate	*die Klimatisierung*
Color	*die Farbe*
Cool	*kühl*
Cork	*der Korken*
Cork (to)	*verkorken*
Crush (to)	*pressen*
Crusher	*die Weinpresse*
Drink (to)	*trinken*
Dry	*trocken*
Estate	*das Gut*
Ferment (to)	*fermentieren/gären*
Fermentation	*die Gärung*
Flavor	*der Geschmack*
Flavor (to)	*würzen*
Flavored wine	*der gewürzte Wein*

Fortified wines	*verschnittene Weine*
Grape	*die Traube*
Grow (to)	*züchten*
Harvest	*die Lese*
Herbs	*die Kräuter*
Humidity	*die Luftfeuchtigkeit*
Label	*das Etikett*
Label (to)	*etikettieren*
Merlot	*der Merlot*
Must	*der Most*
Oak	*die Eiche*
Pinot noir	*der Pinot Noir*
Port	*der Portwein*
Precipitate	*die Ablagerung*
Pulp	*das rückständige Fruchtfleisch*
Red wine	*der Rotwein*
Refine (to)	*raffinieren*
Refrigerate (to)	*kühlen*
Refrigeration	*die Kühlung*
Region	*das Anbaugebiet*
Riesling	*der Riesling*
Rosé wine	*der Rosewein*
Seeds	*die Saat*
Sherry	*der Sherry*
Soil	*der Boden*
Sparkling wine	*der Sekt*
Store (to)	*lagern*
Sugar	*der Zucker*
Sweet	*süß*

Table wine	*der Tischwein*
Tank	*der Tank*
Taste (to)	*probieren*
Tasting	*die Weinprobe*
Varietals	*der Weinverschnitt*
Vermouth	*der Wermuth*
Vine	*die Rebe*
Vineyard	*das Weingut*
Vinifera grapes	*die Vinifera Trauben*
Vintage	*der Jahrgang*
White wine	*der Weißwein*
Wine	*der Wein*
Winery	*die Winzerei*
Yeast	*die Hefe*

ENGLISH-GERMAN GENERAL GLOSSARY*

A

Accent	*der Akzent/die Betonung*
Accept (to)	*akzeptieren*
Acceptable	*akzeptabel*
Accountability	*die Rechenschaft*
Accounting	*die Buchhaltung*
Accounts payable	*die Verbindlichkeiten*
Accounts receivable	*die Forderungen*
Activities	*die Aktivitäten*
Ad	*die Anzeige* (paper)/*der Werbespot* (TV)
Address	*die Adresse*
Administration	*die Verwaltung/die Administration*
Administrative assistant	*der Verwaltungsangestellte*
Admission	*der Eintritt* (cost)/*der Zugang* (permit)
Agenda	*die Agenda/Tagesordnung*
Agree (to)	*zustimmen*
Agreement	*die Zustimmung*
Airport	*der Flughafen*
Airport shuttle	*der Flughafenbus*
American	*amerikanisch*
Amusement	*das Vergnügen/der Spaß*
Amusement park	*der Vergnügungspark*

---

*All nouns referring to persons in this glossary are quoted in the masculine form. In order to get the feminine form, the suffix *-in* is added at the end of the word.

Answer	*die Antwort*
Answer (to)	*antworten*
Answering machine	*der Anrufbeantworter*
Apology	*die Entschuldigung*
Appointment	*der Termin*
Appraise (to)	*schätzen*
Aqua	*hellblau* (color)
Arc	*der Bogen*
Area	*das Gebiet*
Argue (to)	*argumentieren/streiten* (severe)
Arrow	*der Pfeil*
Art	*die Kunst*
Art gallery	*die Kunstgalerie*
Article	*der Artikel*
Ask (to)	*fragen*
Associate	*der Geschäftsfreund* (business))/*der Kollege/der Mitarbeiter*
Asterisk	*das Sternchen*
Attachment	*die Anlage*
Attention	*die Beachtung/die Achtung*
Audio	*das Audio*
Audit	*die Prüfung*
Audit (to)	*prüfen*
Authority	*die Autorität*
Authorize (to)	*die Vollmacht erteilen* (official)
Auto	*das Auto/der Wagen*

B

Background	*der Hintergrund*
Badge	*das Abzeichen/die Marke*

Bag(s)	*die Tasche(n)*
Balcony	*der zweite Rang* (theater)/*der Balkon*
Ballet	*das Ballett*
Bar	*die Bar/die Kneipe*
Bar chart	*das Säulendiagramm*
Bargain (to)	*handeln*
Basketball	*der Basketball*
Bathroom	*das Bad/das Badezimmer/die Toilette*
Bed	*das Bett*
Begin (to)	*beginnen/anfangen*
Beginning	*der Beginn/der Anfang*
Behavior	*das Verhalten*
Bell-shaped curve	*die glockenförmige Kurve*
Benefits	*die Sozialleistungen*
Bill	*die Rechnung/der Geldschein* (money)
Bill of sale	*der Kaufvertrag*
Bin	*der Korb/die Kiste*
Black	*schwarz*
Blackboard	*die Tafel*
Blank	*leer* (empty)/*unausgefüllt* (not filled out)
Blouse	*die Bluse*
Blue	*blau*
Board	*der Vorstand* (company)/*die Tafel* (presentation chart)
Bold	*fettgedruckt* (font)/*kühn* (unafraid)
Bond	*das Wertpapier/die Papierqualität*
Bonus	*der Bonus*

Book	das Buch
Bookmark	das Lesezeichen
Booth	der Schalter
Boss	der Chef
Bottom	der Boden/unten
Box	die Box/der Kasten
Box seat	die Loge
Breakfast	das Frühstück
Brochure	die Broschüre
Brown	braun
Buffet	das Buffet
Building	das Gebäude
Bus	der Bus
Business	das Geschäft
Business card	die Visitenkarte
Business center	das Business Center/das Geschäftszentrum
Busy	beschäftigt
Buy (to)	kaufen

C

Cabinet	der Schrank
Café	das Cafe
Cake	der Kuchen/die Torte
Calculus	die Differential- und Integralrechnung
Calendar	der Kalender
Call (to)	anrufen
Calling card	die Telefonkarte
Camera	die Kamera
Capability	die Fähigkeit
Car	das Auto/der Wagen
Car phone	das Autotelefon

Career	*der Werdegang/die Karriere* (fame)
Cash	*das Bargeld*
Cash a check (to)	*einen Scheck einlösen*
Cat	*die Katze*
Cellular phone	*das Handy*
Center	*das Zentrum*
Central	*zentral*
Central office	*das Zentralbüro*
Central thesis	*die Zentralthese*
Centralization	*die Zentralisierung*
Certified check	*der bestätigte Scheck*
Certified mail	*der Einschreibebrief*
Chair	*der Stuhl/der Sessel/der Vorsitz* (business)
Chairman	*der Vorsitzende*
Chairperson	*die Person, die den Vorsitz hat*
Chairwoman	*die Vorsitzende*
Chalk	*die Kreide*
Change (to)	*wechseln/ändern*
Chart	*das Diagramm*
Check	*der Scheck*
Check (to)	*prüfen/nachsehen*
Check in (to)	*einchecken*
Chicken	*das Huhn/das Hähnchen*
Child	*das Kind*
Children	*die Kinder*
Church	*die Kirche*
Cigar	*die Zigarre*
Cigarette	*die Zigarette*
Circle	*der Kreis*
City	*die Stadt*
Classical music	*die klassische Musik*

Classroom	der Schulungsraum/ das Klassenzimmer
Clear (to)	löschen/verdeutlichen
Clock	die Uhr
Close (to)	schließen/abschließen
Clothing	die Kleidung
Cloudy	bewölkt
Coach (to)	beraten/ trainieren/lehren
Coaching	die Beratung
Coat	der Mantel
Cocktail	der Cocktail
Cocktail party	die Cocktail-Party
Coffee	der Kaffee
Cold	kalt
Cold call	der Überraschungsan- ruf/der unangemeldete Anruf
Color	die Farbe
Color monitor	der Farbmonitor
Column	die Spalte
Comedy	die Komödie
Communicate (to)	kommunizieren/sich unterhalten
Communications	die Kommunikation
Compensate (to)	kompensieren
Compensation	die Kompensation/das Arbeitsentgelt
Compete (to)	konkurrieren
Competition	die Konkurrenz
Competitive price	der konkurrenzfähige Preis
Computer	der Computer
Computer cable	das Computerkabel
Computer disk	die Computerdiskette
Computer monitor	der Computermonitor

Concert	*das Konzert*
Concert hall	*die Konzerthalle*
Concierge	*die Concierge*
Conference	*die Konferenz*
Conference call	*das Konferenzgespräch*
Conference center	*das Konferenzzentrum*
Confirm (to)	*bestätigen*
Confirmation	*die Bestätigung*
Conflict	*der Konflikt*
Connection	*die Verbindung*
Consult (to)	*konsultieren*
Consultant	*der Berater*
Contact (to)	*Kontakt aufnehmen / kontaktieren*
Contract	*der Vertrag*
Contractual obligation	*die vertragliche Verpflichtung*
Converter	*der Konverter/der Transformator*
Convince (to)	*überzeugen*
Cool	*kalt*
Co-owner	*der Mitbesitzer*
Co-partner	*der Partner*
Copier	*der Kopierer*
Copy	*die Kopie*
Copyright	*das Vervielfältigungsrecht /das Copyright*
Corner office	*das Eckbüro*
Cost	*die Kosten*
Country	*das Land*
Course	*der Kursus*
Cover	*der Umschlag*
Cream	*die Sahne*
Crosshatched	*schräg schraffiert*
Cultural	*kulturell*

Culture	*die Kultur*
Curve	*die Kurve*
Customer	*der Kunde*
Customer service	*der Kundendienst*
Customs	*der Zoll*
Cyberspace	*der Cyberspace*

D

Dais	*das Podium*
Dash	*der Schrägstrich*
Data	*die Daten*
Database	*die Datenbank*
Date	*das Datum*
Daughter	*die Tochter*
Day	*der Tag*
Deadline	*der Stichtag/die Deadline*
Deal	*der Handel*
Decentralization	*die Dezentralisierung*
Decide (to)	*entscheiden* (several options)/ *beschließen* (yes or no)
Decision	*die Entscheidung*
Decision making	*der Entscheidungsprozess*
Deferred compensation	*verzögerte Kompensierung/ die Erstattung in Raten*
Delivery	*die Lieferung*
Delivery date	*der Liefertermin*
Demonstrate (to)	*demonstrieren/zeigen*
Demonstration	*die Demonstration*
Department	*die Abteilung*

Design	*das Design/der Entwurf/die Gestaltung*
Desk	*der Schreibtisch*
Diagram	*das Diagramm*
Diagram (to)	*schaubildlich darstellen*
Dial	*die Wählscheibe*
Dial (to)	*wählen*
Dialogue	*der Dialog*
Dinner	*das Abendessen*
Direct (to)	*dirigieren/zeigen/die Richtung anweisen/leiten/führen*
Direct line	*die direkte Leitung*
Directions	*die Richtung* (where)/ *die Anweisungen* (what/how)
Director	*der Direktor*
Directory	*das Telefonbuch*
Disco	*die Diskothek*
Discuss (to)	*diskutieren*
Discussion	*die Diskussion*
Display	*das Display*
Display (to)	*ausstellen/zeigen*
Distribute (to)	*(aus)liefern*
Distribution	*die Auslieferung/die Verteilung*
Doctor	*der Arzt*
Document	*das Dokument*
Dog	*der Hund*
Dollar	*der Dollar*
Door	*die Tür*
Dotted line	*die punktierte Linie*
Down payment	*die Anzahlung*
Download (to)	*downloaden/ herunterladen*

Downsize (to)	*downsizen/abspecken/ gesund schrumpfen* (company)
Drama	*das Drama*
Due	*fällig*

E

Earlier	*früher*
Early	*früh*
Easel	*die Staffelei/der Präsentationsständer*
Edge	*der Rand*
Eight	*acht*
Electrical line	*die elektrische Leitung*
Electricity	*die Elektrizität*
Ellipse	*die Ellipse*
E-mail	*die/das E-Mail*
Enclosure	*die Umzäunung* (property)/ *die Anlage* (attachment)
Encourage (to)	*aufmuntern/ auffordern*
End	*das Ende*
End (to)	*beenden*
Engineer	*der Ingenieur*
English	*das Englisch*
Enjoy (to)	*mögen/sich vergnügen mit/gern machen*
Enterprise	*das Unternehmen*
Entrance	*der Eingang*
Entrepreneur	*der Unternehmer*
Entrepreneurship	*das Unternehmertum*
Envelope	*der Briefumschlag*

Erase (to)	*löschen*
Eraser	*das Radiergummi*
Espresso	*der Espresso*
Evening	*der Abend*
Excel software	*das Excel-Programm*
Exhibit	*die Ausstellung*
Exhibit (to)	*ausstellen*
Exit	*der Ausgang*
Exit (to)	*hinausgehen /beenden*
Expenses	*die Kosten*
Experience	*die Erfahrung*
Exponential	*exponential*
Export (to)	*exportieren /ausführen*
Extension	*die Verlängerung*
Extension cord	*die Verlängerungs-schnur*

F

Facilitate (to)	*unterstützen / verbessern*
Facilitator	*der Vermittler/der Moderator*
Fall (season)	*der Herbst*
Family	*die Familie*
Fax	*das Fax*
Fax (to)	*faxen*
Feedback	*das Feedback*
Feedback (to)	*Feedback geben*
Ferry	*die Fähre*
File	*die Akte/die Ablage*
File (to)	*ablegen*
File cabinet	*der Ablageschrank*
Film	*der Film*
Finance	*das Finanzwesen*

Finance (to)	*finanzieren*
Financial figures	*die finanziellen Daten*
Financial report	*der Finanzbericht*
Find (to)	*finden*
Findings	*die Funde/das Resultat*
First	*zuerst/der/die/das erste*
Fish	*der Fisch*
Five	*fünf*
Flat-panel display	*der Flachbildschirm*
Flight	*der Flug*
Flower	*die Blume*
Folder	*die Akte/der Ordner*
Follow up (to)	*nachfassen*
Food	*das Essen*
Football	*der Fußball*
Foreman	*der Vormann*
Forward (to)	*weiterleiten*
Found	*gefunden*
Four	*vier*
Front	*die Vorderseite*

G

Gain (to)	*gewinnen*
Gallery	*die Galerie*
Gate	*das Tor*
Geometry	*die Geometrie*
Give (to)	*geben*
Glass	*das Glas*
Goal	*das Ziel*
Good	*gut*
Good-bye	*Auf Wiedersehen/der Abschied*

Goods	*die Waren*
Grandparents	*die Großeltern* (plural)
Grant	*die Unterstützung/die Subvention*
Graph (to)	*schaubildlich darstellen*
Graph	*das Schaubild*
Green	*grün*
Grid	*das Raster*
Guarantee	*die Garantie*
Guarantee (to)	*garantieren /fest zusagen*
Guard	*die Garde/der Wachmann*

H

Handout	*die Handzettel*
Hang up (to)	*auflegen*
Hat	*der Hut*
Heading	*die Überschrift*
Health	*die Gesundheit*
Hello	*Hallo*
Help (to)	*helfen*
Helpful	*hilfreich*
Histogram	*das Histogramm/die Säulendarstellung*
History	*die Geschichte/die Vergangenheit*
Hobby	*das Hobby*
Hold (to)	*halten /haben*
Home page	*die Homepage*
Hope (to)	*hoffen*
Horizontal	*horizontal/waagerecht*
Horizontal bar chart	*das horizontale Balkendiagramm*

Horse	*das Pferd*
Hot	*heiß*
Hotel	*das Hotel*
Hour	*die Stunde*
House	*das Haus*
Human resources	*die Personalabteilung*
Husband	*der Ehemann*
Hypertext	*der Hypertext*

I

Ice cream	*die Eiscreme/das Eis*
Idea	*die Idee* (creative thought)/*die Ahnung* (idea of a fact)
Illustrate (to)	*illustrieren/darstellen*
Illustration	*die Illustration/die Darstellung*
Import (to)	*importieren/einführen*
Individual	*individuell*
Inform (to)	*informieren*
Information	*die Information*
Information desk	*der Informationsschalter*
Inside	*innen/innerhalb* (within)
Insight	*die Einsicht/das Wissen*
Install (to)	*installieren*
Installation	*die Installierung*
Insurance	*die Versicherung*
Intelligence	*die Intelligenz*
Intelligent	*intelligent*
International	*international*
International law	*das internationale Recht*

Internet	*das Internet*
Interview	*das Interview*
Interview (to)	*ein Bewerbungsgespräch haben/führen*
Introduce (to)	*vorstellen*
Introduction	*die Vorstellung*
Inventory	*der Lagerbestand/die Inventur*
Invest (to)	*investieren*
Investment	*die Investition*
Invoice	*die Rechnung*
Invoice (to)	*in Rechnung stellen/berechnen*
Issue (to)	*ausstellen*
Item	*die Sache*

J

Jazz	*der Jazz*
Jazz club	*der Jazzclub*
Jewelry	*der Schmuck*
Job	*die Arbeit/die Arbeitsstelle/der Job* (not a career)
Joke	*der Spaß/der Witz*
Joke (to)	*Spaß machen*

K

Karate	*das Karate*
Key issue	*der Hauptpunkt/der Schlüsselpunkt*
Know (to)	*wissen* (a fact)/*kennen* (somebody or a subject)
Knowledge	*das Wissen* (in depth)/*die Kenntnis* (of a fact)

Label	*das Etikett/die Aufschrift*
Label (to)	*etikettieren/beschriften*
Ladies' room	*die Damentoilette*
Language	*die Sprache*
Laptop computer	*der Laptop*
Last	*der/die/das Letzte*
Late	*spät*
Later	*später*
Law	*das Gesetz*
Lawsuit	*die Klage*
Lawyer	*der Anwalt/der Rechtsanwalt*
Layout	*das Layout*
Lead (to)	*leiten/führen*
Leader	*der Leiter/der Führer*
Leadership	*die Leitung*
Leading	*die Leitung/die Führung*
Learn (to)	*lernen*
Left	*links*
Legal	*legal* (within the law) *rechtkräftig* (legally binding)
Legal costs	*die Rechtskosten*
Letter	*der Brief*
Liability	*die Haftbarkeit*
Library	*die Bibliothek*
Light	*das Licht*
Light bulb	*die Glühbirne*
Like (to)	*mögen/wollen*
Limousine	*die Limosine*
Line	*die Leitung*

Linear	*linear*
Line graph	*das Kurvenschaubild*
Link	*die Referenz/der Link*
List (to)	*auflisten/listen*
Listen (to)	*hören*
Literature	*die Literatur*
Local	*lokal/örtlich*
Local call	*das Ortsgespräch*
Location	*der Platz/die Position*
Logarithmic scale	*die Logarithmustabelle*
Log off (to)	*ausloggen*
Log on (to)	*einloggen*
Logo	*das Logo/das Firmenzeichen*
Long-distance	*auf große Entfernung*
Long-distance call	*das Ferngespräch*
Look (to)	*sehen*
Lotus 1-2-3 software	*die Lotus-1-2-3-Software*
Luggage	*das Gepäck*
Lunch	*das Mittagessen*
Luncheon	*das leichte Mittagessen*

M

Magazine	*die Zeitschrift/die Illustrierte*
Mail	*die Post*
Mail (to)	*schicken/senden*
Mail order	*die Postbestellung*
Mailing list	*die Adressenliste*
Mainframe computer	*der Hauptcomputer/der Mainframe-computer*
Make (to)	*machen*
Manage (to)	*managen*

Management	*das Management*
Manager	*der Manager*
Map	*die Karte*
Marker	*der Textmarker*
Market	*der Markt*
Market (to)	*vermarkten*
Market value	*der Marktwert*
Marketing	*das Marketing*
Marketing report	*der Marketingreport*
Materials	*die Materialien*
Mathematics	*die Mathematik*
Maximum	*das Maximum*
Maybe	*vielleicht*
Meat	*das Fleisch*
Media	*die Medien*
Mediate (to)	*verhandeln*
Meet (to)	*(sich) treffen*
Meeting	*die Besprechung/die Sitzung/das Treffen*
Memo	*das Memorandum/die Hausmitteilung*
Men's room	*die Herrentoilette*
Mentor	*der Mentor/der Ratgeber*
Mentoring	*die Beratung/das Mentoring*
Menu	*das Menü*
Message	*die Nachricht*
Message center	*das Nachrichtenzentrum*
Mezzanine	*der erste Rang*
Microphone	*das Mikrofon*
Middle	*die Mitte*
Milk	*die Milch*
Mineral water	*das Mineralwasser*
Minimum	*das Minimum*

Minute	*die Minute*
Mission	*die Mission/das Firmenziel*
Model	*das Modell*
Modem	*das Modem*
Money	*das Geld*
Monitor	*der Monitor*
Month	*der Monat*
Morning	*der Morgen*
Mosque	*die Moschee*
Move (to)	*bewegen*
Movie	*der Film*
Multimedia	*die Multimedia*
Museum	*das Museum*
Music	*die Musik*
Musical	*das Musical*

N

Name	*der Name*
Name (to)	*nennen*
Need (to)	*brauchen*
Negotiate (to)	*verhandeln*
Negotiating	*die Verhandlung*
Network	*das Netzwerk/das Network*
New	*neu*
News	*die Nachrichten*
Newsstand	*das/der Kiosk*
Night	*die Nacht*
Nine	*neun*
No	*nein*
Note	*die Notiz/die Note* (banknote)
Note (to)	*notieren*

Note pad	*der Notizblock*
Number	*die Zahl* (general)/*die Nummer* (specific)
Nurse	*die Krankenschwester/ der Krankenpfleger*

O

Object	*das Objekt*
Objective	*die Objektive/das Ziel*
Offer (to)	*anbieten*
Office	*das Büro/das Amt/die Behörde* (public)
Officer	*der Beamte* (governmental)/*der leitende Angestellte* (company)
Okay (to)	*genehmigen/erlauben*
One	*eins*
Online	*online*
Online service	*der Internet-Service*
On/Off	*an/aus*
Open (to)	*öffnen*
Opera	*die Oper*
Operate (to)	*führen*
Operating system	*das Betriebssystem*
Operations	*der Betrieb*
Operator	*der Führer/der Leiter*
Option	*die Möglichkeit/die Option*
Orange	*orange*
Orchestra	*das Orchestor*
Organization	*die Organisation/die Gesellschaft*
Organization chart	*das Firmenschaubild*
Organize (to)	*organisieren/ordnen* (to put in order)

Orientation	*die Orientierung*
Origin	*die Herkunft*
Outside	*außen /draußen*
Overhead projector	*der Overhead-Projektor*

P

Package	*das Paket*
Package (to)	*verpacken*
Paper	*das Papier*
Page	*die Seite*
Page (to)	*paginieren /die Seitenzahl zuordnen*
Pager	*der Beeper*
Parents	*die Eltern* (plural)
Park	*der Park*
Part	*das Teil* (part)/*der Teil* (part of)
Participant	*der Teilnehmer*
Participate	*teilnehmen*
Partner	*der Partner*
Passport	*der Pass*
Password	*das Passwort*
Past due	*die überschrittene Fälligkeit*
Patent	*das Patent*
Pause (to)	*pausieren / unterbrechen*
Payment	*die Zahlung*
Peer	*der Mitarbeiter/der Kollege*
Pencil	*der Bleistift*
Pension	*die Pension* (governmental)/*die Rente*
Percentage	*der Prozentsatz*
Personnel	*die Personalabteilung*
Pet	*das Haustier*

Philosophy	die Philosophie
Phone	das Telefon
Phone (to)	telefonieren /anrufen (to call someone)
Phone call	der Telefonanruf
Photocopy (to)	fotokopieren
Photograph	das Foto
Picture	das Bild
Pie	die Torte
Pie chart	das Tortendiagramm
Ping-Pong	das Tischtennis
Place (to)	plazieren
Plan (to)	planen
Play	das Spiel
Play (to)	spielen
Please	bitte
Podium	das Podium/das Podest
Point	der Punkt
Point (to)	zeigen
Pointer	der Zeigestock /der Laserpointer
Policeman	der Polizist
Policy/policies	die Police/die Policen
Polygon	das Vieleck
Pork	das Schweinefleisch
Portable	portabel/tragbar
Portable phone	das Handy
Portal	das Tor/das Portal
Porter	der Träger
Position	die Stellung/die Position
Post office	die Post /das Postamt
Postpone (to)	verschieben
Pound key	die Rautentaste/die Nummerntaste

Pound sign	*das Rautenzeichen*
PowerPoint presentation	*die Power-Point-Präsentation*
Present (to)	*zeigen/präsentieren/geben*
Presentation	*die Präsentation*
Presenting	*das Präsentieren*
President	*der Präsident*
Price	*der Preis*
Print (to)	*drucken*
Printer	*der Drucker*
Problem	*das Problem*
Problem solving	*die Problemlösung*
Procedure(s)	*der Vorgang (die Vorgänge)*
Process	*der Prozess*
Procure (to)	*anschaffen*
Produce (to)	*herstellen/produzieren*
Product	*das Produkt*
Production	*die Produktion*
Program	*das Programm*
Promotion	*die Verkaufspromotion*
Property	*das Grundstück*
Proposal	*das Angebot*
Propose (to)	*anbieten*
Provide (to)	*ausstatten/zur Verfügung stellen*
Purchasing agent	*der Einkäufer*
Purple	*purpur*
Purpose	*der Zweck*

Q

Quality	*die Qualität*
Quality control	*die Qualitätskontrolle*

Query	*die Frage*
Question	*die Frage*
Question (to)	*in Frage stellen*
Q&A	*Fragen und Antworten (F&A)*
Quiet	*ruhig*

R

Rain/Rainy	*der Regen/regnerisch*
Rare	*selten*
Reboot	*wieder hochfahren/ rebooten*
Receive (to)	*bekommen/erhalten/ empfangen*
Receiver	*der Empfänger*
Reception	*die Rezeption*
Receptionist	*der Rezeptionist*
Recommend (to)	*empfehlen*
Recommendation	*die Empfehlung*
Reconsider (to)	*(sich) überlegen*
Record	*die Aufnahme* (tape/CD)/*die Quittung* (receipt)
Record (to)	*aufnehmen* (tape)
Recording	*die Aufnahme*
Rectangle	*das Rechteck*
Red	*rot*
Redial (to)	*die Wahlwiederhol- ungstaste drücken*
Reference	*die Referenz*
Reference (to)	*eine Referenz geben*
Referral	*die Empfehlung*
Refreshments	*die Erfrischungen*
Refund	*die Rückerstattung*
Register (to)	*registrieren*

Regression	*der Rückgang*
Regression line	*die rückgängige Kurve*
Rehearse	*proben*
Reject (to)	*ablehnen*
Rent	*die Miete*
Rent (to)	*mieten*
Reorganize (to)	*umorganisieren*
Reply	*die Antwort*
Reply (to)	*antworten*
Report	*der Bericht*
Request (to)	*anfragen*
Reservation	*die Reservierung*
Reserve (to)	*reservieren*
Reserved	*reserviert*
Rest room	*die Toilette/das WC*
Restaurant	*das Restaurant*
Result	*das Resultat*
Resume (to)	*wieder einnehmen* (to resume a position)/ *wieder aufnehmen* (to resume a discussion), etc.
Return (to)	*zurückgeben* (give back)/*zurückbringen* (bring back)/ *zurückgehen* (go back), etc.
Reveal (to)	*enthüllen* (an unknown fact)/*aufdecken* (a mystery)/*aufzeigen* (show)
Right	*rechts*
Right angle	*der rechte Winkel*
Risk(s)	*das Risiko (die Risiken)*
Risk (to)	*wagen* (dare)/*riskieren*

Room	*das Zimmer/der Raum*
Row	*die Reihe/die Matrixreihe* (as a part of a spread sheet)
Rugby	*das Rugby*

S

Salary	*das Gehalt*
Sale(s)	*der Umsatz* (revenue)/ *der Verkauf* (sales)/ *der Ausverkauf* (sale)
Sales call	*der Verkaufsanruf*
Sales report	*der Verkaufsbericht*
Sales tax	*die Verkaufssteuer/die Mehrwertsteuer* (value added tax)
Say (to)	*sagen*
Scale	*die Skala*
Scatter diagram	*das Diagramm*
Schedule	*der Zeitplan*
Science	*die Wissenschaft*
Science fiction	*die Science Fiction*
Screen	*der Bildschirm*
Scuba diving	*das Tauchen*
Search engine	*die Suchmaschine* (Internet)
Season	*die Jahreszeit*
Second	*der/die/das zweite . . .*
Secretary	*der Sekretär/die Sekretärin*
See (to)	*sehen*
Sell (to)	*verkaufen*
Selling	*das Verkaufen*
Seminar	*das Seminar*
Send (to)	*senden /schicken*

Service	*der Service/die Dienstleistung*
Set up (to)	*einrichten*
Seven	*sieben*
Server	*der Server* (computer)
Service	*der Service*
Shaded	*abgedunkelt*
Shadow	*der Schatten*
Ship (to)	*verschiffen/versenden*
Shipment	*die Sendung*
Shipping center	*der Versand*
Shoes	*die Schuhe*
Show (to)	*zeigen*
Sightsee	*die Sehenswürdigkeiten besuchen*
Sign (to)	*unterschreiben*
Six	*sechs*
Skiing	*das Skifahren*
Skill(s)	*die Fähigkeit(en)*
Skirt	*der Rock*
Slice	*die Scheibe*
Slide projector	*der Diaprojektor*
Slides	*die Dias*
Snack	*der Snack*
Snow	*der Schnee*
Snowy	*verschneit*
Soccer	*der Fußball*
Socks	*die Socken*
Software	*die Software*
Solid	*hart*
Solid line	*die durchgehende Linie*
Solve (a problem) (to)	*(ein Problem) lösen*
Son	*der Sohn*
Sound system	*das Soundsystem*

Souvenir	*das Souvenir*
Space	*der Platz/der Raum*
Speak (to)	*sprechen* (to speak)/ *reden* (to give a speech)
Speaker	*der Sprecher* (speaker)/ *der Redner* (person giving a speech)
Special delivery	*die Sonderlieferung*
Specialty	*die Spezialität*
Specification(s)	*die Spezifizierung(en)*
Speech	*die Rede*
Sports	*der Sport*
Spring	*der Frühling*
Square	*das Quadrat*
Stack	*der Stapel*
Star	*der Stern*
Start	*der Start/der Beginn/ der Anfang*
Steak	*das Steak*
Stock	*das Lager* (storage)/*die Aktie* (share)
Stock option	*die Aktienoption*
Stockholder	*der Aktionär*
Stockings	*die Strümpfe*
Stop	*der Stop/der Halt*
Street	*die Straße*
Stress	*der Stress*
Style	*der Stil*
Subject	*das Fach*
Submit (to)	*einreichen*
Suit	*der Anzug* (clothing)/ *die Klage* (lawsuit)
Summer	*der Sommer*
Supervisor	*der Abteilungsleiter*

Supply	*die Utensilien/der Nachschub*
Supply (to)	*versorgen*
Support (to)	*unterstützen*
Surf (to)	*surfen*
Surf the Web	*das Netz/Web surfen*
Switch	*der Schalter* (device)
Switch (to)	*verbinden mit* (telephone)/*ändern* (something)/*schalten* (a device)
Switchboard	*die Vermittlung/die Schaltzentrale*
Synagogue	*die Synagoge*
System(s)	*das System (die Systeme)*

T

Table	*der Tisch /die Tabelle* (chart)
Tailor	*der Schneider*
Talk (to)	*reden*
Tape recorder	*der Kassettenrecorder*
Tax	*die Steuer*
Tax-exempt	*steuerfrei*
Taxi	*das Taxi*
Tea	*der Tee*
Team	*das Team*
Team building	*das Team Building*
Technical support	*der technische Kundendienst*
Telephone	*das Telefon*
Telephone directory	*das Telefonbuch*
Telephone number	*die Telefonnummer*

Telephone operator	*die Telefonvermittlung*
Television	*das Fernsehen* (institution)/*der Fernseher* (set)
Temperature	*die Temperatur*
Ten	*zehn*
Terminology	*die Terminologie*
Text	*der Text*
Thank you	*das Dankeschön*
Theater	*das Theater*
Theory	*die Theorie*
Thesis	*die These*
Three	*drei*
3-D chart	*das dreidimensionale Schaubild*
Ticket	*das Ticket/die Karte*
Tie	*der Schlips/die Krawatte*
Time	*die Zeit*
Time (to)	*zeitlich messen*
Title	*der Titel*
Tobacco	*der Tabak*
Today	*heute*
Tomorrow	*morgen*
Top	*oben* (top of)/*die Spitze* (upper point) *der Deckel* (cover)/*der Kreisel* (toy)
Tour	*die Rundfahrt/die Tour*
Tour bus	*der Tourenbus*
Town	*die Stadt/der Ort*
Trade	*der Handel*
Trade (to)	*handeln*
Trade show	*die Messe*
Trade union	*die Gewerkschaft für Handel*

Trademark	das Warenzeichen
Train (to)	trainieren/schulen
Training	das Training/die Schulung
Transact (to)	vermitteln
Transaction	die Transaktion
Transfer (to)	übertragen/überweisen (money)
Transparency	die Transparenz/die Durchsichtigkeit
Transportation	der Transport
Transportation charges	die Frachtkosten
Travel	die Reise
Travel (to)	reisen
Treasurer	der Schatzmeister
Triangle	das Dreieck
Turn (to)	biegen (street)/drehen (a switch)
Two	zwei
Type	der Stil (style)/die Art (kind)
Type (to)	tippen/schreiben
Typewriter	die Schreibmaschine

U

Umbrella	der Regenschirm
Unacceptable	nicht akzeptierbar/unakzeptabel
Underline	unterstreichen
Understand (to)	verstehen
Understanding	das Verständnis
Underwear	die Unterwäsche
Union	die Gewerkschaft
United States of America	die Vereinigten Staaten von Amerika

| U-shaped | *u-förmig* |
| U-turn | *die Wende* |

V

Value	*der Wert*
Value (to)	*bewerten*
Value added tax	*die Mehrwertsteuer*
Vegetable	*das Gemüse*
Vegetarian	*der Vegetarier/ egetarisch*
Vertical	*vertikal/senkrecht*
Via	*zwischen/über/via*
Vice president	*der Vizepräsident*
Video	*das Video*
Video (to)	*auf Video aufnehmen*
Video conferencing	*eine Videokonferenz haben*
Video recorder	*der Videorekorder*
Virtual reality	*die virtuelle Realität*
Vision	*die Vision/die Voraussicht*
Voice mail	*die Voicemailbox*
Voice recognition	*die Spracherkennung*

W

Wait (to)	*warten*
Waiting room	*das Wartezimmer*
Want (to)	*wollen/mögen*
Warm	*warm*
Warranty	*der Garantieschein*
Watch (to)	*beobachten*
Water	*das Wasser*

Weather	*das Wetter*
Web access	*der Zugang zum Netz*
Week	*die Woche*
Well	*gut*
Well done	*well done* (food)
Wife	*die Ehefrau*
Window	*das Fenster*
Wine	*der Wein*
Wine list	*die Weinkarte*
Winter	*der Winter*
Word software	*das Word-Programm*
WordPerfect software	*das WordPerfect-Programm*
Work (to)	*arbeiten*
Work station	*die Arbeitsstation*
Workbook	*das Arbeitsbuch*
Workshop	*die Werkstatt/der Workshop*
World Wide Web	*das WorldWideWeb/das weltweite Netz*
Write (to)	*schreiben*

X

| X-axis | *die Abzissenachse/die X-Achse* |
| XY scatter | *die XY-Streuung* |

Y

Y-axis	*die Ordinatenachse/die Y-Achse*
Yellow	*gelb*
Yes	*ja*

| Yield | *die Ausschüttung/der Gewinn/die Ernte* |
| You're welcome | *Bitteschön* |

Z

| Z-axis | *die Z-Achse* |
| Zoo | *der Zoo* |

GERMAN-ENGLISH

A

der Abend	*Evening*
das Abendessen	*Dinner*
abgedunkelt	*Shaded*
der Ablageschrank	*File cabinet*
ablegen	*File (to)*
ablehnen	*Reject (to)*
abschließen	*Close (to)*
die Abteilung	*Department*
der Abteilungsleiter	*Supervisor*
das Abzeichen	*Badge*
die Abzissenachse	*X-axis*
acht	*Eight*
die Adresse	*Address*
die Adressenliste	*Mailing list*
die Agenda	*Agenda*
die Ahnung	*Idea* (intuition)
die Akte	*File/Folder*
die Aktie	*Stock (share)*
die Aktienoption	*Stock option*
der Aktionär	*Stockholder*
die Aktivitäten	*Activities*
der Akzent	*Accent*
akzeptabel	*Acceptable*
akzeptieren	*Accept (to)*
amerikanisch	*American*
an/aus	*On/Off*
anbieten	*Offer (to), Propose (to)*
der Anfang	*Beginning*
anfangen	*Begin (to), Request (to)*
das Angebot	*Proposal*
die Anlage	*Attachment*

der Anrufbeantworter	*Answering machine*
anrufen	*Call (to)*
anschaffen	*Procure (to)*
die Antwort	*Answer/Reply*
antworten	*Answer (to)/Reply (to)*
der Anwalt	*Lawyer*
die Anzahlung	*Down payment*
die Anzeige	*Ad (*paper/magazine*)*
der Anzug	*Suit (*clothing*)*
die Arbeit	*Job*
arbeiten	*Work (to)*
das Arbeitsbuch	*Workbook*
die Arbeitsstation	*Work station*
die Arbeitsstelle	*Job*
argumentieren	*Argue (to)*
der Artikel	*Article*
der Arzt	*Doctor*
das Audio	*Audio*
auf große Entfernung	*Long-distance*
auf Video aufnehmen	*Video (to)*
Auf Wiedersehen	*Good-bye*
auflegen	*Hang up (to)*
auflisten	*List (to)*
aufmuntern	*Encourage (to)*
die Aufnahme	*Recording*
aufnehmen	*Record (to)*
die Aufschrift	*Label*
ausführen	*Export (to)*
der Ausgang	*Exit*
ausliefern	*Distribute (to)*
die Auslieferung	*Distribution*
ausloggen	*Log off (to)*
die Ausschüttung	*Yield*
außen	*Outside*
ausstatten	*Provide (to)*

ausstellen	*Display (to), Exhibit (to), Issue (to)*
die Ausstellung	*Exhibit*
das Auto	*Auto*
die Autorität	*Authority*
das Autotelefon	*Car phone*

B

das Bad/Badezimmer	*Bathroom*
das Ballett	*Ballet*
die Bar	*Bar*
das Bargeld	*Cash*
die Beachtung	*Attention*
der/die Beamte	*Officer* (government)
beenden	*End (to), Exit (to)*
der Beeper	*Pager*
der Beginn	*Beginning*
beginnen	*Begin (to)*
die Behörde	*Office* (public)
bekommen	*Receive (to)*
beobachten	*Watch (to)*
beraten	*Coach (to)*
der Berater	*Consultant*
die Beratung	*Coaching/Mentoring*
der Bericht	*Report*
beschäftigt	*Busy*
beschriften	*Label (to)*
die Besprechung	*Meeting*
bestätigen	*Confirm (to)*
der bestätigte Scheck	*Certified check*
die Bestätigung	*Confirmation*
die Betonung	*Accent*
das Bett	*Bed*
bewegen	*Move (to)*

bewerten	Value (to)
bewölkt	Cloudy
die Bibliothek	Library
biegen	Turn (to)
das Bild	Picture
der Bildschirm	Screen
der Bindestrich	Dash
bitte	Please
Bitte sehr	You're welcome
blau	Blue
der Bleistift	Pencil
die Blume	Flower
die Bluse	Blouse
der Boden	Bottom
der Bogen	Arc
die Box	Box
brauchen	Need (to)
braun	Brown
der Brief	Letter
der Briefumschlag	Envelope
die Broschüre	Brochure
das Buch	Book
die Buchhaltung	Accounting
das Buffet	Buffet
das Büro	Office
der Bus	Bus
das Businesscenter	Business center

C

das Cafe	Café
der Chef	Boss
der Cocktail	Cocktail
die Cocktail-Party	Cocktail party
der Computer	Computer

die Computerdiskette	*Computer disk*
das Computerkabel	*Computer cable*
der Computermonitor	*Computer monitor*
die Concierge	*Concierge*
der Cyberspace	*Cyberspace*

D

die Damentoilette	*Women's Room*
das Dankeschön	*Thank you*
die Datei/Datenbasis	*Data base*
die Daten	*Data*
das Datum	*Date*
die Demonstration	*Demonstration*
demonstrieren	*Demonstrate (to)*
das Design	*Design*
die Dezentralisierung	*Decentralization*
das Dia/Dias	*Slide(s)*
der Diaapparat	*Slide projector*
das Diagramm	*Chart/Diagram*
Dialog	*Dialogue*
die Differential- und Integralrechnung	*Calculus*
die direkte Leitung	*Direct line*
der Direktor	*Director*
dirigieren	*Direct (to)*
die Diskothek	*Disco*
die Diskussion	*Discussion*
diskutieren	*Discuss (to)*
das Display	*Display*
das Dokument	*Document*
der Dollar	*Dollar*
das Drama	*Drama*
draußen	*Outside*
drehen	*Turn (to)*

drei	*Three*
das dreidimensionale Schaubild	*3-D chart*
das Dreieck	*Triangle*
drucken	*Print (to)*
der Drucker	*Printer*
die durchgehende Linie	*Solid line*

E

das Eckbüro	*Corner office*
die Ehefrau	*Wife*
der Ehemann	*Husband*
ein Bewerbungsgespräch haben/führen	*Interview (to)*
einchecken	*Check in (to)*
eine Referenz geben	*Reference (to)*
eine Videokonferenz haben	*Video conferencing*
einen Scheck einlösen	*Cash a check (to)*
einführen	*Import (to)*
der Eingang	*Entrance*
der Einkäufer	*Purchasing agent*
einloggen	*Log on (to)*
einreichen	*Submit (to)*
einrichten	*Setup (to)*
eins	*One*
der Einschreibebrief	*Certified mail*
die Einsicht	*Insight*
der Eintritt	*Admission* (cost)
die Eiscreme/das Eis	*Ice cream*
die elektrische Leitung	*Electrical line*
die Elektrizität	*Electricity*
die Ellipse	*Ellipse*
die Eltern	*Parents*

die E-Mail	*E-mail*
der Empfänger	*Receiver*
empfehlen	*Recommend (to)*
die Empfehlung	*Recommendation/ Referral*
das Ende	*End*
das Englisch	*English*
enthüllen	*Reveal (to)*
entscheiden	*Decide (to)*
die Entscheidung	*Decision*
der Entscheidungsprozess	*Decision making*
die Entschuldigung	*Apology*
die Erfahrung	*Experience*
die Erfrischung	*Refreshment*
der erste Rang	*Mezzanine*
der Espresso	*Espresso*
das Essen	*Food*
das Etikett	*Label*
etikettieren	*Label (to)*
das Excel-Programm	*Excel software*
exponential	*Exponential*
exportieren	*Export (to)*

F

das Fach	*Subject*
die Fähigkeit	*Capability/Skill*
die Fähre	*Ferry*
fällig	*Due*
die Familie	*Family*
die Farbe	*Color*
der Farbmonitor	*Color monitor*
das Fax	*Fax*
faxen	*Fax (to)*
das Feedback	*Feedback*

Feedback geben	*Feedback (to)*
das Fenster	*Window*
das Ferngespräch	*Long-distance call*
das Fernsehen	*Television*
fettgedruckt	*Bold* (font)
der Film	*Film/Movie*
der Finanzbericht	*Financial report*
die finanziellen Daten	*Financial figures*
finanzieren	*Finance (to)*
das Finanzwesen	*Finance*
finden	*Find (to)*
das Firmenschaubild	*Organization chart*
das Firmenzeichen	*Logo*
das Firmenziel	*Mission*
der Fisch	*Fish*
der Flachbildschirm	*Flat-panel display*
das Fleisch	*Meat*
der Flug	*Flight*
der Flughafen	*Airport*
der Flughafenbus	*Airport shuttle*
die Forderungen	*Accounts receivable*
das Foto	*Photograph*
fotokopieren	*Photocopy (to)*
früh	*Early*
früher	*Earlier*
der Frühling	*Spring*
das Frühstück	*Breakfast*
die Frachtkosten	*Transportation charges*
die Frage	*Query, Question*
fragen	*Ask (to)*
Fragen und Antworten (F&A)	*Q&A*
führen	*Direct (to), Lead (to), Operate (to)*
der Führer	*Operator/Leader*

die Führerschaft	*Leadership*
die Führung	*Leading*
fünf	*Five*
der Fund	*Finding*
der amerikanische Fußball	*Football*
der Fußball	*Soccer*

G

die Galerie	*Gallery*
die Garantie	*Guarantee*
garantieren	*Guarantee (to)*
der Garantieschein	*Warranty*
das Gebäude	*Building*
geben	*Give (to)*
das Gebiet	*Area*
gefunden	*Found*
das Gehalt	*Salary*
gelb	*Yellow*
das Geld	*Money*
das Gemüse	*Vegetable*
genehmigen	*Okay (to)*
die Geometrie	*Geometry*
das Gepäck	*Luggage*
das Geschäft	*Business*
der Geschäftsfreund	*Associate*
die Geschichte	*History*
das Gesetz	*Law*
gesund schrumpfen	*Downsize (to)*
die Gesundheit	*Health*
die Gewerkschaft	*Union*
die Gewerkschaft für Handel	*Trade union*
gewinnen	*Gain (to)*

das Glas	*Glass*
die Global-Software	*Word software*
die glockenförmige Kurve	*Bell-shaped curve*
die Glühbirne	*Light bulb*
die Großeltern	*Grandparents*
grün	*Green*
der Grund	*Purpose*
das Grundstück	*Property*
gut	*Good/well*

H

die Haftbarkeit	*Liability*
das Hähnchen	*Chicken*
das Hallo	*Hello*
halten	*Hold (to)*
der Handel	*Deal/trade*
handeln	*Bargain (to)/trade (to)*
das Handy	*Cellular phone/portable phone*
der Handzettel	*Handout*
hart	*Solid*
der Hauptcomputer	*Mainframe computer*
das Haus	*House*
die Hausmitteilung	*Memo*
das Haustier	*Pet*
heiß	*Hot*
helfen	*Help (to)*
hellblau	*Aqua*
der Herbst	*Fall* (season)
die Herkunft	*Origin*
die Herrentoilette	*Men's room*
herstellen	*Produce (to)*
herunterladen	*Download (to)*
heute	*Today*

hilfreich	*Helpful*
hinausgehen	*Exit (to)*
der Hintergrund	*Background*
das Histogramm	*Histogram*
das Hobby	*Hobby*
hoffen	*Hope (to)*
die Homepage	*Home page*
hören	*Listen (to)*
horizontal	*Horizontal*
das horizontale Balkendiagramm	*Horizontal bar chart*
das Hotel	*Hotel*
das Huhn	*Chicken*
der Hund	*Dog*
der Hut	*Hat*
der Hypertext	*Hypertext*

I

die Idee	*Idea* (creative thought)
die Illustration	*Illustration*
illustrieren	*Illustrate (to)*
importieren	*Import (to)*
in Frage stellen	*Question (to)*
in Rechnung stellen/ berechnen	*Invoice (to)*
individuell	*Individual*
die Information	*Information*
der Informationsschalter	*Information desk*
informieren	*Inform (to)*
der Ingenieur	*Engineer*
innen/innerhalb	*Inside*
installieren	*Install (to)*
die Installierung	*Installation*
intelligent	*Intelligent*

die Intelligenz	*Intelligence*
international	*International*
internationales Recht	*International law*
das Internet	*Internet*
der Internet-Service	*Online service*
das Interview	*Interview*
investieren	*Invest (to)*
die Investition	*Investment*

J

ja	*Yes*
die Jahreszeit	*Season*
der Jazz	*Jazz*
der Jazzclub	*Jazz club*

K

der Kaffee	*Coffee*
der Kalender	*Calendar*
kalt	*Cold*
die Kamera	*Camera*
das Karate	*Karate*
die Karte	*Map*
der Kassettenrekorder	*Tape recorder*
die Katze	*Cat*
kaufen	*Buy (to)*
die Kenntnis	*Knowledge (of a fact)*
das Kind	*Child*
die Kinder	*Children*
das Kiosk	*Newsstand*
die Kirche	*Church*
die Klage	*Suit (lawsuit)*
die klassische Musik	*Classical music*
die Kleidung	*Clothing*

die Kommunikation	*Communications*
kommunizieren	*Communicate (to)*
die Komödie	*Comedy*
kompensieren	*Compensate (to)*
die Kompensierung	*Compensation*
die Konferenz	*Conference*
das Konferenzgespräch	*Conference call*
der Konferenzzentrum	*Conference center*
der Konflikt	*Conflict*
die Konkurrenz	*Competition*
der konkurrenzfähige Preis	*Competitive price*
konkurrieren	*Compete (to)*
konsultieren	*Consult (to)*
Kontakt aufnehmen	*Contact (to)*
der Konverter	*Converter*
das Konzert	*Concert*
die Konzerthalle	*Concert hall*
die Kopie	*Copy*
der Kopierer	*Copier*
der Korb	*Bin*
der Korbball	*Basketball*
Kosten	*Cost/Expenses*
die Krankenschwester	*Nurse*
die Krawatte	*Tie*
die Kreide	*Chalk*
der Kreis	*Circle*
der Kuchen	*Cake*
kühl	*Cool*
die Kultur	*Culture*
kulturell	*Cultural*
der Kunde	*Customer*
der Kundendienst	*Customer service*
die Kunst	*Art*
die Kunstgalerie	*Art gallery*

der Kursus	Course
die Kurve	Curve
das Kurvenschaubild	Line graph

L

der Lagerbestand	Inventory
das Land	Country
der Laptop	Laptop computer
das Layout	Layout
legal	Legal
das leichte Mittagessen	Luncheon
leiten	Lead (to)
der leitende Angestellter	Officer (company)
der Leiter	Leader
lernen	Learn (to)
das Lesezeichen	Bookmark
das Licht	Light
der Liefertermin	Delivery date
die Lieferung	Delivery
die Limosine	Limousine
linear	Linear
die Linie	Line
links	Left
die Literatur	Literature
die Logarithmustabelle	Logarithmic scale
die Loge	Box seat
löschen	Erase (to)/clear (to)
lösen (ein Problem)	Solve (a problem) (to)
die Lotus-1-2-3-Software	Lotus 1-2-3 software

M

| machen | Make (to) |
| das Management | Management |

managen	*Manage (to)*
der Manager	*Manager*
der Mantel	*Coat*
die Marke	*Badge*
das Marketing	*Marketing*
der Marketingreport	*Marketing report*
der Markt	*Market*
der Marktwert	*Market value*
die Materialien	*Materials*
die Mathematik	*Mathematics*
das Maximum	*Maximum*
die Medien	*Media*
die Mehrwertsteuer	*Value-added tax*
das Menü	*Menu*
der Mentor	*Mentor*
die Messe	*Trade show*
die Miete	*Rent*
mieten	*Rent (to)*
das Mikrofon	*Microphone*
die Milch	*Milk*
das Mineralwasser	*Mineral water*
das Minimum	*Minimum*
die Minute	*Minute*
der Mitarbeiter	*Peer*
der Mitbesitzer	*Co-owner*
das Mittagessen	*Lunch*
die Mitte	*Middle*
das Modell	*Model*
das Modem	*Modem*
mögen	*Enjoy (to)/like (to)*
die Möglichkeit	*Option*
der Monat	*Month*
der Monitor	*Monitor*
der Morgen	*Morning*
morgen	*Tomorrow*

die Moschee	*Mosque*
die Multimedia	*Multimedia*
das Museum	*Museum*
das Musical	*Musical*
die Musik	*Music*

N

nachfassen	*Follow up (to)*
die Nachricht	*Message*
die Nachrichten	*News*
das Nachrichtenzentrum	*Message center*
die Nacht	*Night*
der Name	*Name*
nein	*No*
nennen	*Name (to)*
das Netz surfen	*Surf the Web*
das Netzwerk/Network	*Network*
neu	*New*
neun	*Nine*
nicht akzeptierbar	*Unacceptable*
notieren	*Note (to)*
die Notiz	*Note*
der Notizblock	*Note pad*
die Nummer	*Number* (specific)

O

oben	*Top*
das Objekt	*Object*
die Objektive	*Objective*
öffnen	*Open (to)*
online	*Online*
örtlich	*Local*
die Oper	*Opera*

das Operationssystem	*Operating system*
orange	*Orange*
das Orchestor	*Orchestra*
die Ordinatenachse	*Y-axis*
die Organisation	*Organization*
organisieren	*Organize (to)*
die Orientierung	*Orientation*
das Ortsgespräch	*Local call*
der Overhead-Projektor	*Overhead projector*

P

das Packet	*Package*
paginieren	*Page (to)*
das Papier	*Paper*
der Park	*Park*
der Partner	*Partner/ co-partner*
der Pass	*Passport*
das Passwort	*Password*
das Patent	*Patent*
pausieren	*Pause (to)*
die Personalabteilung	*Human resources/ personnel*
der Pfeil	*Arrow*
das Pferd	*Horse*
die Philosophie	*Philosophy*
planen	*Plan (to)*
der Platz	*Location/space*
plazieren	*Place (to)*
Podest	*Podium/dais*
Podium	*Podium/dais*
die Police/Policen	*Policy/policies*
der Polizist	*Policeman*
die Post	*Mail/Post office*

das Postamt	*Post office*
die Postbestellung	*Mail order*
die Power-Point-Präsentation	*PowerPoint presentation*
die Präsentation	*Presentation*
das Präsentieren	*Presenting*
präsentieren	*Present (to)*
der Präsident	*President*
der Preis	*Price*
proben	*Rehearse*
das Problem	*Problem*
die Problemlösung	*Problem solving*
das Produkt	*Product*
die Produktion	*Production*
die Produktionsabteilung	*Operations*
produzieren	*Produce (to)*
das Programm	*Program*
der Prozentsatz	*Percentage*
der Prozess	*Process*
prüfen	*Audit (to)/check (to)*
die Prüfung	*Audit*
der Punkt	*Point*
die punktierte Linie	*Dotted line*
purpur	*Purple*

Q

das Quadrat	*Square*
die Qualität	*Quality*
die Qualitätskontrolle	*Quality control*

R

der Rabatt	*Bonus*
das Radiergummi	*Eraser*

der Rand	*Edge*
das Raster	*Grid*
der Ratgeber	*Mentor*
der Raum	*Space*
die Rautetaste	*Pound key*
das Rautezeichen	*Pound sign*
die Rechenschaft	*Accountability*
die Rechnung	*Invoice/bill of sale*
der rechte Winkel	*Right angle*
das Rechteck	*Rectangle*
rechts	*Right*
die Rede	*Speech*
reden	*Talk (to)*
die Referenz	*Reference/link*
der Regen	*Rain*
der Regenschirm	*Umbrella*
registrieren	*Register (to)*
regnerisch	*Rainy*
die Reihe	*Row*
die Reise	*Travel*
reisen	*Travel (to)*
die Rente	*Pension*
reservieren	*Reserve (to)*
reserviert	*Reserved*
die Reservierung	*Reservation*
das Restaurant	*Restaurant*
das Resultat	*Result/finding*
die Rezeption	*Reception*
der Rezeptionist	*Receptionist*
die Richtung	*Directions*
die Richtung anweisen	*Direct (to)*
das Risiko (Risiken)	*Risk(s)*
riskieren	*Risk (to)*
der Rock	*Skirt*
rot	*Red*

die Rückerstattung	*Refund*
der Rückgang	*Regression*
die rückgängige Kurve	*Regression line*
das Rugby	*Rugby*
ruhig	*Quiet*
die Rundfahrt/Tour	*Tour*
der Rundfahrtenbus	*Tour bus*

S

die Sache	*Item*
sagen	*Say (to)*
die Sahne	*Cream*
die Säulendarstellung	*Histogram*
das Säulendiagramm	*Bar chart*
der Schalter	*Booth/switch*
der Schatten	*Shadow*
schätzen	*Appraise (to)*
der Schatzmeister	*Treasurer*
das Schaubild	*Graph*
schaubildlich darstellen	*Diagram (to)/graph (to)*
der Scheck	*Check*
die Scheibe	*Slice*
schicken	*Mail (to)*
der Schlüsselpunkt	*Key issue*
der Schmuck	*Jewelry*
der Schnee	*Snow*
der Schneider	*Tailor*
schräg schraffiert	*Crosshatched*
der Schrank	*Cabinet*
schreiben	*Write (to)*
die Schreibmaschine	*Typewriter*
der Schreibtisch	*Desk*

der Schuh/die Schuhe	*Shoe(s)*
der Schulungsraum	*Classroom*
schwarz	*Black*
das Schweinefleisch	*Pork*
die Science Fiction	*Science fiction*
sechs	*Six*
sehen	*Look (to), See (to)*
die Sehenswürdigkeiten besuchen	*Sightsee*
die Seite	*Page*
Seitenzahl zuordnen	*Page (to)*
der Sekretär/die Sekretärin	*Secretary*
selten	*Rare*
das Seminar	*Seminar*
senden	*Send (to)*
die Sendung	*Shipment*
senkrecht	*Vertical*
der Server	*Server (computer)*
der Service	*Service*
sieben	*Seven*
die Sitzung	*Meeting*
die Skala	*Scale*
das Skifahren	*Skiing*
der Snack	*Snack*
die Socken	*Socks*
die Software	*Software*
der Sohn	*Son*
der Sommer	*Summer*
die Sonderlieferung	*Special delivery*
das Soundsystem	*Sound system*
das Souvenir	*Souvenir*
die Spalte	*Column*
der Spaß	*Joke*

Spaß machen	*Joke (to)*
spät	*Late*
später	*Later*
die Spezialität	*Specialty*
die Spezifizierung	*Specification*
das Spiel	*Play*
spielen	*Play (to)*
der Sport	*Sports*
die Sprache	*Language*
die Spracherkennung	*Voice recognition*
das Sprachspei chersystem	*Voice mail*
sprechen	*Speak (to)*
der Sprecher	*Speaker*
die Stadt	*City/town*
die Staffelei	*Easel*
der Stapel	*Stack*
der Start	*Start*
das Steak	*Steak*
die Stellung	*Position*
der Stern	*Star*
das Sternchen	*Asterisk*
die Steuer	*Tax*
steuerfrei	*Tax-exempt*
der Stichtag	*Deadline*
der Stil	*Style/type*
der Stop	*Stop*
die Straße	*Street*
der Stress	*Stress*
die Strümpfe	*Stockings*
die Stunde	*Hour*
die Subvention	*Grant*
die Suchmaschine	*Search engine*
surfen	*Surf (to)*

die Synagoge	*Synagogue*
das System	*System*

T

der Tabak	*Tobacco*
die Tabelle	*Table (*chart*)*
die Tafel	*Blackboard*
der Tag	*Day*
die Tasche	*Bag*
das Tauchen	*Scuba diving*
das Taxi	*Taxi*
das Team	*Team*
der Team-Aufbau	*Team building*
der technische Kundendienst	*Technical support*
der Tee	*Tea*
der Teil	*Part*
teilnehmen	*Participate*
der Teilnehmer	*Participant*
das Telefon	*Phone/telephone*
der Telefonanruf	*Phone call*
das Telefonbuch	*Directory*
telefonieren	*Phone (to)*
die Telefonkarte	*Calling card*
die Telefonnummer	*Telephone number*
die Telefonvermittlung	*Telephone operator*
die Temperatur	*Temperature*
der Termin	*Appointment*
die Terminologie	*Terminology*
der Text	*Text*
das Theater	*Theater*
die Theorie	*Theory*
die These	*Thesis*

das Ticket	*Ticket*
tippen	*Type (to)*
das Tischtennis	*Ping-Pong*
der Titel	*Title*
die Tochter	*Daughter*
die Toilette	*Rest room*
das Tor	*Gate/portal*
die Torte	*Pie*
das Tortendiagramm	*Pie chart*
tragbar	*Portable*
der Träger	*Porter*
trainieren	*Train (to)*
das Training	*Training*
die Transaktion	*Transaction*
die Transparenz	*Transparency*
der Transport	*Transportation*
das Treffen	*Meeting*
treffen (sich)	*Meet (to)*
die Tür	*Door*

U

überlegen (sich)	*Reconsider (to)*
der Überraschungsanruf	*Cold call*
die Überschrift	*Heading*
die überschrittene Fälligkeit	*Past due*
übertragen	*Transfer (to)*
überzeugen	*Convince (to)*
u-förmig	*U-shaped*
die Uhr	*Clock*
umorganisieren	*Reorganize (to)*
der Umsatz	*Sale(s)*
der Umschlag	*Cover*

die Umzäunung	*Enclosure (*around property*)*
unausgefüllt	*Blank (*not filled out*)*
unten	*Bottom*
unterbrechen	*Pause (to)*
das Unternehmen	*Enterprise*
der Unternehmer	*Entrepreneur*
das Unternehmertum	*Entrepreneurship*
unterschreiben	*Sign (to)*
unterstützen	*Support (to)/facilitate (to)*
unterstreichen	*Underline*
die Unterwäsche	*Underwear*
die Utensilien	*Supply*

V

der Vegetarier	*Vegetarian*
verbinden mit	*Switch (to)*
die Verbindlichkeiten	*Accounts payable*
die Verbindung	*Connection*
die Vereinigte Staaten von Amerika	*United States of America*
die Vergangenheit	*History*
das Vergnügen	*Amusement*
der Vergnügungspark	*Amusement park*
die Vergünstigungen	*Benefits*
das Verhalten	*Behavior*
verhandeln	*Mediate (to), Negotiate (to)*
die Verhandlung	*Negotiating*
verkaufen	*Sell (to)*
das Verkaufen	*Selling*
der Verkaufsanruf	*Sales call*

der Verkaufsbericht	*Sales report*
die Verkaufspromotion	*Promotion*
die Verkaufssteuer	*Sales tax*
die Verlängerung	*Extension*
die Verlängerungsschnur	*Extension cord*
vermarkten	*Market (to)*
vermitteln	*Transact (to)*
der Vermittler	*Facilitator*
die Vermittlung	*Switchboard*
verpacken	*Package (to)*
die Verschickungsabteilung	*Shipping center*
verschieben	*Postpone (to)*
verschiffen	*Ship (to)*
verschneit	*Snowy*
die Versicherung	*Insurance*
versorgen	*Supply (to)*
das Verständnis	*Understanding*
verstehen	*Understand (to)*
vertikal	*Vertical*
der Vertrag	*Contract*
vertragliche Obligation	*Contractual obligation*
das Vervielfältigungsrecht	*Copyright*
die Verwaltung	*Administration*
der Verwaltungsangestellte	*Administrative assistant*
die verzögerte Kompensierung	*Deferred compensation*
via	*Via*
das Video	*Video*
der Videorekorder	*Video recorder*
das Vieleck	*Polygon*
vielleicht	*Maybe*
vier	*Four*
die virtuelle Realität	*Virtual reality*

die Vision	*Vision*
die Visitenkarte	*Business card*
der Vizepräsident	*Vice president*
die Vollmacht erteilen	*Authorize (to)*
die Vorderseite	*Front*
der Vorgang	*Procedure*
der Vormann	*Foreman*
der Vorsitz	*Chair* (business)
der Vorsitzende	*Chairman/chairperson*
die Vorsitzende	*Chairwoman*
der Vorstand	*Board* (company)
vorstellen	*Introduce (to)*
die Vorstellung	*Introduction*

W

waagerecht	*Horizontal*
der Wagen	*Car*
wagen	*Risk (to)*
wählen	*Dial (to)*
die Wählscheibe	*Dial*
die Wahlwiederholung- staste drücken	*Redial (to)*
Waren	*Goods*
das Warenzeichen	*Trademark*
warm	*Warm*
warten	*Wait (to)*
das Wartezimmer	*Waiting room*
das Wasser	*Water*
wechseln	*Change (to)*
der Wein	*Wine*
die Weinkarte	*Wine list*
weiterleiten	*Forward (to)*
well done	*Well done* (food)
die Wende	*U-turn*

der Werbespot	Ad (TV)
der Werdegang	Career
die Werkstatt	Workshop
der Wert	Value
das Wertpapier	Bond
das Wetter	Weather
wiederaufnehmen	Resume (to)
wiederhochfahren	Reboot
der Winter	Winter
das Wissen	Knowledge (in depth)
wissen	Know (to)
die Wissenschaft	Science
der Witz	Joke
die Woche	Week
wollen	Want (to)
das WordPerfect-Programm	WordPerfect software
das WorldWideWeb	World Wide Web

X

| die X-Achse | X-axis |
| die XY-Streuung | XY scatter |

Z

die Z-Achse	Z-axis
die Zahl	Number (general)
die Zahlung	Payment
zehn	Ten
zeigen	Point (to)/show (to)
der Zeigestock	Pointer
die Zeit	Time
zeitlich messen	Time (to)
der Zeitplan	Schedule

die Zeitschrift	*Magazine*
zentral	*Central*
das Zentralbüro	*Central office*
die Zentralisierung	*Centralization*
die Zentralthese	*Central thesis*
das Ziel	*Goal*
die Zigarette	*Cigarette*
die Zigarre	*Cigar*
das Zimmer	*Room*
der Zoll	*Customs*
der Zoo	*Zoo*
zuerst	*First*
der Zugang	*Admission (permit)*
der Zugang zum Netz	*Web access*
zuletzt	*Last*
zurückgeben	*Return (to)*
zustimmen	*Agree (to)*
die Zustimmung	*Agreement*
zwei	*Two*
zweite	*Second*
der zweite Rang	*Balcony* (theater)

INDEX

NOTES

NOTES

NOTES

NOTES

NOTES

NOTES

NOTES

NOTES